UNSEEN CH

DISABLED CHARACTERS IN
20TH-CENTURY BOOKS FOR GIRLS

EDITED BY

HELEN A. AVELING

Bettany Press 2009

First published in Great Britain
by Bettany Press, 2009.
8 Kildare Road London E16 4AD.

Text © the authors 2009.

The rights of the authors to be identified
as the author of this work has been asserted
by them in accordance with the
Copyright, Designs and Patents Act 1988.

British Library Cataloguing in Publication Data.
A catalogue record for this book is available
from the British Library.

This book is sold subject to the condition that it
shall not, by way of trade or otherwise, be lent,
re-sold, hired out, or otherwise circulated
without the Publisher's prior consent in any
form of binding or cover other than that in
which it is published and without a similar
condition including this condition being imposed
on the subsequent purchaser.

All rights reserved.

ISBN 978 0 9552973 7 3

Printed and bound in Great Britain by
CLE Print Ltd, Huntingdon, Cambridgeshire.

CONTENTS

	List of Illustrations	iv
	Notes on Contributors	v
	Acknowledgments	viii
	Introduction HELEN A. AVELING	1

STEREOTYPES

I.	Modelling Illness in the Early 20th Century HELEN A. AVELING	19
II.	Beyond Beauty: Stigmatizing Social Behaviour in UK & North American Young Adult Fiction LINDA DICK	49
III.	Stereotyping in the Late 20th Century LOUISE NORLIE	81

ROLE MODELS

IV.	Not Always Cured Or Killed: Disability in Early 20th-century Girls' School Stories HELEN A. AVELING	117
V.	A Choice Of Virtues DEBORAH KENT	153
VI.	"I don't want to be different": Diabetes in Contemporary Young Adult Fiction MEREDITH GUTHRIE	179

INCLUSION & SEGREGATION

VII.	Doing Not Dreaming: Disability & Mental Health in Elsie J. Oxenham's Books JU GOSLING & JULIE NEWMAN	219
VIII.	Changes at the Chalet School: Illness & Disability in the Chalet School Series JU GOSLING	259
IX.	My Sibling the Other REBECCA R. BUTLER	303

LIST OF ILLUSTRATIONS

FACING PAGE

G. W. Goss: *The Rescue of Sadie, from*
The Only Day Girl, *Dorothea Moore,*
Nisbet, London & Edinburgh, 1923. 16

H. Coller: *Morag Tackles Winifred, from*
The Girls of St Bride's, *Dorita Fairlie Bruce,*
Oxford University Press, London, 1923. 114

Lewis Parker: *Sally Starts School, from*
Mine for Keeps, *Jean Little,*
Little, Brown & Company, Canada, 1962. 216

NOTES ON CONTRIBUTORS

Helen A. Aveling was born in Malawi in 1958 and grew up in England, where she had an extremely enjoyable childhood and schooldays. Cerebral palsy has been as much an integral part of her life as her love of books. Helen is a graduate of Essex University, where she studied English Literature, and was the first woman in her family to get a degree. Collecting books was a natural extension of Helen's love of them, and she has an impressive collection of children's books. In 1995 Helen was a founder-member of the New Chalet Club (for fans of Elinor M. Brent-Dyer) and she has contributed many articles to their journal as well as publishing articles elsewhere.

Rebecca R. Butler holds a BA in English Literature and an MA in Children's Literature, both from the University of Roehampton, the National Centre for Children's Literature. She is a wheelchair user, and has a special interest in the presentation of disabled characters in children's books. Rebecca works as a tutor, writer, conference speaker and literary critic. She has appeared on such television programmes as the BBC's Newsnight, and featured in DVD presentations for various charities. Rebecca has also won civic awards for her voluntary work, and lives in south-west London.

Linda Dick is married with two grown daughters and two grandchildren, and lives in Allegan, Michigan, on the banks of the Kalamazoo River. Linda is a part-time professor at Western Michigan University and at Kalamazoo Valley Community College, specialising in literature and creative writing. An avid reader, Linda also enjoys sailing on Lake Michigan and going to the beach. Her published writing credits include short poems and personal essays, as well as literary biographies for such well-known characters as Summer in *Missing May* and *White Fang*. Linda's current creative writing projects include two historical novels for young adults.

Ju Gosling was brought up in Essex and now lives in London. She wrote her MA disseration on the Chalet School series, and went on to examine the genre of girls' school stories for her PhD in Communications and Image Studies. In 1994 Ju founded Bettany Press, together with author and academic Rosemary Auchmuty. Since then she has published a range of titles connected with twentieth-century girls' literature, including non-fiction, original titles and reprints of rare books. Ju also works as an artist and writer, and is active in the Disability Rights and Disability Arts movements.

Meredith Guthrie graduated from Bowling Green State University with her PhD in American Culture Studies in 2005. She is now a lecturer in Communications at the University of Pittsburgh. Her areas of study include girl culture, the media, and the impact the media and marketing have on girls' body images, and she is now developing a book about the impact of popular culture on young adolescent girls. When she's not teaching or writing, Meredith spends her time chasing her young daughter, Sydney, while she chases the dog, Steve. In rare moments of calm, she likes to read novels. She hopes to pass on her love of reading to Sydney (since Steve is a lost cause).

Deborah Kent grew up in Little Falls, New Jersey. New Jersey was one of the first states to encourage the integration of blind students into mainstream schools, and when she entered eighth grade Deborah was able to transfer from a special class for blind children in the neighbouring city of Paterson to her local public school. After receiving a BA in English at Oberlin College, she earned a Master's degree from Smith College School for Social Work. In the mid-1970s she decided to leave her job in community mental health for a year to pursue her life-long dream of becoming a writer, and moved to a town in Mexico where she completed her first young adult novel. Since then Deborah has published an extensive range of both fiction and non-fiction. She is also active in the National Federation of the Blind.

Julie Newman is a disabled woman who lives in East London and is a campaigner for Disability Rights and Civil Liberties. She has a BA in Social Psychology from Sussex University and a Post-Graduate Diploma in Counselling and Interpersonal Skills from the Institute of Education at the University of London. She has worked as a Mental Health professional, and comes from a Nursing and Public Sector background. Her current work includes film-making, photography and documenting the work of Disabled Artists. She has a keen interest in social history.

Louise Norlie is the nom de plume of a New Jersey writer who has experienced disability since she was born in 1982 in Chicago, Illinois through living with osteogenesis imperfecta (also known as 'brittle bone disease'). Louise attended Fairleigh Dickinson University, but was not part of the literary community there as she took the practical path of studying business which has led to her current position in the government sector. Her writing has been published widely on the internet and in print, in publications such as *Disability Studies Quarterly*, *Audacity Magazine*, *Ragged Edge Magazine* and *Life is Full*. She has also published essays on the works of Herman Melville, Edgar Allen Poe, James Hogg, H. P. Lovecraft, and Susan Sontag. Louise recently completed her first novel, and is also an active member of a local writers' group. Her hobbies include playing the piano and listening to classical music.

ACKNOWLEDGMENTS

This book would never been completed if it had not been for the seven contributors, so my sincere thanks to them.

A deep thank you also goes to Ju Gosling for never giving up in her belief that Bettany Press would one day publish the book. She has also picked me up more times than I care to count and topped up my confidence levels more than once.

Thanks are also due to my many PAs who have shown interest in the concept of the book, as well as listening to me spout forth whenever I hit what I felt was a brick wall; to my friend and university lecturer Kay Stevenson, who looked at the early drafts of my chapters from an academic perspective; and to Joy Wotton for proof-reading assistance.

Above all, I owe thanks to my many book-collecting friends and dealers, particularly Sue Sims for selling me a copy of Dorita Fairlie Bruce's *Girls of St Bride's* in March 1994.

Helen A. Aveling
Chatham 2009

FOR MY PARENTS, WHO WOULD HAVE BEEN SO PROUD,

AND MY SISTER WHO IS!

INTRODUCTION

HELEN A. AVELING

According to my mother, as a child I read almost anything that had words on it, and devoured books at a fantastic speed. The 1970s were my reading heyday as a child; Barbara Willard and her *Mantlemass* books joined writers such as Rosemary Sutcliff. A different but also favourite series was Joan Lingard's 'Kevin and Sadie' series, set in the Northern Ireland of the 1960s and begun in 1970, about a boy and girl from opposite sides of the religious divide who fall in love and have to cope with the animosity as well as the turbulent life of the 1960s. At the time I probably did not realise just how radical the books were in terms of children's fiction, but they drew me back time after time, and were the closest to reality that I remember reading about .

As well as a myriad of more modern books, including Elinor M Brent-Dyer's Chalet School books (their publication spanned the period from 1925 to 1970), I grew up with the 'classic' girls' fiction of books like Johanna Spyri's *Heidi* (1880), Louisa Alcott's *Little Women* (1868) and their sequels, and Susan Coolidge's *Katy* series (1872-91). However, I never connected with the treatment of disability and illness within these. Instead, I responded to the characterisation of Clara, Beth, Katy and her Cousin Helen as if they were real people. I loathed Cousin Helen with an intensity only matched by my hatred of Pollyanna; failing to see the 'learning curve' that Katy went through in order to transmute her into a socially acceptable woman. I saw through the veil of illness that surrounded Beth to her timid personality, and completely ignored Clara's wheelchair, failing to grasp why everybody was so glad when she started to walk. Brent-Dyer often follows the nineteenth century and early twentieth century's passive portrayal of illness and disability (see Ju Gosling's detailed discussion in Chapter VIII.), but once again I failed to connect with it, seeing only the character and not their impairment.

As I outline in my chapter 'Not Only Cured or Killed: Disability in Early Twentieth-century Girls' School Stories' (p117), the very beginning of this book is traceable to a weekend in April 1994, when I shared my excitement at the discovery of someone who I considered to be a unique disabled character in terms of children's fiction, and specifically in terms of girls' fiction: Dorita Fairlie Bruce's Winifred Arrowsmith. My excitement, and that of my many book-collecting friends — most of them being non-disabled — caused me to wonder whether Winifred was a one-off, an aberration, in terms of school stories for girls. Winifred remains disabled throughout a three-book series written in the 1920s and 1930s, returning to her old school as an adult to become an eminently competent wheelchair-using secretary. At this point, my idea for a book was vague. All I wanted to do was to see whether my impression, gained through my childhood reading, that Winifred was atypical was correct, and that there were no more realistic portrayals of a character with a physical impairment in the twentieth century than her.

After a lengthy period of my own research, in 2003 I advertised on the English Department of the University of Pensylvania's email list, inviting self-defined disabled women to contribute to this book. Their remit was to examine the way in which physical and mental or emotional impairment is shown and used in children's fiction. The books examined here are those written specifically for, and largely read by, girls in the twentieth century.

I wanted most, or all, of the contributors to be women with disabilities, thus giving a unique slant to the publication. In keeping with feminist research methodology, I also wanted to forefront individual perspectives on the books being examined, and to highlight the contributors' personal responses to the fictional portrayals of disability and illness as former twentieth-century girl readers.

The decision to commission chapters from disabled women was a very conscious one. There is little in the way of writing by women with impairments about how they see the portrayal of disability or illness in fiction as a whole, and even less when it comes to stories for girls. The studies of disability, children's fiction and women's lives have, to date, existed almost in isolation from each other. This book seeks to bring them together, enabling personal commentary from disabled women on subjects which resonate for us as individuals. We are not seeking to present a definitive understanding of any of the books discussed here, instead we are saying: "This book is important to me and this is why." The book thus straddles three distinct disciplines, Women's Studies, Disability Studies and Children's Studies.

The book is structured into three sections as follows: 'Stereotypes'; 'Role Models' (including Winifred Arrowsmith); and 'Inclusion & Segregation'. Within each section, chapters fall into what, for convenience, I call the 'Early Period', 'Middle Period' and 'Modern Period' of the twentieth century. The 'Stereotypes' section examines the way in which disabled characters have reflected wider cultural stereotypes of disability in twentieth-century books for girls. In 'Role Models', writers look at how, or if, a disabled character is used by the author to put forward a model — idealised or realistic — for their readers to emulate. Finally, the 'Inclusion & Segregation' section looks at whether or not disabled characters are included within the wider community in the books being discussed. The time period for the three Early Period chapters is relatively static, being the years 1908-1939. The Mid-Period chapters tend to fall between the late 1930s to the 1950s in terms of their start dates, with the Modern Period chapters starting between 1970s and the early 1990s. The reason for this variation can be accounted for by the choice of books chosen by each chapter writer, as well as their particular focus and field of study.

For the most part, each writer was given a free hand in their selection of material to examine. There was one over-riding criteria which had to be applied throughout, being the use of the Social Model of Disability[1] in our analysis. This was important if the characters were to be treated holistically, rather than being a rag-bag of symptoms. As women with impairments, all of the contributors have been percieved as 'conditions', 'complaints' or 'afflictions' at some point in our lives; this renders us invalid as people and as women with a wide range of skills; and perpetuates the disabling response to us as individuals. We are reclaiming our validity as part of the human race and as part of society, and we seek to find evidence of this in childrens' fiction, especially fiction written entirely or primarily for girls.

The book's format is similar to one which has been

used by Jo Campling in *Images of Ourselves* (1981) and Jenny Morris in *Able Lives* (1989), in that it provides a vehicle for all eight writers to explore the subject of their choice in a way that brings out what matters to them as women with impairments. This, I believe, creates a valuable starting point, as it provides a personalised interpretation of not only how, for example, cerebral palsy in Jean Little's *Mine for Keeps* (1962) is developed as a theme, but what the societal environment was like at the time when the book was first published. It also provides a means to compare books that are more than fifty years old with those that were published in the last years of the twentieth century, and allows us to chart the progress — or lack of it — of positive and realistic characterisation of disability over the same time span from the perspective of disabled women ourselves. Who better to assess the realistic portrayal of a character with any impairment than people living with one?

Without wanting, or intending, to be elitist in any way, I and my co-writers have, for the most part, avoided the area covering learning and/or behavioural impairments. This is partly for the reason that none of us have sufficient experience on which we can draw to assess the portrayal of these themes, but the reality is that writers for children have even more readily avoided this subject in their fiction than they have avoided physical and mental or emotional impairments. Writers for children have always tended to home in on the 'physically obvious' in their fiction, it being easier to construct a character within these parameters even if the author has limited direct experience of the particular disabling condition or impairment. Thus the majority of books referenced in this study feature characters with sensory or mobility impairments or long-term health conditions, and little or no intellectual problems. The representation of learning and behavioural impairments in children's literature deserves its own study by someone far more experienced in the field than I, and I sincerely hope it will come in time as it is an extremely neglected field of study.

In choosing the title for this book, *Unseen Childhoods: Disabled Characters in Twentieth-century Books for Girls*, I sought one that would encapsulate the diverse nature of the essays contained in it, but one which would also highlight the fact that, to a greater or lesser extent, anyone with a disability remained invisible in wider twentieth-century society. Those who have a socially invisible impairment fare equally badly when others are later confronted with their access needs. They are condemned for not behaving 'normally' at these times, and censored for 'letting the side down' as if it is their fault that their body is not the same as the social group which calls itself 'normal'. Along with many disabled women, I refuse to label myself as 'impaired', or 'physically challenged': so far as I am concerned I simply have a body that is a law unto itself and gets around on wheels. The closest I come to a label is when I describe my dexterity as being 'haphazard' and my speech as 'distorted'.

Nevertheless, wider society wants to label us, and seems to need to create categories to place us in so that they are comfortable. This, in much of the twentieth century, led to many children with a disability being shut away in institutions, hidden from sight, forgotten (or ignored) by their families — as a doctor in 1960 suggested to my family that they did with me. Those children then lived their lives unseen by wider society, prevented by the culture of the day from taking part in any ordinary events with their peers in the outside world. It is unsurprising, then, that they were also for the most part invisible within fiction.

Historically, it has not just been people with impairments who have gone unseen through childhood. The same can be said of girls. In every patriarchal society throughout recorded time, it has been men and boys who have been important in the culture — girls have come a poor second to their brothers. Even in the later years of the twentieth century and on into this one, many cultures continue to favour boys over girls, sometimes with huge societal implications for the future. Girls have been taught that they do not matter, that they are on this planet only to serve and to please men. They have been taught to be silent and passive even when it is a difficult skill to learn, and literature has often been the means by which this lesson is taught.

If you are a woman with a disability, it can often feel as if you are doubly invisible and invalidated. We do not count in the scheme of things, being instead an object or obstacle that those around us have to contend with. People rarely ask us for opinions — we are apparently not thought capable of rational thought — or whether we mind being excluded from society's activities. Yet we have as much experience as other people, be it positive or not, as much right to be heard and listened to. I doubt if any contributor to this book would claim to know all there is to know about life with whatever impairments and access needs that they have — I certainly do not— but we do have the experience of our own life to bring to the feast of knowledge and common sharing. If we are kept away from this feast then society is losing a horseshoe nail[2], and our lives are rendered meaningless and insignificant.

Lois Keith's book, *Take Up Thy Bed And Walk* (2001), explored the 'classic' nineteenth-century books for girls in an innovative way by examining the six books under consideration in terms of death, disability and cure, the three lasting vehicles used to teach Victorian girls to become little women in every way. This book picks up these threads and follows them through a wide-ranging selection of books throughout the twentieth century and (just) into the twenty-first century. We see whether, or how, representation changes over the century, and watch as society's changes are eventually reflected in the fictitious portrayal of disability and illness.

Despite each chapter being written in isolation, when assembled they flow from each other in a manner that I had not wholly expected. There is little overlapping in content, yet they lock together like a jigsaw, and this, I hope, will enhance the overall impact this book has.

In Chapter I., 'Modelling Illness in the Early 20th Century', I examine a selection of books where TB is either a dominant or a sub-theme to look at how illness, one of the classic devices in early stories for girls, was handled on both sides of the Atlantic Ocean. The chapter goes on to look at several LM Montgomery titles, and notes the more honest treatment of North American heroines compared with their contemporaries in Britain, where writers sensationalised the most minor ailment.

In Chapter II., 'Beyond Beauty: Stigmatizing Social Behaviour in UK & North American Young Adult Fiction', Linda Dick traces social attitudes to disability in children's fiction with specific reference to the post-war obsession with beauty and its equation with physical perfection. Dick uses books originally printed in both North America and Britain and focuses on titles from the late 1950s through to the mid-1960s, discussing authors as diverse as Meriol Trevor, Judy Blume and Rosemary Sutcliff.

Louise Norlie, in her chapter 'Stereotyping in the Late 20th Century' (Chapter III.), examines the use of stock characters in titles from the 1980s through to the early years of the 21st century. As a contributor with lifelong experience of disability, Norlie tests her own hypothesis regarding the believability of disabled characters.

In Chapter IV., 'Not Always Cured or Killed: Disability in Early 20th-century Girls' School Stories', I look at a range of school stories from the period 1915–39. Winifred Arrowsmith proved not to be the only disabled character who was allowed to remain disabled, although she and Sadie Vanhessel from *The Only Day Girl* by Dorothea Moore are by far the most believable and realistic.

Deborah Kent's 'A Choice of Virtues' (Chapter V.) traces her responses as a visually impaired child in the 1950s to finding a positive and believable blind character, Susan Oldknow, in LM Boston's Green Knowe series. Kent then compares this to her response to the more traditionally passive portrayal of a blind person, the character Mary, in Laura Ingalls Wilder's better-known 'Little House on the Prairie' series.

In Chapter VI., Meredith Guthrie discusses American books written for diabetic girls in ' "I don't want to be different": Diabetes in Contemporary Young Adult Fiction'. Guthrie examines similar themes to Linda Dick, but from the perspective of 'self-help' books — not too dissimilar to Victorian chapbooks — which also address the ever-important issues (to teenage girls, at least) of self-image and boyfriends.

Chapter VII., 'Doing Not Dreaming: Disability

and Mental Health in Elsie J. Oxenham's Books', Ju Gosling and Julie Newman revisit the prolific 'Abbey' (and connected) books. Oxenham is unique both in her inclusion of mental and emotional health as a plot line, and her rejection of medicalised treatments in favour of folk dancing, crafts, nature and, crucially, friendship as a means of gaining health.

In Chapter VIII., 'Changes at the Chalet School: Illness and Disability in Elinor M Brent-Dyer's Chalet School Series', Ju Gosling reviews the treatment of ill-health and disability in Elinor M Brent-Dyer's 58-book series. She examines the shift on the author's part from the comparatively positive portrayals in the early titles of the 1930s and 1940s to the more markedly stereotyped and negative characters in the books of the 1950s and 1960s, and looks at the extent to which characters are included in or excluded from the wider school community.

Finally, Chapter IX., 'My Sibling The Other', is a discussion by Rebecca R. Butler about the literary representation of the psychological impact on a child of having a sibling who is disabled. This in turn throws light on how the disabled sibling is represented. Two of the three titles discussed here are intended for a younger readership than the majority of those discussed throughout the book, but all of the books have a wide range of reading ages.

Collating the chapters provided me with a unique overview of disabled child characters across the century. What struck home to me most was the fact that, despite pronounced advances for the better in Britain and North America in terms of society's approach to disability and to those of us whose bodies work differently to the accepted norm, few of these advances have been reflected in book form. The years immediately following 1981, designated as the International Year of Disabled People by the United Nations, saw the publication of books for children where disability was featured, but, as this book shows, they were of variable quality in terms of the portrayal of disability or impairment. Over the remaining years of the century standards rose, but, as can be seen in the following chapters, there remains much room for improvement, even within the tiny minority of books aimed at child and young adult readers that deal with disability in some form.

It is probably impossible to discuss, however briefly, the range of books available to children without mentioning Harry Potter. This series, perhaps more than any other, has made it socially acceptable for adults to read children's books in public. Authors such as Philip Pullman and Lemony Snickett have also contributed to the blurring of the edges of the categories. This has reinvented the world of books insofar as the popularity of reading in all age groups has vastly increased. However, the sad thing in terms of the inclusion of believable disabled characters is that, apart from Snickett, these authors have not included disabled characters in any great numbers — or, mostly and including JK Rowling, at all.

The authors here discuss a few exceptions, and there are others that do not appear in this book, such as Veronica Robinson's *David in Silence* (1965), a story centred around a deaf teenager moving to a new area; Gina Wilson's *A Friendship of Equals* (1981); Ian Strachen's *The Flawed Glass* (1989), about a young Scots girl with what appears to be cerebral palsy; and Jane Stemp's *Waterbound* (1995)[3]. However, viewing the century as a whole, it makes me wonder whether we are going to have to wait at least another generation before the overall situation changes in the world of fiction, and particularly within children's fiction. I also wonder whether the consumption of books where disabled characters are stereotyped, or most often are invisible, will have cemented out-moded ways of characterising anyone whose body — or mind — is different to such an extent that the young authors of today will reproduce exactly the same type of books for tomorrow's children?

The issue of how long a book remains in print is also very pertinent in respect of children's and young adult fiction. Less than a third of the fifteen titles discussed in the three late-20th/early 21st-century chapters are listed on Amazon UK with the certainty of "Buy New" against the title. I also conducted a straw poll of availability on Amazon UK of the four books mentioned above. *David in Silence* (1965) was listed as last being published by Pan in 1999, and is wholly unavailable. *A Friendship of Equals* (1981), which appears to have been printed only once, is also listed as being unavailable. *The Flawed Glass* (1989), listed as having been last published in 1991, is listed as "available as new and used"; as is *Waterbound* (1995), which is listed as last being published in 1996.

My personal experience of Amazon UK's definition of 'available' when there is no "Buy New" beside the entry always cautions me to double-check elsewhere before purchasing online through them, so I checked the websites of two major British bookshop chains, Waterstones and WH Smith. Both only listed *The Flawed Glass* as being available, with WH Smith's entry giving a different publisher and date to that of Amazon,[4] and a caveat that availability would be four weeks or more. When I then checked for the book on Little, Brown & Co's website I drew a total blank, as I also did on Pan

Macmillan's site. This begs the question of how likely it would be that one would actually get a new copy of *The Flawed Glass* through Amazon UK, or whether the only copies now available are ex-library ones. (Which in turn suggests that they are no longer available in libraries either.)

Today, there is a real chance that disabled characters will be entirely absent from children's and young adults' choice of reading material. If not, then their reading is likely to be peopled with characters who in some cases will be more artificial than those who come from the early years of the twentieth century. This will be the case whether or not readers mix with their disabled peers at school and socially. Young — and not-so-young — disabled readers will also continue to struggle to find fictional representations of characters 'like them'. Yet only when there are truly believable disabled characters in fiction, both for adults and children, will those of us who live with bodies and minds that work differently be members of society on a completely equal footing with everyone else.

NOTES

1) The Social Model of Disability emphasizes dignity, independence, choice and privacy. Furthermore, it perceives the individual holistically rather than labeling them with medical terms. One of the key concepts of the Social Model is that society disables people, and that this occurs when a person is excluded because of their access needs from something that other people in society take for granted. For example, using the Social Model, a wheelchair user who is unable to use a bus or enter the cinema is disabled because the bus does not have a lowered floor and the cinema a ramp, and not because of their impairment. The medical terminology of the Medical Model is paternalistic and exclusive, thus putting barriers in the way of the person with an impairment; it has a 'cannot do' labeling which pigeon-holes the individual, while the Social Model adopts the 'can do' approach to impairment, looking for streamlined ways around any difficulties, including the individual at every opportunity.

2) "For the want of a nail, the shoe was lost; for the want of a shoe the horse was lost; and for the want of a horse the rider was lost, being overtaken and slain by the enemy, all for the want of care about a horseshoe nail." (Benjamin Franklin).

3) Robinson, Veronica, *David in Silence*, André Deutsch (special edition for RNID), London, 1965; Wilson, Gina, *A Friendship of Equals*, Faber, London, 1981; Strachen, Ian, *The Flawed Glass*, Methuen, London, 1989; Stemp, Jane, *Waterbound*, Signature (imprint of Hodder), 1995.

4) Strachen, Ian, *The Flawed Glass*, Little, Brown & Co, London, 1990.

REFERENCES

Alcott, Louisa, *Little Women*, 1868.

Campling, Jo, *Images of Ourselves: Women with Disabilities Talking*, Routledge & Kegan Paul Ltd, London, 1981.

Coolidge, Susan, *What Katy Did*, 1872.

Keith, Lois, *Take Up Thy Bed and Walk: Death, Disability and Cure in Classic Fiction for Girls*, The Women's Press, London, 2001.

Little, Jean, *Mine for Keeps*, Little, Brown & Co, Canada, 1962.

Morris, Jenny, *Able Lives: Women's Experience of Paralysis*, Women's Press, London, 1989.

Spyri, Johanna, *Heidi*, originally published in Switzerland in 1880.

STEREOTYPES

EARLY PERIOD

I. MODELLING ILLNESS IN THE EARLY 20TH CENTURY

HELEN A. AVELING

"The sickly female is ... either literally too good for this world, in which case her illness is but an entry into the heavenly home where she really belongs, or she is the example of everything wrong with the world, in which case her illness is an extension of her corruption." (Herndl, Diane Price, *Invalid Women: Figuring Feminine Illness in American Fiction and Culture*, 1840-1940, p51).

In this chapter I shall look at LM Montgomery's 'Anne of Green Gables' and 'Emily' series, alongside Eleanor H Porter's *Pollyanna* and *Pollyanna Grows Up* and Frances Hodgson Burnett's *The Secret Garden* and E Nesbit's *Harding's Luck*, all of which are promoted and sold as 'Children's Classics' intended for readers between 9-12 years old.

In addition, I will take a brief look at *Betty Trevor* by Mrs George de Horne Vaizey, now available to read online at Project Gutenberg. These are all books in which a cure is effected, though in *Betty Trevor* it is a very tenuous one for the character with tuberculosis (TB). I will trace any shifts in the treatment of illness and disability to test the notion that their usage acts as ciphers to represent other things, such as the acquisition of more socially acceptable behaviour. I will also note differences, and similarities, between the ways in which illness is cured in books first published in Canada, the United States and Great Britain.

As Heather Munro Prescott (2004) observes, the motifs of children's illness are there to teach girls, in particular, how to be little women rather than harum-scarum tomboys. She goes on to say that, as "rates of child illness and mortality declined in the mid-twentieth century, public discussion of child sickness and death became less common, particularly in literature aimed at children and adolescents" (pp25-36).

The period 1900-39 is therefore a period of transition, with writers of children's fiction creating a 'Never-Never' land in which they could either opt to reflect the changing times, or could continue to use illness and death as a means to impart 'lessons'. Prescott also reveals that in the United States from 1910 onwards, stories emerged featuring, as one of their threads, the treatment and prevention of TB. These stories tended to be of the type that used the 'Never-Never' land to instruct their readers, and presented them with an idealised backdrop to the actual tale with healthy activities wining the battle against TB and other illnesses. Quite often these stories were written for boys, but there were stories for girls which "also tended to advocate developing strong, healthy bodies" (ibid, p36), as well as teaching them to be "so much softer and weaker" than men (Nesbit, E, *The Railway Children*, p217).

TURN-OF-THE-CENTURY BRITISH WRITERS

Writers in Britain often deliberately cushioned their readers from reality, propagating the male perspective which decreed that middle- and upper-class women were delicate flowers to be protected and cherished. Under no circumstance were girls and young women to be allowed the freedom to be themselves; instead, all hints of independence and autonomy of thought were to be crushed in favour of a compliant child-woman who accepted the controlling aspects of her life as normal. This was part of the British Victorian concept of 'The School of Pain'. During the learning of 'correct' or socially acceptable patterns of behaviour, fictional girls and boys often experienced a period where they were physically immobilised through illness or accident.

This continued until (in the case of girls) they had learned not to be a tomboy; not to seek independence of action; to be obedient to others (mainly men); and to seek to please at the expense of their own wants and needs. Once the child had learned whatever he or she needed to learn, the disability or illness vanished. The Victorians coupled this learning process with an intense evangelical message: that only by the intervention of God would the learning be made easier. Jonathon Gathorne-Hardy (1977) reports that in 1843 Mrs Ellis advocated: " '[t]he first thing of importance [to women] is to be content to be inferior to men — inferior in mental power in the same proportion that [they] are inferior in bodily strength.'"[1] Although Mrs Ellis was writing in the middle of the nineteenth century, the sentiments were still very clearly in operation during the first decade of the twentieth century.

An example of this is Mrs George de Horne Vaizey's *Betty Trevor* (available online at Project Gutenburg). Originally published in 1907, and with a slightly older readership than the other books in this chapter, the book clearly supports the notion that no matter how genteelly poor the family is, the daughters of the family become schooled in the correct reactions and aspirations in order that they will be good wife-material. All tomboy acts are put away forever by their teens, leaving their childhood firmly in the past. With the friendly support of her new friend Cynthia Alliot, who is slightly older than Betty, seventeen-year-old Betty learns to be a lady, with the emphasis on the linkage between a firm adherence to the social norms for a 'young lady' and a belief in God and in His plans for each person. Cynthia is portrayed as a hybrid between the two stereotypes: the docile woman; and the former tomboy who understands Betty's and her younger sisters' need for excitement in their life and who acts as a 'teacher' long before illness threatens.

The book ends with Cynthia as a standard invalid, enduring her illness quietly (p255). Betty has had to watch her good friend and mentor as she is isolated from the world for the sake of her health. It is not only Betty for whom Cynthia is a 'improving influence', however. Miles, two years Betty's senior, falls under Cynthia's influence and secretly falls in love with her. He is in no (financial) position to say anything about this to Cynthia at that point, and instead takes up a post as a mining surveyor in Mexico. At the end of the book Miles, on his first furlough home for six years, visits Cynthia. The visit begins with a warning to him from Mrs Alliot, Cynthia's mother.

> "You will be surprised to find Cynthia looking so well. She has put on flesh during the last few months, and the sea air has given her a colour. Last winter she was painfully thin. It has been a long uphill struggle, but now at last we begin to see definite improvement. The doctors are confident that it will be a complete cure if we are

very careful during the next two or three years. The great thing is to live in pure bracing air, and to keep her happy and cheerful. Anything that caused agitation or worry of any kind, would have a deleterious effect. She has a very sensitive nature, and things go deeply with her, more deeply than with most girls. Her father and I hide all worries from her, even our anxiety about herself. We, and all the friends who love her, must unite in doing everything in our power to spare her during these all important years. I know you will understand the position." (p296)

Miles sees his old friend lying on a couch:

with her golden mane wound smoothly round her head, with blue shadows under the sweet eyes, and hollows where the dimples used to dip in the rounded cheeks. At the first glance the air of delicacy was painfully pronounced, but as she smiled and flushed, the old merry Cynthia looked at him once more. (p299)

Although Cynthia reveals some of her frustration at being an invalid, she immediately pushes it away, as though she is somehow not *permitted* to have these emotions. She has joined the countless other invalids in their silent enduring of their illness, and it is threatening to swamp her. Is it only because of Miles' visit that she feels she can let her true emotions surface briefly? Perhaps.

She coughed again, and brushed her hair from her brow, evidently fatigued by her own emotion. The dainty finish and grace of her appearance, which had been the greatest charm in Miles' eyes long ago, was accentuated by her illness into a fragility which made her seem more like a spirit than a flesh-and-blood woman to his unaccustomed eyes. (pp299-300)

After the visit, Miles declares his love for Cynthia to her mother, despite Mrs Alliot's warning that Cynthia can "never be well". This is an expression which resonates with any Chalet School collector — or indeed any other girls' school-story writer[2] — as it is authorial sleight-of-hand for indicating that the character is not expected to live, or if they do live it will be as a complete invalid.

'THE SCHOOL OF PAIN' AND POLLYANNA

Writers from the early years of the twentieth century onwards increasingly secularised the concept, often reducing the 'The School of Pain's' message to the level of a didactic lecture or a device that simply carried the story forward. Books lost the powerfully spiritual element of the mid- to late-Victorian novels, such as Susan Coolidge's *What Katy Did* (1872) and Louisa May Alcott's *Little Women* (1868-9), where belief in God's omnipotence led the girl to make sense of the 'lessons' taught by illness by admitting that she needed His help.

Eleanor H Porter's aggravatingly pious *Pollyanna* (originally published in the United States in 1913) to some extent *is* a twentieth-century extension to the religious 'School of Pain', but somehow this overt emphasis on the child's belief jars on me in a way that neither Mrs March's or Cousin Helen's beliefs do. Why is this so?

A simplistic answer might be that Porter was a less skilled writer, but I think it goes deeper than that. Pollyanna's belief in God is real enough, but her insistence that there has to be something to be 'glad' about, even in the face of overwhelming odds, is what makes it grate on me.

The only time that Pollyanna cannot initially find anything to be glad about comes when she overhears the doctor's diagnosis that she will remain confined to bed following her accident towards the end of the book. It is only at this point that the character becomes a real person, transforming from a proto-plaster saint. Pollyanna gives in to the one thing that she banished from Beldingsville: despair. During this period of despair and subsequent hospitalisation, Pollyanna is enrolled in the same 'School of Pain' that Katy Carr was in before her, and finds it just as hard as Katy did, although she is cured as a result of surgery rather than by a transformation of attitude. Frustratingly, she is not shown in the hospital except through a letter to her Aunt Polly, and by the time that this is written Pollyanna is rapidly approaching her return to Beldingsville 'cured' and ambulant and is characteristically upbeat.

Porter does rectify that to a degree in *Pollyanna Grows Up* (1915), when nurse Della Weatherby tells her sister, Ruth Carew, that she needs a 'dose' of Pollyanna.

> "Her 'Glad Game'. I'll never forget my first introduction to it. One feature of her treatment was particularly disagreeable and even painful. It came every Tuesday morning, and very soon after my arrival it fell to my lot to give it to her. I was dreading it, for I knew from past experience with other children what to expect: fretfulness and tears, if nothing worse. To my unbounded amazement she greeted me with a smile and said she was glad to see me: and, if you'll believe it, there was never so much as a whimper from her

lips through the whole ordeal, though I knew I was hurting her cruelly.

"I fancy I must have said something that showed my surprise, for she explained earnestly: 'Oh, yes, I used to feel that way too, and I did dread it so, till I happened to think 'twas just like Nancy's wash days, and I could be gladdest of all on Tuesdays, 'cause there would not be another one for a whole week.'" (p10)

However, even this does not satisfy me, since it seems as if Pollyanna is perpetually acting a part in some play rather than being honest to herself. This is an example of how the application of 'The School of Pain' does not work properly in the twentieth century. Pollyanna hovers very close to being a prig, and though part of the problem is the dated language, it is largely because Porter does not employ the entire concept of the 'The School of Pain' in either of the Pollyanna titles still in print.

THE SECRET GARDEN AND AN ALTERNATIVE TO 'THE SCHOOL OF PAIN'

Frances Hodgson Burnett's *The Secret Garden* (published in Britain in 1911) deals with illness in a very different way. Burnett sees both children as suffering from an illness that is present to teach the child a 'lesson', but she does not employ any standard variant of the 'The School of Pain'. It is true that Colin imagines himself in pain, but his pain is self-induced and self-propagating.

Ten-year-old Mary Lennox is a thoroughly unpleasant child when she arrives at Misselthwaite Manor. Sent from India to Yorkshire after her parents' death, Mary is described as having a:

little thin face and a little thin body, thin light hair and a sour expression. Her hair was yellow, and her face was yellow because she had been born in India and had always been ill in one way or another. (p7)

We are told in this opening description that Mary had been "a sickly, fretful, ugly little baby" who had turned into "a sickly, fretful, ugly toddling thing" (p7). Mary's demeanour on her journey to England had been that of a spoilt child, earning her the slightly derisive soubriquet "Mistress Mary" which Burnett uses throughout the book, and she retreats into her shell of an autocratic "Missie Sahib", making her isolation on the journey to Britain even more complete.

The two children are very alike in the way that they are initially drawn. Both are unbelievably self-absorbed: examples include Mary's tantrum when her Ayah is not there to dress her; and Colin's fits of temper when he imagines that he feels another lump on his spine. Both are demanding: Mary in her insistence that Martha dress her; Colin in his determination that nobody sees him.

Colin Craven, like his father, is described in terms of his perceived impairment. Even after he has shed his "little Rajah" manner, Colin's name is permanently linked in my mind with his wheelchair or his perceived hunched back, while his father can be summed up by this description of a man who "was not so much a hunchback as a man with high, rather crooked shoulders, and he had black hair streaked with white. ... His face would have been handsome if it had not been so miserable." (p101)

Colin, on the other hand:

had a sharp, delicate face, the colour of ivory, and

he seemed to have eyes too big for it. He had also a lot of hair which tumbled over his forehead in heavy locks and made his thin face seem smaller. He looked like a boy who had been ill, but he was crying more as if he were tired and cross than as if he were in pain ... [and] Mary could not help noticing what strange eyes he had. They were agate grey and they looked too big for his face because they had black lashes all round them. (pp108-9)

This first description feminises Colin and turns him into a girl-like character. It is so successful that, simply by substituting the masculine pronouns for feminine ones, it gives a very convincing feminine description. I have explored the feminising of a young boy in Chapter IV: 'Cured Or Killed: Role Models In Early Twentieth Century Girls' School Stories', but there is a critical difference between the portrayals of Tom McGregor and Colin Craven. Colin has *imagined* himself to be ill, while Tom has not. Tom is genuinely ill; Colin is a hypochondriac. Just as Tom is a 'sweet' little child, Colin is the opposite. From his bed Colin terrorises the household in his father's long and frequent absences to the extent that the housekeeper, Mrs Medlock, is less than open about his presence in the house when telling Mary about her new home.

It takes Mary over six months (or half a book) before she meets her cousin, and then it is through inquisitiveness and a kind of positive disobedience, two things that the Indian Mary is unlikely to have indulged in previously. Mary's healing has begun, and she has gained permission from her uncle to have her "bit of earth" (p104) by the time that she meets Colin. As her first conversation with Colin progresses, Mary has figuratively to put her foot down and assert herself in order to preserve the secret nature of the garden when Colin says that he will instruct the staff to take him to the walled garden. Mary's response is one of fear and panic; fear that the garden will be taken from her, and panic that all she has gained in confidence and health will be destroyed by her cousin's autocratic manner. Both children had had beautiful mothers, and although to an adult reader Mary's mother is a silly, Society-obsessed woman, her neglected daughter regarded her as very beautiful:

> Memsahib, Mary used to call her that oftener than anything else, was such a tall, slim, pretty person and wore such lovely clothes. Her hair was like curly silk and she had a delicate little nose which seemed to be disdaining things, and she had large laughing eyes (pp8-9),

while the resented, and curtained-off, portrait of Colin's mother reveals a:

> picture of a girl with a laughing face. She had bright hair tied up with a blue ribbon and her gay, lovely eyes were exactly like Colin's unhappy ones, agate grey and looking twice as big as they really were, because of the black lashes all round them. (p117)

The contrast between the mother and her child, whether it is Colin or Mary, is very marked. On a purely physical level Mrs Lennox has the attractiveness that her daughter lacks, while Colin's agate grey eyes are cheerless and dull in contrast with his mother's. This contrast is used repeatedly to highlight the relative illness of the children. Burnett is using the attractiveness of the respective mothers as a goal that their child has to achieve if they are to succeed in life.

In Mary's case, simple exercise and fresh air propel her along the path away from illness of the psyche to physical health and therefore physical attractiveness, while Colin's journey away from illnesss is slightly more complex. He has to undergo two transformations; first, he must shed the pseudo-feminine invalid persona that Burnett initially uses in her physical description of the boy. Here Burnett is tapping into the American tradition of the sickly female, so Colin has to shed this in order to become masculine. At the same time he, like Mary, has to learn to shed his autocratic and unchildlike manner in order to adopt a child's malleable persona: Colin to grow up to 'be a man' and Mary to be — what? The final description of Colin is of

> a tall boy and a handsome one. He was glowing with life and his running had sent splendid colour leaping to his face. He threw the thick hair back from his forehead and lifted a pair of strange gray eyes — eyes full of boyish laughter and rimmed with black lashes like a fringe. (p250)

while the last description of Mary is far more passive, coming a few pages earlier than the one of Colin. Susan Sowerby tells Mary

> "...I'll warrant tha'rt like thy mother too. Our Martha told me as Mrs. Medlock heard she was a pretty woman. Tha'lt be like a blush rose when tha' grows up, my little lass, bless thee."... Mary had not had time to pay much attention to her changing face. She had only known that she looked 'different' and seemed to have a great deal more hair and that it was growing very fast. But

remembering her pleasure in looking at the Mem Sahib in the past she was glad to hear that she might some day look like her. (p234)

The passivity of this description brings the brief appearance of Mrs Lennox's suggested frivolity and her doll-like image to mind: a very different portrayal of Mary than we have been accustomed to. Thus, Colin will be an active man to Mary's passive woman. I feel let down by Burnett at this point; even when Mary was at her most obnoxious, she was at least *doing* something active, even if it was throwing a tantrum! The very last reference to Mary is when she comes running out of the walled garden — behind Colin. Is this what the transformation is all about for Mary, just becoming a means to help someone else?

A casual examination of a web page containing details of most of the many reissues of *The Secret Garden*[3] shows that there are very few covers that show Colin, and all that do mask his wheelchair completely. For me, as a wheelchair-user, this typifies the fact that, while a wheelchair can be, and for me is, a very useful 'bit of kit', society at large is so disconcerted by anything that isn't in the usual realm of things that it is blanked out, ignored and discounted. I am still the Invisible Woman, despite the push towards complete political correctness. I do not need Harry Potter's Cloak of Invisibility or the Psammead's ability to grant wishes — all I need is my wheelchair!

In the same way, Colin's wheelchair is not only ignored by the boy himself until he has a need for it, but it is ignored by Burnett and all the illustrators of the story since 1911. In fact, so thoroughly does Burnett ignore it that I have not been able to spot one full description of it in the entire book, even though I have to own to cheating a little by using the online Project Gutenberg copy and searching for "wheeled chair" and "chair-carriage". The nearest I have got to a full description of Colin in his wheelchair are the occasional phrases, such as when Colin was "carried down-stairs and [was] put in his wheeled chair ... [with] his rugs and cushions" (p179), which Colin later tore "off his lower limbs and disentangle himself" in order to show Ben Weatherstaff that he is not deformed (p191). Otherwise Burnett has Colin either in bed or reclining on a sofa.

In the final pages of the story, the chair, like Mary, is completely ignored by Burnett and the Cravens. Both are left behind in Colin's grand march home, as he walks side by side with his father. Does Dickon push the empty chair (which had been the means by which Colin got out of doors), accompanied by the sidelined Mary, back to the house? Or is it left in the now-not-secret garden, or even worse, is an anonymous servant told to take it to wherever the family stored unwanted things?

E NESBIT AND THE 'CURE'

For me, *Harding's Luck* by E [Edith] Nesbit — first published in Britain in 1909 — is a classic 'cure' story. Despite growing up in the working-class slums of 1900s London, Dickie is a very innocent and trusting character who has been left two family items by his father, a seal and an old-fashioned rattle that Dickie calls "Tinkler". They are clues to his true identity, as well as magical devices that enable Dickie to go back in time and be Master Richard Arden, the son of a comparatively wealthy man. This also helps Dickie to restore the family fortune in the twentieth century. The fantasy element is continued because Master Richard is not lame in the past. When it is time for "Master Richard" to walk for the first time after a long illness, Dickie needs encouraging, for:

> [i]n the old New Cross days he had not liked to look at his feet. He had not looked at them in these new days. Now he looked. ...
> "I dreamed that I was lame! And I thought it was true. And it isn't! it isn't! it isn't!" (pp85-86)

This reinforces the common perception that all disabled people want a cure and to be 'just like everyone else'. When Dickie wakes up from that first "dream", he has forgotten that he is lame until he trips as he gets up. He then has a "sickening sideways fall" (p98), as his weak leg gives way under his weight. Dickie ultimately chooses to return to his past life and to live out his days as Master Richard Arden. In this way Nesbit continues to reinforce the reader's belief that all disabled people hanker after a 'cure'.

In this book and its companion, *House of Arden* (1908), Dickie's choices directly influence his changes in fortune in both the twentieth and the seventeenth centuries. The chapters set in early Stuart times are the triggers for Dickie's actions in the twentieth century. Early on in the book, Dickie gets involved with Beale, a man with a slightly dubious set of morals. However, Dickie 'improves' Beale over the course of the book, in the same way as Cousin Helen 'improves' Katy. He therefore has the satisfaction of knowing that all will be happy ever after in the twentieth century, before he returns to the seventeenth century for the last time, "for Dickie is not lame" there. (p280)

In its online synopsis of *Harding's Luck*, Amazon

describes the book as "a story of injustice, poverty, deformity, magic, romance, suspense, sacrifice, and triumph over adversity that comes to its point with a fateful twist."[4] The wording in the synopsis is a damning one for the twenty-first century, as the inclusion of the word "deformity" is anachronistic at best. It is helping to perpetuate the negative portrayal of anyone whose body functions differently to the so-called norm, and simply reinforces the Medical Model of Disability. Surely the synopsis would be just as informative without that word? It would certainly be less insulting!

LUCY MAUD MONTGOMERY AND TB

LM (Lucy Maud) Montgomery's most widely available books in paperback today are her eight-book 'Anne of Green Gables' series, first published between 1908 and 1939, and her 'Emily' trilogy of books, first published between 1923 and 1927 (all published initially in Canada). The titles containing the name "Anne" are easily identifiable as part of the 'Anne' set, but two titles, *Rainbow Valley* and *Rilla of Ingleside*, require the reader/collector to know of their existence in order to complete their collection. My early 1980s 'Anne' Puffin paperbacks do not list them at all, and it was only when researching this chapter that I became aware of their place in the 'Anne' series.

When, in *Anne of the Island* (1915), Ruby Gillis develops TB, she loses her 'Gillis-ness', to misquote Mrs Rachel Lynde, becoming a suffering invalid in denial. The entire Gillis family is in total denial regarding Ruby's ever-declining health, and maintain the fiction that Ruby will be able to go back to teaching in the autumn. They do not want to admit either that Ruby is ill, or that the Avonlea society's perception of this is slowly stripping Ruby of all her personality, leaving just the illness to define this once active and lively girl. Ruby plays her part in the pretence, saying sharply when Anne asks if she is well: "... I'm perfectly well. I never felt better in my life. Of course, that congestion last winter pulled me down a little. But just see my colour. I do not look much like an invalid, I'm sure." (Montgomery, LM, *Anne of the Island*, p108). This denial lasts up to her last evening with Anne. Only then does she drop the pretence, admitting to her old school friend that she is afraid of dying.

The vocabulary used to describe Ruby, in both life and in death, is hauntingly familiar to me as a collector of Elinor M Brent-Dyer's Chalet School books, with her frequent use of TB as a descriptor. Ruby's features have become drawn, chiselled and sharp, creating an appearance that is stereotypical of late-nineteenth/early-twentieth century invalids. It would not matter what book one picks up from this era: if there is a character with TB, the illness siphons off their personality, leaving the TB as the identifying characteristic. Ruby does not own her TB: instead, it owns her. She is swamped by it to the point where Montgomery is able to say that Ruby:

> was even handsomer than ever; but her blue eyes were too bright and lustrous, and the colour of her cheeks was hectically brilliant; besides, she was very thin; the hands that held her hymn-book were almost transparent in their delicacy. (p100)

This is not the Ruby Gillis whom Anne went to school with; instead, it is Ruby transformed by illness. Anne finds it hard to reconcile the two, and even more so when the other is dead, for Ruby:

had always been beautiful; but her beauty had been of the earth, earthy; it had had a certain insolent quality in it, as if it flaunted itself in the beholder's eye; spirit had never shone through it, intellect had never refined it. But death had touched it and consecrated it, bringing out delicate modellings and purity of outline never seen before. (p135)

In one of the other 'Anne' books, *Anne of Windy Poplars* (1936, published in the UK as *Anne of Windy Willows*), one of Anne's new friends in Kingsport (where she is teaching prior to her marriage) treats Anne to a family history session in an old graveyard. Miss Valentine Courtaloe says quite proudly that her family were "very consumptive. Most of us died of a cough" (p47), before going into dizzying accounts of the many and varied characters who were laid to rest in the family plots. The apparent casualness of the announcement struck me until I remembered that, for anyone living in the years before the Second World War and the discovery of penicillin, TB was an unpleasant fact of life. Although as a Chalet School collector I knew this, somehow my knowledge had never made the transition across the Atlantic and into my reading of the 'Anne' books.

Elsewhere, Montgomery treats illness as a much more minor theme, as in her 'Emily' trilogy, originally published in Canada between 1923 and 1935. The daughter of parents who both died of TB or TB-associated illnesses, Emily Starr has had ten years of running wild and enjoying the freedom of not attending school. She has been schooled instead by her father, much to the disapproval of his servant Ellen Greene. Emily is periodically described as having the *potential* for developing TB — TB was not then understood to be infectious — which is why she has not been sent to school. Emily's late father's servant, Ellen Greene, informs the newly orphaned ten-year-old that she is "queer" and too accustomed to older company (*Emily of New Moon*, 1923, p30). This is just before taking her downstairs to meet her Murray relations, who are a little surprised by the "alien, level-gazing child" who showed that she was "anything but meek and humble" with her "slight, black, indomitable little figure" (p36).

Coming to the trilogy as an adult, I found it difficult to lose myself in the tale of a young orphan being brought up by her mother's family. I found it hard, too, to convince myself that Montgomery herself knew what to make of this creation of hers. From research, I know that these three books, targeted predominantly at readers aged 9-12 (as with the 'Anne' series), are autobiographical in a way that the 'Anne' books are not. Certainly one of the hindrances to my enjoyment of the trilogy is Montgomery's ambivalence and uncertainty as to what to do about Emily's health. Ellen badgers the child to remember her hat in the opening pages of *Emily of New Moon*, saying that she can't "monkey with colds the way some kids can" (p12). The very first description of Emily is of a child with a:

> long, heavy braid of glossy, jet-black hair ... In all else [her father] thought, she was like the Starrs — in her large, purplish-grey eyes, with their very long lashes and black brows, in her high, white forehead — too high for beauty — in the delicate modelling of her pale, oval face and sensitive mouth. (pp12-13)

The description of Emily's "glossy" hair is far removed from the more usual portrayal of a sickly child — or even one who is at risk of TB — although her delicate, pale face and sensitivity echo nineteenth-century descriptions of the 'consumptive'. This dichotomy follows Emily throughout her experiences in the three books, as if Montgomery cannot make up her mind whether to make the character consumptive or not. Emily herself frequently refutes this perception by (mainly) her Aunt Ruth Dutton, saying "I am *not* consumptive" when her aunt suggests it (p321).

Montgomery indicates her ambivalence about Emily's health by allowing her infinitely more freedom to be an ordinary child than the British Victorian/Edwardian writers would have dared to do, and indeed uses the device of Emily's health to create the space for her to enjoy her freedom. However, she also appears to have changed her own perceptions of TB to some extent. Compare Ruby Gillis' description (written eight years earlier) with that of Emily's father who:

> had lain on the sitting-room lounge all day. He had coughed a good deal, and he had not talked much to Emily, which was a very unusual thing for him. Most of the time he lay with his hands clasped under his head, and his large, sunken, dark-blue eyes fixed dreamily and unseeingly on the cloudy sky that was visible between the boughs of the two big spruces in the front yard. (p10)

Despite this, Mr Starr later summons up the strength to lift the ten-year-old Emily into his lap. TB has not swamped him in the way that it had Ruby Gillis, and even allowing for the fact that we see Douglas Starr through his daughter's eyes, he is fitter than Ruby. *Ruby* had not had the energy to do more than leave her needle sticking in an uncompleted piece of embroidery on the afternoon of her death (*Anne of the Island*, 1925, p135). In the first book in the trilogy, Emily even survives an attack of measles, despite sinking into delirium on the fifth day. As a result of the delirium, she is instrumental in solving an eleven-year-old mystery — without the drama which would have accompanied that feat in the hands of a British writer of the same era.

Although Montgomery uses Emily's 'potential' for developing TB to allow her more freedom as a child, when later boarding with her unsympathetic Aunt Ruth while she attends High School, Emily is constantly being reminded that she is susceptible to TB whenever her aunt wants (or needs) to feel she is 'in control'. On reading the trilogy, I feel that Ruth Dutton uses the real or imagined threat of TB as a control mechanism, helping her to feel that this strange niece *can* be controlled. The first meeting between Emily and her Murray relations really sets the tone for Ruth Dutton's complete lack of comprehension of the complex personality of this unusual child. Emily has to tolerate her aunt's somewhat futile attempts to rule her life while she is in Shrewsbury, partly because Ruth clings to the idea that, because both Emily's parents died because of TB, Emily herself is a delicate flower who must be shielded from all draughts while in her care.

> "Em'ly Starr, put that window down at once. Are you crazy?"
> "The room is so close," pleaded Emily.
> "You can air it in the daytime, but never have that window open after sundown. I am responsible for your health now. You must know that consumptives have to avoid night air and draughts."

"I'm not consumptive," cried Emily rebelliously.
"Contradict, of course."
"And if I were, fresh air any time is the best thing for me. Dr Burnley says so. I hate being smothered." (*Emily Climbs*, 1925, p104)

It is not just her family who persist in regarding Emily as being in imminent danger from TB. At the beginning of *Emily Climbs*, Emily finds herself in a position where she is trapped and unavoidably overhears neighbours of her Aunts Elizabeth and Laura disparaging her, but the climax of this conversation comes when one of them says, rather dismissively, " 'But then she probably won't live through her teens. She looks very consumptive. Really, Ann Cyrilla, I do feel sorry for the poor thing.' " (p75)

However, by the beginning of *Emily's Quest* Montgomery has finally decided that Emily is *not* consumptive, and this is reflected in the accident that the nineteen-year old Emily has when she trips over a basket of mending left on the stairs. The effect is similar to Katy Carr's accident in that Emily has a vague back injury which leaves her in bed for months, but Montgomery adds a very painful foot injury that leads to septicaemia and the threat of amputation. Montgomery allows a short fever followed by months of pain and the risk of permanent lameness, but as the spring arrives, so Emily's recovery begins. There is no drama and the entire winter of illness occupies only four pages of narrative (*Emily's Quest* 1935, pp62-65) — very different to many of Montgomery's British contemporaries who, I suspect, could have turned four pages into four chapters.

CONCLUSION

The stereotypical way in which an ill or disabled person in children's fiction is just a collection "made up of scraps and patches" (Montgomery, 1923, p39) frequently robs them of all individuality. I set out on this chapter wondering how true that assertion was in the dozen books that I have chosen to reference. I was surprised to discover that it was the way in which those "scraps and patches" were used that influenced how the character was drawn, rather than there being changes influenced by the country or year the books were first published.

In terms of the books in which there was reference to TB, it is clear to me that Mrs George de Horne Vaizey romanticises the situation, relying on Victorian language and values to convey the positive influence of the 'sufferer'. If anybody had asked me to describe the archetypal 'pale and interesting invalid', I know I would have come up with a description similar to the illustration by EP Kinsella in *Betty Trevor*. This illustration of Cynthia saying goodbye to Miles (perhaps for ever) shows a young woman in long frilly clothes lying on a chaise longue, propped up with cushions and with a shawl round her shoulders. The lightness in shading of Cynthia's clothing echoes Vaizey's description, but it also draws one's eyes to the invalid, just as Montgomery's description of Ruby focuses the reader's mental image.

However, in her description of Ruby, Montgomery does not use the slightly cloying phrasings of her British counterpart. Ruby *is* fair-haired, as Cynthia is, and wears a "white shawl wrapped about her thin shoulders" (Montgomery, 1925, p129) the last time that Anne sees her, but there is a freshness and vitality in the description that is missing in

Vaizey's account of Cynthia's farewell to Miles Trevor. Perhaps it is because Ruby and Anne are outside, despite it being late evening, but there is a residual spark in Ruby that Cynthia has extinguished in herself. Ruby does not apologise for feeling afraid and resentful that her life is at its end in the way that Cynthia does, so despite being swallowed up by her illness, there is something that sparkles in Montgomery's final descriptions of Ruby. There is also a vibrancy in Emily from the very first page of *Emily of New Moon* to the final page of *Emily's Quest* that refuses to be suppressed, and this makes the Canadian books far more relevant and appealing to the modern readership.

In assessing *The Secret Garden,* I have to take issue with Frank Eyre (1971) and his assertion that the book belongs "in spirit to the last century" and Frances Hodgson Burnett "could only by strict interpretation of date be considered as [a] twentieth-century writer".[5] The reason I take issue is that, in comparison with E Nesbit's two books, Burnett's book does not contain the constant authorial comments that are a feature of many of Nesbit's published stories. It also presents illness of the psyche in a holistic way rather than taking a dogmatic approach, so that as Mary explores the huge gardens at Misselthwaite Manor, she begins to heal without the intervention of religion or medicine. (This approach to mental and emotional health is further reflected in Oxenham's books; see Chapter VII for details.) Admittedly, once Colin goes outside and starts to think of other things than his imagined ill-health, the children attribute the changes in Colin to "Magic", but this is not the author applying religion or the belief that everything is attributable to God.

If any of the books that I have selected qualify for

Eyre's disparaging assessment, it is, in my opinion, the 'House of Arden' pair. Published in Britain about the same time as *The Secret Garden*, these two books by E Nesbit are full of authorial judgments which overlay and interrupt the story to such an extent that I am surprised publishers still publish and sell these two interlinked stories. They also contain the stilted language that I associate with books given as Sunday School Prizes earlier in the century.

Despite all this, I still find (and always have found) Nesbit's two books far less irritating than pious Pollyanna and her infernal Glad Game! I know why this is so. The Glad Game has always felt affected, while Dickie's attempts to speak "proper" are on one level innocent and harmless. Pollyanna is brought up short when she is the invalid, but unfortunately it does not last, and she is soon back talking in platitudes to ill people as if this is the only way that an invalid can understand. It is this stereotype that all the other authors manage to dodge, even Nesbit and Vaizey: that of an invalid being 'done to'. Anyone with any kind of speech difficulty will immediately understand the subtle difference between being talked *to* rather than *at*, and this is what Porter in the guise of Pollyanna does not do. The character somehow manages to leave me feeling that I have been spoken/read *at*, and this is what makes her Game so irritating.

In conclusion, therefore, I feel that Lucy Maud Montgomery is the most sucessful in offering a unsentimental portrayal of illness, with Frances Hodgson Burnett a close second, considering the culture that they were living and writing in. These writers give us memorable characters who happen to be ill/dying, and manage not to smother the character with the illness, however vague it may be.

The other three sucuceed to a lesser degree, with, predictably (as she is not to my knowledge in print) Mrs George de Horne Vaizey coming last. All the characters have their good points in terms of portrayal, but out of all of them, it is Emily and Mary who linger most in my mind.

AUTHOR DATES

Frances Hodgson Burnett 1849-1924

Mrs George de Horne Vaizey 1857-1917

E Nesbit 1858-1924

Eleanor H Porter 1868-1920

LM Montgomery 1874-1942

NOTES

1) Mrs Williams Ellis, *The Women of England*, 1843, in Gathorne-Hardy, *The Public School Phenomenon*, p 253.

2) See for example May Wynne's *Peggy's First Term* (1922).

3) www.fantasticfiction.co.uk/b/frances-hodgson-burnett/secret-garden.htm

4) www.amazon.co.uk

5) Frank Eyre, *British Children's Books in the Twentieth Century*, p19.

REFERENCES

Burnett, Frances Hodgson, *The Secret Garden*, Penguin Books, London (first published in USA in 1909, and in Great Britain by William Heinemann in 1909).

de Horne Vaizey, Mrs George, *Betty Trevor*, Religious Tract Society, London (online at www.gutenberg.org/etext/21117), 1907.

Eyre, Frank, *British Children's Books in the Twentieth Century* (originally published as *20th-century Children's Books* in 1959 for The British Council by Longmans, Green and Co), revised and enlarged edition, 1971.

Gathorne-Hardy, Jonathon, *The Public School Phenomenon* (first published by Hodder and Stougton 1977), Penguin Books, London, 1979.

Herndl, Diane, *Invalid Women: Figuring Feminine Illness in American Fiction and Culture 1840-1940*, University of North Carolina Press, Chapel Hill, NC, 1993.

Montgomery, LM, *Anne of the Island*, Puffin, London (first published in Great Britain by Harrap 1925).

Montgomery, LM, *Anne of Windy Willows*, Puffin, London (first published in Great Britain by Harrap 1936; US title *Anne of Windy Poplars*).

Montgomery, LM, *Emily Climbs*, Puffin, London (first published in Great Britain by Harrap 1925).

Montgomery, LM, *Emily of New Moon*, Puffin, London (first published in Great Britain by Harrap 1923).

Montgomery, LM, *Emily's Quest*, Puffin, London, (first published in Great Britain by Harrap 1927).

Nesbit, E, *The House of Arden*, 1908.

Nesbit, E, *Harding's Luck*, T. Fisher Unwin, London (first impression 1923), 1926.

Nesbit, E, *The Railway Children*, Puffin, London (first published 1906).

Porter, Eleanor H, *Pollyanna* Harrap & Co, London (first published in USA 1913.

Porter, Eleanor H, *Pollyanna Grows Up*, Harrap & Co, London (first published in USA 1915 and in Great Britain in 1927).

Prescott, Heather Munro, 'Stories of Childhood Health and Disease' in Meckel, Richard A, Golden, Janet, Prescott, Heather Munro, *Children and Youth in Sickness and in Health: A Historical Handbook and Guide*, Greenwood Press, Westport, CT, 2004.

www.fantasticfiction.co.uk/b/frances-hodgson-burnett/secret-garden.htm

MIDDLE PERIOD

II. BEYOND BEAUTY: STIGMATIZING SOCIAL BEHAVIOUR IN UK & NORTH AMERICAN YOUNG ADULT FICTION

LINDA DICK

BORN in 1951, I grew up in white, middle-class America. I always had plenty to eat, a nice home, good clothes and loving parents. All of the children in my school were 'normal', in that none of them exhibited any obvious physical or mental impairments. And because I never saw impairments in the children that I went to school with, I did not have an incentive to seek out books with disabled protagonists. What creates that sense of 'normality', when in fact there is nothing normal about a segregated society? Many times, "the terms used to describe people with disabilities can be a litmus test of attitudes towards them" (Kilham, 2001). When I go back to my childhood and ask the question — where are the disabled children in my childhood? I find that they only appear briefly in fiction, and then as watered-down characterizations intended to be more of a plot device or window dressing in books like *Heidi* (1880) and *The Secret Garden* (1909), or as syrupy sweet renditions in books such as *Pollyanna* (1913) — all of which were originally published decades before I read them.

While I never feel as if the characters in these books are truly ill or disabled:

stories about child health and disease give us

> insight into the social milieu in which they [are] written. They tell us much about ... what values the society hope[s] to transmit to children and adolescents.... [Sometimes] the images of the sick and suffering child are used as a metaphor for larger social ills. Historically, high rates of child illness and death prompted culturally sanctioned responses. (Meckel, 2004, p25)

Even in *Heidi* and *The Secret Garden*, the strong message is that if you are good and pure, work hard enough and be a good girl or boy, then your impairment will fall away from you as if it were an old snake skin. A whole and perfect new body is revealed, one that conforms to the natural world of 'normality'. I see this as a plot device because "as rates of child illness and mortality decline in the mid-twentieth century, public discussion of child sickness and death becomes less common, particularly in literature aimed at children and young adults" (ibid, p25).

> the reform activity of the early twentieth century [in the United States which] culminates in a view of childhood that children be sheltered from the unpleasant aspect of the adult world. This attitude is reflected in the children's literature of the 1920s and 1930s, which tends to avoid harsh social realities caused by war and economic uncertainty. (Meckel, 2004, p36)

'Baby boomer' children of the white middle-class were placed in an insular world, protected from the vulgarities of anything not beautiful and perfect, thus invoking the Greek model of perfection. Therefore children with a motor or cognitive impairment were removed from this idealized landscape, both in practice and in literature. The appearance of Clara in *Heidi* and Colin in *The Secret Garden* were not realistic renditions of the disabled child in society, but simply plot devices to allow for the wholesome goodness and purity of the protagonist to shine. This is why the books continued to be popular with parents and educators for so long.

SOCIAL CONDITIONS

The white middle-class world of the early to mid-twentieth century saw the rise of the institution and 'special' schools, which caused several things to happen. Disabled people were removed from the public sphere, but they were often also given the tools that were needed to operate in a culture that had as its primary ideal personal mobility, independence and self-sufficiency, i.e. (segregated) training and work. As the post-World War II family moved from the urban to suburban, a shift in family structure can also be blamed for the non-acceptance of the infirm or disabled. Gone were the extended family units, replaced by the nuclear ideal family unit of a father, a mother, a son and a daughter all housed in the little white house on Main Street with a picket fence in middle-class America. Keeping up with the Joneses didn't include a wheelchair ramp up the front lawn to the front porch. Such an addition to the home of a disabled child or adult was perceived as being ugly, and so not appropriate for what society constituted as 'normal'.

This ideal of what constituted beauty/normality was transmitted to the public sphere through television programmes such as "Leave it to Beaver"; through advertisers' use of glamorous people; and through Hollywood images of what was supposed to be beautiful and normal — even today, all of these still inform and build the public attitude about what constitutes 'normal'. Schriner points out that, "to the extent that society fully accommodates a condition, it ceases to be a disability as defined under the human variation model" (Schriner, 2001). Thus the American landscape informed by marketing, Hollywood and television became a landscape of non-acceptance for the 'non-normal'.

This idealized world based on upward mobility in a capitalistic society does not accommodate a condition that doesn't fit into the mould of normal, nor does it make room for any child with a disfiguring physical attribute or cognitive impairment. At the same time, upward economic mobility allows for medical intervention to occur, and the idealized perception that medical science can fix anything feeds into the idealized notion of what is beautiful and normal. So while disabled people were shunned, they were also seen to be beginning to enjoy the greatest benefits from medical intervention since the beginning of the twentieth century — advancements which were viewed as being necessary to allow them to become independent and self-sufficient citizens.

DEFINING DIFFERENCE

As a college professor who specializes in teaching children's literature, I have been curious for a long time as to how the disabled child sees or does not see themself reflected in the classroom library. With the lack of availability of disabled protagonists, the disabled child suffers a lack of self-worth. They become one of the 'Other', an outsider. When a young adult feels as if they are on the fringe of society due to an impairment, their ego is doubly impacted. "Adolescence is a period of development that involves preparation for social roles associated with young adulthood..." (Palisano, 2007), which is often the subject of the young adult novel.

If we re-visit some background information on the history of illness and mortality in the United States, then perhaps a pattern may emerge as a comparison model when looking at impairment in young adult literature in the years 1940-1980. Pre-1900, the rate of illness and child mortality in the United States was approximately 20%. Of the remaining 80%, many children suffered life-long impairments due to multiple illnesses, accidents or 'abnormalities' at birth. With the rise of the institutions and special schools in the twentieth century, many of these disabled children were removed from the public sphere (Meckel, 2004, p14). Childhood disability became an uncommon sight since, alongside segregation of disabled children, medical progress caused "...children to [experience] their greatest improvement in life expectancy by 1930" (Meckel, 2004, p16).

How, then, did this shape the mindset of the public with regard to physical and mental impairment in young adults by the middle of the century? When the disabled child disappeared from the public landscape, so did they disappear from the literary landscape, as parents of 'normal' children strove to insulate the next generation from the disturbing or ugly sight of things not defined as aesthetically pleasing by the cultural norms and expectations of white middle-class American post-World War II life.

ART AS A CULTURAL MIRROR

In reviewing the presence of impairment in young adult literature between the years 1940-1980,

I went in search of books that portray disabled protagonists. I wanted to know how the culture in the story perceived the impairment. By using the text as a mirror for the cultural values in place at the time that the books were published, these cultural values and what the stigma of disability meant for that time-frame might be revealed. I was curious, therefore, to see the disabled protagonist in action within the literary world, and to discover what social constructions were in place which regulated the ability or impairment of the protagonist.

After an overview of the literature under review, I found some basic questions to pose:

> How does the disabled protagonist function within the literary world? Through independence? Through the help of others? Through the functionality of environment?
>
> What does the disabled protagonist think about his/her own impairment? How are the cultural norms reflected by the characterization of the literary players in the text? How is the disabled protagonist or character stereotyped?
>
> How does the characterization of a disabled protagonist move the plot forward? Is the disabled protagonist a plot device or window dressing?

LITERARY INVESTIGATION — AN OVERVIEW

In a survey of books from 1940 to the late 1980s, I found hundreds to select from, most of them now out of print. I used two main bibliographic sources for my search: *Notes From A Different Drummer* by Barbara H. Baskin, published in 1977; and *Accept Me As I Am* by John B. Friedberg, published in 1985. Friedberg's book is especially helpful because it categorizes books by impairment. After reading a couple of dozen books that are still in print, I settled on the following list for inclusion in the discussion that follows:

Deenie by Judy Blume (1973)
The Young Unicorns by Madeleine L'Engle (1968)
Mine for Keeps by Jean Little (1962)
Warrior Scarlet by Rosemary Sutcliff (1957)
The Rose Round by Meriol Trevor (1963)

In the texts listed above, I found some interesting impairment classification distinctions. The first classification is that of the 'temporary impairment'. Deenie fits into this category quite nicely because she will only be impaired for four years, and then her stint as a disabled child will be over. The second classification can be described as the 'acquired impairment'. Emily in *The Young Unicorns* (1968) is blinded when she is about eleven years old, and will spend the rest of her life without sight.

The third classification is that of children who are born with 'motor or cognitive impairments'. For Sally, in *Mine for Keeps* (1962), the motor impairment is cerebral palsy. Deenie and Sally are products of medical and technological intervention in that they wear mechanical devices such as braces that help to restrict Deenie's spinal curvature and assist Sally with her mobility.

Drem in *Warrior Scarlet* (1957), and Theo in *The Rose Round* (1963), also experience what might be considered impairments from birth, both having limited use of and growth in one arm and hand.

As an adult, I now experience an 'invisible' illness, Meniere's Disease, which affects the balance of the inner ear. Suddenly, going to a concert or a movie theatre can throw me into a state of equilibrium topsy-turvy. My ability to drive or even walk across the room can be eliminated or greatly reduced within an hour of the attack. Yet, for all practical purposes, I look just fine. 'Normal'. And this is how people react to me on first meeting me. For me, my new normal is to carry around a supply of Dramamine, because the irritated vestibular canal triggers the brain's vomit reflex without much warning. While my impairment may not be noticeable to others, we cannot help but compare our own physical and mental traits to people we come into contact with, be they real or literary. It is a natural ethnocentric trait which started out as a survival method in early man. Yet as time goes by, and we recognize the differences in people around us, accepting the differences seems to be difficult.

Drawing on my own experience, I have specifically avoided including books like *The Planet of Junior Brown* (1971), which deals with mental illness, because visible physical impairment is so much easier for people to react to and either reject or accept almost instantly. That is not to say that less visible impairments — which also includes illnesses such as diabetes and epilepsy — are less important, but they will not be discussed here.

HOW DOES THE DISABLED PROTAGONIST FUNCTION WITHIN THE LITERARY WORLD?

Deenie is the protagonist in Judy Blume's novel of the same name, first published in 1973. She is living in a middle-class family in New Jersey, and has just entered the seventh grade. As a pretty and popular twelve-year-old, Deenie is self-assured in her world of school and cheerleading tryouts, and is not so sure about her mother's aspiration that Deenie becomes a fashion model. The fact that Deenie is poised on the edge of the fashion industry acts as a telling signifier of American society and the culture's fascination with the body beautiful.

The month that Deenie tries out for cheerleading, she is diagnosed with scoliosis. Left untreated, Deenie will have a curved spine which will leave her with an unacceptable appearance within mainstream society. As Deenie is entering her teenage years, though, adolescence weighs in as another self-esteem issue that she will be faced with during the four years of wearing a 'Milwaukee Brace', a device that screams of difference and abnormality. Deenie finds early on that wearing the brace greatly limits her mobility. She can't easily retrieve items dropped on the floor; nor sit comfortably at a table to eat or write; and she can't disguise the brace altogether — even though she wears it under her clothing, parts of the brace do show. Deenie finds it necessary to rely on the help of others in order to function and to continue to complete day-to-day tasks. While Deenie's father treats her as if nothing has changed, her mother is constantly bemoaning the loss of the modelling career that Deenie didn't want anyway.

Deenie's mother reflects the perception of society that people get what they deserve. When she sees Deenie in the Milwaukee Brace for the first time, she cries: "Oh, my God!...What did we ever do to deserve this?" (p85) She resonates the idea that:

> the association of physical abnormality with moral taint is as deeply ingrained in Western

culture as is the compassionate view [to help the sick] .... Until well into modern times, the superstition persisted in Europe that the deformed were works of the Devil. (Katz, p19, 1981)

The impression Deenie's mother has of the entire affair is that Deenie is sick, when Deenie doesn't feel ill at all and keeps insisting she is *not* sick. Deenie ends up confronting this idea of illness versus deformity for several chapters, as she encounters the different people in her world while wearing the brace.

In a shopping spree, trying to find clothes to fit over the brace, Deenie becomes overwhelmed and exasperated. She just wants to go home and wear her older sister's hand-me-downs. Her mother, typical for the time frame, puts guilt on Deenie by saying "We're all trying to help you, ... but if you won't help yourself there isn't much we can do." (p99) It is noteworthy, however, that Deenie's parents are able to afford to seek medical intervention, which reflects the changing attitudes that began to occur after 1930 towards medicine and intervention.

Deenie's teachers react in practical ways, helping Deenie to see her new status as being as normal as possible given the fact that she is now wearing a brace, which Deenie indignantly describes as: "Right now I feel like I'm in a cage and no undershirt's going to change that!" (p89) The vice-principal of the school, however, sees Deenie in the category of 'handicapped child'. Due to the brace, Deenie is now eligible to ride the 'special bus'. Deenie wants no part of the special bus, and continues to move forward with as little change to her daily routine as possible.

Within Deenie's circle of friends, her girlfriends

especially seem to play into the idea that scoliosis isn't so bad. They think, as Deenie initially does, that she can just have an operation and then everything will be all fixed up just fine. They even chip in to buy Deenie a pretty pink nightgown for the expected hospital stay. When the hospital stay doesn't materialize and Deenie is faced with wearing the brace, she is more of an enemy to her appearance than anyone else around her.

Deenie's self-perception is that she is now a freak, an outcast. In this, she reflects what Rothschile observes in "...that the standards for physical integrity and perfection as well as for beauty appear to be very strict in Anglo-Saxon countries, especially among the middle classes, with any deviation from the highly admired state of perfection being punishable by social stigmatization." (Katz, p20, 1981) Deenie reacts both to herself with this world view, and to her perception of what she thinks others are thinking about her new status as 'Other'.

After Deenie's diagnosis, and while she is waiting for the Milwaukee Brace to be made, she has an opportunity to walk by Old Lady Murray, who runs a vending stand near the bus stop. Old Lady Murray's body demonstrates the results of untreated scoliosis, and she has a hunch-backed appearance. In the past, Deenie has avoided looking Old Lady Murray in the face. When Deenie and her friends stop at the stand after a movie, Deenie shows her changing views on impairment with:

> "I didn't look away from Old Lady Murray like usual. Instead I said 'Hello' to her, which I've never done before. She said 'Hello' back and I could see her gold front tooth .... I studied the bump on her back and wondered if she always had it or if it grew there when she got older." (p59)

In a typical reaction and an effort to gain back some control over her life, Deenie cuts off her long, beautiful hair. She is reduced at times to accepting unsolicited help from her father, and to calling for her mother to help her because she couldn't reach her sanitary napkin supply at the onset of her menstrual cycle.

When her friends come over to visit after the brace is in place, they "were being careful not to look directly at [Deenie]." (Blume, 1973, p96) They don't have the vocabulary to express their feelings until Janet says "but if you want to know the truth ... it was a real shock, even though we knew the doctors would have to do something because you can't grow up with a crooked spine." (p98)

One of Deenie's biggest concerns is how the boy she likes will react to the brace. This is probably the only part of the story that I don't quite believe, because it seems almost too good to be true. Buddy accepts Deenie without reservation and never even comments on the Milwaukee Brace. He ends up kissing her at a party, thus finally pushing Deenie to the acceptance that wearing a Milwaukee Brace isn't going to ruin her entire adolescent life. The lack of conversation about the brace with Buddy is not as realistic as the conversation between Deenie and her girl friends. The brace is Deenie's major focus on fearful rejection at the moment that this boy kisses her, with no conversation before or after about the device. Does this imply that with such a beautiful face, devices like a Milwaukee Brace fade out of view in the eyes of the beholder? This re-enforces the Cinderella syndrome that beauty conquers all. Had Deenie been covered with acne or eczema, would the outcome have been the same? This reader thinks not.

The character of Sally, in *Mine for Keeps* (1962),

also reflects many of the same societal attitudes that the character of Deenie portrays with regard to how she is perceived. She is hindered further, however, because she experiences more of a motor impairment than Deenie. Deenie has the same chance as her peers of living a long life without disability as a result of her Milwaukee Brace, but Sally will need to wear her leg braces for the rest of her life if she is to stay mobile and so will have to cope with these attitudes for much longer.

THE HELP OF OTHERS

In Madeleine L'Engle's book, *The Young Unicorns* (1968), the protagonist Emily is blinded at the age of eleven. The book opens about a year later, with a slightly unconvincingly well-adjusted Emily getting about just fine. She is the heroine of the novel, solving a mystery that ultimately solves the crime which resulted in her blindness. She has exuberance, poise, self-confidence and all the attributes of a well-adjusted adolescent. While the plot line is a little like a young female Sherlock Holmes, the character of Emily shows only traces of vulnerability in her new status as a disabled person. She has helpers all around her who help to make her world of darkness secure and safe. It is her blindness, however, that plays an important part of the climax and the seemingly trite plot device — which depends on Emily's very blindness to succeed — just isn't convincing.

The reason that Emily's situation is not believable is because the reader never sees Emily go through any of the adjusting frustrations that we see Deenie struggle through. Emily is an accomplished pianist, and perhaps her already finely tuned hearing has helped her advancement in the adjustment stage —

in any case, Emily explodes upon the page well-adjusted and the star of the centre stage. At the same time, Emily is always dependent on the support of others.

Drem, of Rosemary Sutcliff's *Warrior Scarlet* (1957), is at the opposite end of the spectrum from Emily. Drem, whose right arm never fully develops and is "withered", must seek out the help of another in order to fulfill his dream to slay a wolf with a spear. Right arms are spear-throwing arms, and Drem must seek out the help of an adult who has had an injury to his own right arm. The injured adult becomes a role model for Drem, and helps Drem learn to throw the spear left-handed.

It is interesting that Drem, who is suffering from a possible birth trauma and who will therefore ultimately be expelled from the clan, works closely with a man who has lost the use of his own right arm through an accident and who is fully accepted by the clan. Therefore, the views in this Bronze Age society contain a double standard. If a boy can prove his manhood during his coming-of-age ceremony, then he is always a man no matter what may befall him later in life. Drem, though, faces the prospect of not being allowed to complete the coming-of-age ceremony, and so of being condemned to a life as a child in the eyes of the people.

While this social construction is based in part on a survival strategy (people must hunt to eat, people must throw a spear to hunt, thus Drem will never hunt), Drem must overcome this stigma and gain his coming-of-age ceremony through an alternative method. The alternative is to learn how to throw a spear with his left hand. The big question is, will his clan allow it? Drem never thinks of himself as being impaired. He has had an under-developed arm all his life, so he has never known the full use of it, and therefore he does not miss it except in the socially constructed coming-of-age ceremony — where suddenly the use of the right arm is paramount to success and acceptance.

The attitudes of the people that surround Drem are varied. His mother accepts Drem without reservation. Drem's grandfather has a closed mind, and states that Drem will never be a warrior or a man. Caught between these two polar opinions about his abilities, Drem seeks his own answers and solutions both within and without the confines of the tribe. When Drem ultimately does complete his manhood task, albeit a year later than expected, he is rewarded with a renewed sense of self-worth and the newly won respect of his grandfather.

This is a very rewarding story to read because there is no self-pity. The society of the tribe itself, while a little hesitant about Drem's abilities, nevertheless do not block his attempts to gain the full status of a man. This is an uncompromising situation where the evidence of stereotype is far removed from the centre of life. The community for the most part accepts Drem and his impairment so long as he can fulfill the requirements of earning his manhood in the traditional way. The question of right arm or left arm as a spear-throwing arm becomes the main focus, not the withered arm itself. And the help that Drem receives comes from another disabled person.

THE ENVIRONMENT

Jean Little's *Mine for Keeps* (1962) forefronts functionality of the environment as being crucial for the story's forward momentum. When the novel opens, Sally, who has cerebral palsy, is looking forward to moving back home after being institutionalized for seven years in a special school. Through the story line, the reader learns that Sally experienced problems with her speech and mobility prior to entering this. In the special school environment, all of the children were working under similar conditions — the school was full of wheelchairs, children with braces, and multitudes of helpers.

As Sally contemplates her old life at the school that she is leaving and approaches her new life at home, the reader has a glimpse into the world of the special school as Little describes Sally's thoughts:

> It wasn't just the girls either. Room 9 itself had become more Sally's home than the place where she spent her holidays. She knew exactly how it looked early in the morning when the other three girls were asleep and everything was still. What with sixty children and nearly as many people on the staff, the school was only quiet when almost everyone was asleep. It was anything but quiet at night in that room, with Miss Jonas and the helpers trying to hustle them all into bed at once. 'Lights Out' rang at half past eight and there never seemed to be enough time to finish before that bell. People hurried everywhere, helping to undo buttons and brush teeth, taking children to the toilet, bringing them back, dodging wheelchairs, unbuckling braces and giving orders which went unheard in the uproar ... They were all supposed to dress and undress themselves if they could, but whenever Miss Jonas had her back turned, Sal could get one of the helpers to whisk a few buttons for her. (p6)

Sally thinks she is ready to move back home, but she is not ready for the mainstream of life that accompanies her return to her family:

the thought of getting ready for bed in a strange house, the thought of facing days without a bell to tell her when to do things, the thought of not having the other girls around, suddenly piled up into what looked like a mountain of troubles to Sally. (p7)

Despite having been institutionalised, when Sally does return home, her parents treat her the same as they do the rest of their children, and she is expected to get herself up and dress herself without help. While the reader doesn't respond to Sally as being a spoiled child, she is accustomed to having assistance with her buttons and zippers without having to ask. At home, mother has purchased pull-on skirts and shirts for Sally. But Sally doesn't take the time even to notice the style of clothing that her mother lays out for her the first morning. Instead, she stays in bed sulking and wishing that she were back in the special boarding school.

As Sally emerges from her insular world of boarding school and enters the realm of the public sphere, she experiences for the first time her full range of capabilities. Her family does not coddle her, but expects her to pull her weight with chores and schoolwork. One of the issues that comes up is Sally's return to the public classroom. The teacher is not prepared for Sally's mobility difficulties, and therefore does not recognize that she can't get up out of her chair as fast as everyone else for the daily opening activity, which involves standing and reciting before class begins. Sally also can't keep up with the oral math test that is administered because she can't write as fast as others, and therefore falls behind in recording her answers. She ends up inadvertently cheating, which sends her into an emotional tailspin. Her impairment seems invisible to the teacher because he does not try to adjust the routine to allow for Sally's working with leg braces, nor does he realize that Sally's hand/motor coordination is not the same as everyone else in the class.

From Sally's perspective, however, even settling down at her desk is a trying task when:

> for the next few minutes, she was too busy to notice whether anyone was staring at her or not. She had to get her crutches stowed out of the way, and then undo the knee-locks on her braces and get turned around so that her feet were under the desk instead of sticking out blocking the aisle. The lock on the left brace jammed. Sally tugged at it angrily. Her fingers, stiff with tension and damp with perspiration, slipped on the smooth steel. She wiped her palm on her skirt, gave one more tug, and the lock clicked open. Her knees bent. She swung her feet under her desk and sighed thankfully. (p39)

Just as she gets settled:

> Clang! A bell rang suddenly and every child in the room, except Sal, stood up. Sally stared wildly at the empty desks all around her and at the forest of plaid skirts, blue jeans, jumpers and slacks that had risen on every side. (p40-41)

The students have risen to sing, but Sally is left stranded in her seat.

When Sally finally comes to terms with her cheating behavior with the teacher, they both recognize that the situation could have had a different outcome if a little thought had gone into the activity prior to it beginning. This particular segment of the text implies that disabled children were not common in the classroom at the time, and therefore 'scaffolding' of the activities for Sally was not considered. Mr. Mackenzie, the teacher, admits that "first of all ... I want to say how sorry I am that you have had so difficult a day. I could have made it much easier for you if I had used my head" (p50).

Had a child come into the classroom with a broken leg, on wooden crutches, then the teacher's reaction probably would have been quite different and a certain amount of modified activity would have been arranged without a second thought. Of course, there should have been no difference at all. However, it does indeed make a difference to Mr. Mackenzie, and reflects the attitudes of the society within which this text is situated. By the 1960s, disability has become invisible in the mind because it is largely invisible in the public school. Sally is the only child in her classroom (if not the school) wearing leg braces.

Sally finally begins to come to terms with her own abilities when she takes on the responsibility of raising a small dog. The dog gives Sally another being to concentrate on, and the episodes of feeling sorry for herself begin to fade away. Sally begins to explore creative ways in which to become more independent and mobile, even with the limitations of braces and crutches. The safe and cozy environment of the special school finally fades from her consciousness, and gives way to the development of a safe and cozy, but different environment at home.

WHAT DOES THE DISABLED PROTAGONIST THINK ABOUT THEIR OWN ABILITIES?

Adolescents who are categorized as disabled or handicapped can suffer social stigmatization from both peers and adults. Deenie sees herself as a freak once she is fitted with the Milwaukee Brace. Told all her life how beautiful her face and hair are, she now feels that the brace is detracting from her beauty, despite the brace functioning to preserve her 'normal' appearance for the future. Her close girl friends, while shocked at the sight of the brace, are still accepting of Deenie as a close friend. Deenie's big test comes when she confronts Buddy, a boy who she has a crush on. Buddy responds by kissing Deenie at a party, thus squashing any thought she might still harbor about her attractiveness to boys at a time in her life when this is becoming an important self-image issue.

Emily in *The Young Unicorns* (1968) does not have a self-image issue at all. She is portrayed as being beautiful in mind, spirit and body. Being blind does not change Emily's physical appearance, only her way of navigating the world, which she does with humour and self-control. With a self-assuredness that at times seems conceived as a plot device, Emily nevertheless sails through her world without any problems.

Sally, in *Mine for Keeps* (1962), suffers from her own lack of self-confidence at the beginning of the story, which is reinforced by her sister's beliefs about what Sally can and can't do. Her parents, however, give Sally the tools she needs to overcome her fears of coping with the new situation of living at home for the first time in seven years. Sally, while always very comfortable with her impairment, does learn to have a better self-appreciation for her own skills and talents in overcoming obstacles such as standing up to her sister when it comes to feeding the dog.

In Sutcliff's *Warrior Scarlet* (1957), Drem faces the world undaunted by his undeveloped right arm and unusable hand. At the beginning of the story, he does not feel incapacitated at all. There are several scenes, however, which show the restrictions that Drem does operate under, like stringing a bow when this task normally takes two hands. When Drem is faced with his own limitations, he meets them face on and conquers them one at a time, unlike Theo in Trevor's *The Rose Round*, who constantly bends to the pressure of others to hide and ignore his own unusable arm and hand. Theo has very little self-esteem, and it is only through the words and actions of the protagonist, Matthew, that Theo begins to assert his own will upon his own destiny.

In life as well as in literary characterization, not only does the disabled adolescent have to deal with the issues associated with their impairment, but the stigma of the vocabulary of disability itself can be demeaning to an ego and self-image. When I was growing up in the 1950s and 1960s, my childhood vernacular included words like "crippled" and "crazy" to describe those visual and invisible attributes associated with motor and cognitive impairments. As a child, I probably would have shrunk away from Drem's "withered" arm or Theo's gloved hand. My mother would have told me not to stare, thus creating a sense of shame in me for those people who don't fit into the Greek model of perfection, as promoted by Hollywood and the glamour magazines so prominent in the mid twentieth century.

The attitude of the pre-baby boomer generation was to shun what was not 'whole' or 'complete'. Anyone who has been the brunt of teasing for anything can understand this mindset. Being 'whole' and 'complete' equals being white, middle- or upper-class, with no disfiguring physical attributes, and with your cognitive abilities fully intact and measured each year by good report cards for children or by promotions in the workplace for adults. The social measure of success is determined by forward movement, both mentally and physically. Being self-sufficient while fitting into the mould of what society calls 'normal' is the measuring stick by which all of the characters under review are measured. The closer the protagonist is to 'normal', the more accepting the characters in the literary world become.

This is quite evident in Emily in *The Young Unicorns*, who is blind but otherwise pretty and wholesome.To this extent Drem, who is operating under the most dogmatic social norms, displays the strongest courage and the highest self-esteem out of all the characters under review. Shown initially as a strong boy who is thrown into turmoil over his coming-of-age ceremony, he works independently and successfully to overcome the stigma that his clan has placed on him. He successfully throws off the stigma and becomes accepted as he is, without any change to his physical form. Instead, he invokes a change in social acceptance, which none of the other characters under review accomplish.

Not that this is a goal for the other characters. Most of the books discussed here tend to show the change that occurs within the character to become more accommodating to the social structure itself, by learning how to operate within it with a disability or impairment. While they all do so successfully, it is only Drem who actually changes the social construction of acceptance itself without himself or his attitudes changing at all. His initial determination to go through the coming-of-age ceremony holds steady throughout the book, when he is finally successful in killing his first wolf with a spear in his left hand. Therefore, tradition breaks and Drem becomes a new hero for which younger boys may now look up to in generations to come as the left-handed spear thrower.

In the context of Western culture's obsession with beauty, one might apply the same ideas to physical appearance, whether of the face or of the overall package. Both Deenie and Sally are concerned about their physical appearance and motor functions within the confines of braces. Emily in *The Young Unicorns* (1968) is hardly concerned with her physical appearance at all. She is a self-assured young teen, seemingly well-adjusted to her new dark world. Drem, while he is not concerned with the physical beauty of his arm (or lack thereof), *is* concerned with the functionality of his other arm in order to obtain the status of a man. Therefore, beauty doesn't concern Drem, but functionality does. It is the acceptance of his clan to let him use his left arm at all to obtain this status which is the main stumbling block that he faces.

HOW ARE THE CULTURAL NORMS REFLECTED BY CHARACTERIZATION?

Societal norms are often reflected in the views of characters within the novels. Theo — a supporting character rather than the protagonist — suffers under the cruel and misguided disgust of his mother and ridicule of his close family members which continues into his adult life, infantilising him and rendering him more as a peer to Matthew. This treatment begins when Theo is born with an underdeveloped right arm and hand. While his arm is small, like a child's, his hand is "...a small knobbly uneven thing with a sort of thumb and what looks like a couple of stumps of fingers, growing in odd places." (Trevor, 1963, p89.) His mother equates his impairment with ignorance and stupidity, which reflects some of the cultural values present in the 1940-1980 time frames. Matthew, the protagonist, views Theo in a variety of accepting ways. He shows a natural curiosity about Theo's hand, and reflects some of societal viewpoints when he asks Theo: " 'Don't you like them to be sorry for you?' " Theo says:

> "No … the way most people are sorry for anyone is to treat him as somehow different from themselves, a poor thing, not a person … They don't think, of course … If they did they might realize that not having a body like theirs doesn't mean one doesn't have a mind and feelings like theirs.'" (pp42-43)

Matthew is slightly nauseous the first time he sees Theo's hand, but when he looks again he sees that "…after all, it is only a piece of flesh and bone that has not grown the right shape" (p89).

Theo, who works in a school for disabled children, strives to move the school to his manor home where his mother is in residence. While Theo will inherit the manor home upon her death, he is also made to feel that he is never welcome there. His mother can't stand the sight of Theo, nor of Theo's hand. Indeed, Theo must wear a glove on that hand whenever he is in his mother's presence. In a confrontation between the two, where Theo is explaining to his mother that he wants to bring the school children home, she exclaims:

> "Bring your little imbeciles to Woodhall? What an idea!" cried Madam.
> "They're not imbeciles, Mamma."
> "Cripples, it's just as bad! How can you ask that of me, you who know what distress it has always

caused me to see you, my eldest son, crippled as you are? It is like your senselessness to demand such a thing of your mother." (p71)

While Theo never seems to become completely comfortable with his hand, and he continues to let the opinions of others rule his actions for most of the novel, he does finally stand up to his mother and brings the children home to live and begins a new school there, finally becoming truly adult.

HOW IS THE DISABLED PROTAGONIST OR CHARACTER STEREOTYPED?

Within any of the books under discussion, the question of stereotyping is difficult to discuss, mainly because all of the characters with the exception of Theo are main characters, protagonists. They are therefore fully developed characters with flaws and imperfections that fall within the realm of any human being's flaws and imperfections. Thrown over this is a layer of disability. In the case of Drem in *Warrior Scarlet* (1957), he is the only boy in the tribe with an undeveloped arm. There are not many instances of children being born with impairments within this clan. Therefore an abnormality of only one does not constitute a stereotype within his fictional world, and his story is not one that is commonly told in ours.

Deenie and Sally are somewhat stereotyped, both by themselves and others in their world. Deenie expects everyone in her inner circle to look at her as she looks upon herself, as a freak. When she finds that this is not quite what everyone's attitude is, her own attitude about what constitutes a freak changes. Not only does she strive to continue to be part of her mainstream cohort, she also begins to include those others who are in her class and living on the fringe — the old friend Susan who now rides on the special bus, and the Creeping Crud, aka Barbara Curtis, who has eczema — back into her own social world.

In an effort to bridge the world of 'normal' and other, Deenie herself erases the line of social and fictional demarcation that does not, of course, exist in reality. Faced with the fact that her mobility is greatly reduced, she must learn to accept help from others. In the locker room, Barbara (who has the eczema) helps Deenie by doing up Deenie's shoe laces. As the two girls walk into the gym, the gym teacher tells all the girls to choose partners. Deenie's immediate reaction to this is to bond with Barbara as "... me and Barbara looked at each other and grabbed hands" (Blume, 1973, p 114). Prior to this, Deenie had felt nothing but abhorrence in touching Barbara's hands. Again, this blurring of boundaries between 'normal' and 'abnormal', and the acknowledgment that we are all 'normal', does not echo society's stereotypes.

Sally, however, is in the world of the 'Other', and has been in this world all of her life. It is only as a young adolescent that she comes to terms with what that means. Looking at the mainstream world of her classmates, and trying to fit herself into that world, means that Sally has to make some adjustments to her world view. Having to learn to ask for help is usually a painful lesson to learn, because everyone likes to think of themselves as being self-sufficient, however delusional this might be.

Within Sally's world, the non-disabled reader makes initial assumptions about a character who wears leg braces and who must use crutches to get around, such as believing that Sally cannot function as fully as someone without braces and crutches.

Mindy, Sally's sister, demonstrates those assumptions when she decides to take over the job of feeding Sally's new dog, Susie. In the Copeland household, everyone is responsible for their own pet. When Sally claims she can feed her own dog, Mindy replies, "But you can't, honey," (Little, 1962, p76), meaning that Sally can't bend over and pick Susie's bowl up off the floor to fill it. Their father, however, has made other arrangements, by making a small cart for Sally to use so that she won't have to reach right to the floor: her inability to bend does not mean she is incapable of feeding her pet. The reader is made aware of alternative solutions by providing the cart for the food dish.

When I see how Jean Little characterizes the supporting characters in *Mine for Keeps* (1962), I believe that the reactions of the children in Sally's classroom accurately portray what my feelings might have been if a child wearing leg braces and using crutches had become part of the classroom that I was in. In some other respects, I can identify with Sally being the new girl in class, because every couple of years *I* was the new girl in class. My father's upward climb on the corporate ladder moved us every two years during my entire school career. We always moved during the summer so as to not interrupt my schooling. However, this left me without any friends to play with during those summer moves. I entered the classroom in the fall as the new kid on the block, and was forced to forge new bonds of acceptance and friendship in every instance within a group of children who, for the most part, had been a cohort since kindergarten or first grade.

Therefore, I totally understand Sally's trepidation in facing a new school situation, and I would have been like Libby and offered to be friends right away.

Understanding Sally's situation as the new kid on the block would have placed us in this category of 'other', and in unity stands strength. Within Sally's new classroom, some students are curious, some are helpful and some are indifferent. The level of acceptance, however, is something that is earned from within. Sally is given the courage and strength to forge ahead in her new life when she takes on the responsibility of raising her small dog, Susie. Susie transfers Sally's focus from being the new kid on the block to something more important to Sally, the welfare of her new pet companion — one who is totally dependent upon Sally for everything. Once this shift occurs, "School was different on Monday. Sal was full of thoughts of Susie ..." (p74).

It is a different story in Trevor's *The Rose Round* (1963). While Theo is not the protagonist, he is a strong supporting character. He is placed in the middle of being stereotyped as an imbecile by his mother and his uncritical acceptance by young Matthew; both of which render him child-like. The juxtaposition of the mother and Matthew, and their reactions to Theo, offer the reader a clear view of what a stereotype is, and the negative effects that label causes Theo to suffer under.

The messages of the culture are pressed home through the interaction of peers and adults alike, as demonstrated in the books under review. While teasing and shunning are the most common ways for children to inflict emotional scars upon each other, this does not occur in any of the books except *The Rose Round* (1963). It is difficult to judge if these texts are accurate portrayals of real life. The fictional characters are well-developed and placed in literary situations meant to highlight the protagonists' strengths and weaknesses from an inner perspective, as opposed to suppression by outside forces such as teasing and shunning.

The characters in the few books discussed here display cultural constructions common for the time frame in which the books are published. Deenie and Sally are seen to benefit from mechanical devices (medical intervention). Emily succeeds through the help of a close support group at home. Theo, with his under-developed hand, gains enough self-esteem to help children who suffer from the stigma of being 'crippled'. Drem, the most successful of all protagonists under discussion, devises solutions to gain his social status and acceptance by his clan as a man. The affluence of any given family (with the exception of Drem's family) paves the way for such social mainstreaming to occur.

While medical advances — and increasing wealth in society (poverty is the single biggest cause of impairment) — make impairment less common, medical and technological advances and economic growth also allow disabled people to function more fully as self-sufficient members of society. As functioning citizens, the population of disabled citizens has become a voice and advocate for more equitable treatment in the social/public sphere, closing the gap between impairment and social stigma as experienced in the early part of the century. In Drem's case his physical impairment was unchanged, but the social stigma of using the left hand to throw a spear is overcome by his determination to become a man within his clan. It is this text, therefore, that stands out as the most important display of how social construction can be changed. It is significant that Sutcliff (1920-1992) had a form of arthritis and was a wheelchair user from an early age.

For Sally and Deenie, despite their own self-loathing of braces and how these affect their appearance, they each nevertheless make full use of their aids to become mobile citizens in a mobile world. Emily and Theo are at opposite ends of the spectrum of acceptance, which reflects the ideology of the twentieth century in general.

In looking at my parents' generation, my own generation and my children's generation, it is easy to trace the social changes that have occurred which are also reflected in the books under review. These social constructions have gone from non-acceptance as in the case of Theo, to the success of Drem in changing viewpoints with his accomplishments. As the ADA act of 1990 moved the public consciousness closer and closer to eradicating the social constructions of impairment and recognizing instead abilities, so too will the literature of the next generation reflect those changes in social constructions of acceptance and non-stigmatizing behaviour.

NOTES

1) The Social Model of Disability emphasizes dignity, independence, choice and privacy. Furthermore, it perceives the individual holistically rather than labeling them with medical terms. One of the key concepts of the Social Model is that society disables people, and that this occurs when a person is excluded because of their access needs from something that other people in society take for granted. For example, using the Social Model, a wheelchair user who is unable to use a bus or enter the cinema is disabled because the bus does not have a lowered floor and the cinema a ramp, and not because of their impairment. The medical terminology of the Medical Model is paternalistic and exclusive, thus putting barriers in the way of the person with an impairment; it has a 'cannot do' labeling which pigeon-holes the individual, while the Social Model adopts the 'can do' approach to impairment, looking for streamlined ways around any difficulties, including the individual at every opportunity.

REFERENCES

Beuf, Ann Hill, *Beauty is the Beast: Appearance-Impaired Children in America*, University of Pennsylvania Press, Philadelphia, 1990.

Blume, Judy, *Deenie*, Laurel-Leaf, New York, (first published in USA by Bradbury Press), 1973.

Burnett, Frances Hodgson, *The Secret Garden*, Penguin Books, London (first published in USA in 1909, and in Great Britain by William Heinemann in 1909).

Duffy, Yvonne, 'Beauty Queen or Poster Child?', *Belles Lettres*, 4[2], 18, 1989.

Katz, Irwin, *Stigma: A Social Psychological Analysis*, Hillsdale, Lawrence Erlbaum Associates, New Jersey, 1981.

Kilham, Chris, 'Depictions of Disability: A Way With Words', *Australian Journal of Early Childhood*, Volume 26 Issue 1, p26, 2001.

L'Engle, Madeleine, *The Young Unicorns*, Bantam Doubleday Dell Books for Young Readers, New York, (first published in USA by Farrar, Straus, Giroux, 1968).

Little, Jean, *Mine for Keeps*, Little, Brown & Company (first published in Canada by Little, Brown & Company, 1962).

Meckel, Richard A., Golden, Janet, Prescott, Heather Munro, *Children and Youth in Sickness and in Health: A Historical Handbook and Guide*, Greenwood Press, Westport, 2004.

Palisano, Robert J., Copeland, Wendy P., Galuppi, Barbara E., 'Performance of Physical Activities by Adolescents with Cerebral Palsy', *Physical Therapy*, 871, 77, 2007.

Porter, Eleanor H., *Pollyanna* Harrap & Co, London (first published in USA 1913).

Schriner, Kay, Scotch, Richard K, 2001, 'Disability and Institutional Change', *Journal of Disability Policy Studies*, Volume 12 Issue 2, p100.

Spyri, Johanna, *Heidi*, originally published in Switzerland in 1880.

Sutcliff, Rosemary, *Warrior Scarlet*, Farrar, Straus and Giroux, (first published in Great Britain by Oxford University Press 1958).

Trevor, Meriol, *The Rose Round*, Bathgate, Bethlehem Books, (first published in Great Britain by Hamish Hamilton, 1963).

LATE PERIOD

III. STEREOTYPING IN THE LATE 20TH CENTURY

LOUISE NORLIE

ALTHOUGH I was a voracious reader as a child, I made no particular effort to find books that focused on a disabled character. Well aware that my impairment placed me in the minority — I was generally the only disabled person in my school — I expected that these books were not written with disabled readers in mind. I also assumed that, rather than placing a disabled character within a storyline that would otherwise interest me, the focus would be on the disability itself if a book *did* contain a disabled character. Such books would offer little that I did not already know: having lived with osteogenesis imperfecta since birth, I have not known life from any other perspective. Perhaps these books were written to teach a lesson or to 'inspire' readers. Disabled characters would not be portrayed in the same way as others.

Supporting my assumption were books with 'token' disabled characters. During the course of many years of reading, characters that used wheelchairs cropped up here and there, generally as background in a school setting. I was not impressed by how they were portrayed. They were present only for the sake of diversity. Their personalities were never even considered, because the presence of their disability was used to satisfy the requirement of describing them. From this, I further assumed that any disabled character, even one central to the story itself, would not emerge as particularly vibrant.

There was also a more personal reason for such paranoia. I knew, all too well, about stereotypes. I sensed them when people spoke to me or about me. While out in public, strangers often approached my parents to ask about my impairment. They acted as if I were invisible and could not speak for myself. They acted as if my impairment was public property, giving them the right to interrogate and judge me. If they spoke to me or about me after learning about my "challenges," they called me an "inspiration". They encouraged me by claiming that "I was doing so well" (how did they know?), that I must "keep trying," and that I did not "seem disabled" (was having a disability a 'bad' thing that I must 'overcome'?). Such words as "determined", "inspiration", "overcome" and "courage" took on a life of their own, as stereotypical patterns that pigeonholed me into acting out a role that I did not want to play.

In my everyday life, I aspired to be treated as an individual, not merely as an example of a person with osteogenesis imperfecta. Unfortunately, stereotypes often affected my interactions with others. I also witnessed them in television shows and films. Sensitive to condescension and labeling, I could specify the nature of these misconceptions from an early age. Noting how pervasive they were, I doubted that stereotypes were entirely avoided in children's fiction, and was reluctant to risk finding what I did not want to read.

What makes an individual? As cursory definitions, one could cite emotional depth, various personality traits, and uniqueness. Young adult fiction does not usually take the form of a 'character study', being usually driven by plot. Nevertheless, it is most enjoyable when plot is driven by character and characters have distinct personalities. This helps the reader to care about the characters and to relate to them as people. Individuality makes them seem real, just like people we know. For example, the popular 'Sweet Valley' series, created by Francine Pascal, involves the adventures of identical twins Jessica and Elizabeth. Jessica is wild and impetuous, while Elizabeth is sensible, studious and serious. Invariably, plots involve Jessica's mischievous adventures and consequent dilemmas, from which Elizabeth grudgingly rescues her. The twins often resort to switching identities in the course of their exploits. Their memorable personalities are reflected in both dialogue and plot.

Eventually I read some well-known novels with disabled characters, such as *Izzy, Willy-Nilly* by Cynthia Voigt (1983) and *Freak the Mighty* by Rodman Philbrick (1993). In spite of my reservations, I hoped to find absorbing characters and plots that were not just about disabilities. But upon reading these and others, my feelings were mixed. While I was pleased to find instances where disabled characters are fully human, involving and real, there were instances where I found just what I suspected, or worse. I found disabled characters who are either oversimplified and clichéd, or distorted and unrealistic. Even when the personalities of the characters are realized, certain formulas are used in the plot. An impairment is shown to decrease the value of the character's lives, and disability is shown as something that would go away if the characters tried hard enough.

Various stereotypes ranged from the subtle to the blatant. One could posit that subtle stereotypes are not really stereotypes at all — they are simply the author's choice in telling the story. This theory is hard to accept in the face of repetitions of certain aspects of character or plot. A strong presence of stereotypes is clearly revealed by identifying common trends in multiple fictional examples.

THE IMPORTANCE OF DETERMINATION

Recipes for the depiction of disabled characters emerge from a simple combination of words. Certain terms are used regularly in newspaper and magazine articles about disabled people. The hackneyed concepts of courage, determination, and 'overcoming disability' have expanded to become foundations for both storylines and characters. Determination, for example, can be the saving grace of an otherwise 'useless' disabled person, or it can make a disabled person so fierce and tough as to be practically inhuman.

In *Phoning a Dead Man* by Gillian Cross (2001), determination is taken to a remarkable extreme. It becomes the central, if not the only, personality trait of Annie. In this mystery thriller, Hayley's brother John is reported dead after carrying out one of his demolition tasks in Russia. Annie, John's fiancée, decides to travel to Russia as she believes there is more to the mystery than meets the eye. She uses a wheelchair, and requests that Hayley join her as an assistant. Various adventures ensue as a complex intrigue is unraveled.

Annie is exceedingly self-confident. 'Overcoming' or being cured of her disability is not an issue. She is an admirably proficient traveller, and knows exactly how to manage. The details of her experiences in airports and airplanes are realistic; Annie's character is not. In the opening scenes of the novel, Hayley and her parents are mourning for the death of John. Remarkably, Annie, John's friend and fiancé, does not betray much sorrow. This could be explained by Annie's suspicion that John is not really dead and that she has no doubts about the success of her endeavour to find him. Even so, Annie shows no sympathy for the grieving family. Her sole objective is to reach Russia to investigate John's demise.

From the first moment we encounter Annie, intense willpower and unfeeling harshness are her primary attributes. They influence everything from her speech to her appearance. The book is filled with physical descriptions of Annie that contribute to this effect, sometimes verging on the ludicrous. Annie's face is "like a weasel's, sharp and fine-boned" (p14), her face is "as sharp as a hatchet"(p61), while her "small, sharp face [is] keen and attentive" (p4), with eyes that are "fierce [and] probing" (pp14-15). Other parts of her body are described using equally severe metaphors. Her fingers are "small and bony [but grip] like iron" (p39). Her hands are "twisted together in her lap, viciously tight" (p75). Annie's actions are similar. When she speaks, she "snaps" (p73). When she looks, she "glares" (p73). Perhaps Annie is thin and angular, but why "hatchet"? Why "weasel"? Why are "fierce" and "sharp" the most frequent descriptions of her?

During the course of the narrative, Annie continues to be completely void of feeling. She is undaunted in her confrontations with unscrupulous Russian mobsters. She is oblivious to Hayley's sorrow, fatigue, or bewilderment. Her lack of empathy makes her seem almost cruel. And while her emotional depth is lacking, Annie is a super-woman in all other ways. The author seems intent on making Annie super-efficient at anything and everything. This is true in small and large moments in the story. Even when Annie answers the phone, the author states that "it hardly had time to ring before Annie answered" (p4). Arriving in a Russian airport, she does not pause for a second to observe her surroundings. Instead, Annie goes "into hyperdrive" (p32) and her "narrow face sharpened, concentrating" (p32). While Hayley is naturally fatigued by the difficult journey, Annie is tireless and "would snap and hustle and rattle out orders too fast for anyone to keep up with her." (p52) She is constantly demanding, "rapping out instructions" (p32) and interrupting others at will.

What is the purpose of this? I can only guess. In striving to demonstrate that Annie is competent and resilient 'in spite of' her disability, the author protests too much. Annie's personality is so distorted that she becomes completely unbelievable as an individual. While it is admirable that Annie's impairment does not make her powerless, she has become a caricature of robotic fierceness. Need a capable disabled person, resolved to accomplish certain goals, lack emotions and even a hint of fallibility? The bizarre portrayal of Annie creates a character that no one can relate to.

When it comes to the necessity for a disabled person to be determined, a reader can do no better than to turn to Rowena Edlin-White's *Clo and the Albratross* (1996). In this novel, Clo's athletic sister, Beth, is severely injured in a car accident. She has a reversible brain injury and it is necessary for her to use a wheelchair. Clo has to push her sister around town where she finds problems with accessibility.

Beth becomes the titular "albatross" after her injury, lifeless and empty. In her sister's opinion, Beth with physical impairments is little more than an inconvenience. The plot revolves around Clo's agonies of embarrassment and discomforture; Beth herself is of no importance, a powerless victim surrounded by a hostile environment. People "point and shake their heads sadly at one another" (Edlin-White, *Clo and the Albatross*, p63) when they see Beth. Children mock her, taunting "spazzo, crippo" (p 64). During these incidents, Beth closes her eyes and pretends to be asleep. Clo is angry because her sister is "playing the helpless invalid" (p66).

Moments after these confrontations, Beth is allotted dialogue that reveals she is alert and aware of her surroundings. Therefore Beth is indeed an apathetic and lazy invalid, just as her sister suspects with bitterness. As expected, determination is all she needs to recover from her disability and to become a real person again. Inspired by her friend Kim, who proclaims that "if a rather dotty old teacher hadn't taken me on, I'd still be in a wheelchair today" (p154), Beth's mobility begins to return through rigorous exercise.

After this change in Beth's outlook, she is given a slightly increased level of participation in the narrative. She also admits to her former faults. When faced with mockery and discrimination, she pretended not to notice because "it was easier than getting involved" (p99). She never "really tried to help" Clo (p95). But even when there are additional scenes of Beth interacting with others, her individuality is a matter of irrelevance. Only determination distinguishes her in the later half of the book, and it is seen to work miracles. At the novel's finale, Beth is able to walk short distances and is on the road to a complete recovery. Once this achievement occurs, Clo proclaims that the albatross is no more and "Beth's alive" again (p153). In Kim's case as well as Beth's, disability is a simple case of mind over matter. According to this book, a physical impairment can be mended with coaching; a disabled person without "determination" and an unwavering pursuit of improvement is not a person at all, merely an inert burden.

THE NEED TO 'OVERCOME' IMPAIRMENT

The stereotype that people can 'overcome' their disability with enough self-control occurs elsewhere. In several novels, impairments diminish in order to create a mawkish or melodramatic conclusion. Courageous disabled characters are seen to muster a heroic level of concentration and grit. Their triumph is in the moment when their impairments vanish. For this to occur, all that is needed is willpower and optimism.

A common premise in these stories is that a character with a mild physical impairment wishes to 'overcome' some aspect of their disability. This concept acts as a subplot that parallels the main plot. In *Willow King* (Platt, 1998), Katie, who has uneven legs, fights to save the life of a horse born with crooked legs. At the end of the story, she has trained the horse to be a champion racer. Because of her disability, she is the only one to "see into his heart and spirit." (p184)

At a victory celebration, Katie summons the confidence to dance although there is a chance that she may trip. She remembers "how valiantly King had fought for his life on the day he was born and all the courage and determination he had showed since then"(p192). Predictably, Katie dances perfectly, having learned how to dispense with her disability from her experience with the horse. In this story, the horse is likewise an "overcomer." With the appropriate amount of courage, the horse with crooked legs is able to perform an astonishing physical feat. The tale of his racing triumph falls into the usual formulaic pattern reflected in human characters with impairment.

The concept of the 'overcomer' takes centre stage in *The Ghost of Grania O'Malley* by Michael Morpurgo (1996). In this novel, Jessie has mild cerebral palsy. She aspires to reach the summit of Big Hill, a hill near her home. When she attempts this climb in the beginning of the book, the language indicates that her cerebral palsy can be ignored if she tries hard enough. Jessie is described as "willing her fumbling feet forward"(p5). She feels "her legs weakening all the while [but she] fought them, forcing them on" (p7). She stumbles and falls, but is helped to her feet by the ghost of Grania O'Malley, a female pirate from the 16th century. The disembodied voice of the ghost declares with confidence that Jessie will accomplish her goal as long as she does not "sit there feeling sorry" for herself (p8). As a result of this encouragement and her resolve to succeed, Jessie reaches the summit, although she is bruised and bloodied in the process.

The main conflict of the story is whether Big Hill will be destroyed by developers who wish to mine it, or whether it will remain untouched as part of the local heritage. Jessie and her cousin Jack oppose the destruction of the hill. At the book's climax, the pair hasten to stop the diggers. For the first time, Jessie charges ahead of her cousin, "fending off Jack's questions with the same grim determination that drove her tottering legs" (p144). Jessie "couldn't understand why she wasn't falling over, but somehow she wasn't" (p145). Under the necessity of the moment, Jessie's disability disappears. As in the film *Forrest Gump*, where the boy's leg braces fly off when he eludes bullies with startling speed, Jessie runs faster than she imagined possible. Predictably, she accomplishes the treacherous climb once more as she and Jack lead the protestors to the hill-top.

The character of Jessie is developed by insights into her fears about the relationship of her parents and her feelings for her cousin Jack. She emerges as a real person; her involvement with the ghost and the hill protest shows that her life does not revolve around her impairment. In *Willow King*, Katie's character is not developed outside of her rather bland combination of niceness and bravery. Nevertheless, the stereotype surrounding these characters is a particularly bothersome and naive one. With enough effort, determination, and courage, these disabled characters can make their impairments disappear.

There is another problematic element in these stories — 'overcoming' their disability is a central ambition of the characters. The reality that many people must live with their impairments and are quite happy to do so is not acknowledged or accepted. While it is quite possible that a character such as Katie in *Willow King* would long to dance gracefully and that Jessie would aspire to climb Big Hill, it is surely more than a coincidence that the aspirations of these disabled characters involves some physical feat. Their personal goals are intrinsically related to their impairments, which magically fade under the pressure of the moment. This stereotype is facilitated by the use of third-person narration, which distances the reader from the characters and makes it easier to create formulaic motivations.

COMPENSATING FOR IMPAIRMENT

Kim, in *Clo and the Albatross*, exclaims that "I've got a gammy leg but I can make good pots; Gary's got cerebral palsy but he knows more about computers than you or I will ever know!"(Edlin-White, p125). This summarizes a prevalent stereotype for disabled characters: the existence of a compensatory ability. According to several novels, a disabled person must have some other special talent, a hidden strength that acts as a redemption for their otherwise blighted existence. What if Gary only had average abilities on the computer? What if Gary was just an ordinary guy without any particular talents? That is a situation that many authors of children's literature do not confront.

A discussion of 'compensatory ability' would not be complete without considering *Freak the Mighty* (Philbrick, 1993). This novel enjoys wide popularity, and to this day is required reading for children in many American schools. It is undeniably entertaining and includes many important ideas, particularly about the power of friendship. However, behind its clever wordplay, fantasy, and humour lurks a wide range of the usual stereotypes, with 'compensatory ability' at its most prominent.

This story details the friendship between learning disabled Maxwell and physically disabled Kevin, nicknamed "Freak". Both have tremendous compensatory abilities that verge on the legendary. Although Maxwell is mocked as having "no brain" (p76), he has extraordinary height and strength.

His feet are "humongous" (p12), greater than the largest adult-size shoe. He is so massive that adults are terrified of him, even though he is only in the eighth grade. Kevin is just the opposite, tiny in size but powerful in his mind.

Maxwell is the narrator of the story, and Kevin is portrayed from his point of view. Kevin has an unspecified physical impairment where he is "growing on the inside but not the outside" (p89). He is "kind of twisted in a way that means he can't stand up straight and makes his chest puff out" (p8). Like Annie in *Phoning a Dead Man*, Kevin is fierce and demanding. He has "weird fierce eyes" (p4) — also called "death-ray eyes" (p3) — and is seen "strutting around the sidewalk, giving orders" (p7). On occasion, he threatens to hit others with his crutch. Even more untiring and vigorous than Annie, Kevin is "so full of ever-ready energy you can practically hear his brain humming" (p44).

Kevin's compensatory abilities are far more fabulous than Maxwell's. Maxwell considers him to be "possibly the smartest human being in the whole world" (p32). Kevin has a precocious knowledge of everything, from science to history to language. He identifies fireworks using chemical nomenclature, bandies obscure and erudite vocabulary, brandishes terminology from *Star Trek*, and memorizes the dictionary. At Christmas, Kevin presents Maxwell with a dictionary that he developed using his own newly coined definitions. Needless to say, although Kevin is captivatingly eccentric, he is not convincing or plausible for a twelve-year-old.

Both boys are on the outskirts of society. Due to his disability and his compensatory intelligence, Kevin is an outlandish outsider. Maxwell is also an outcast due to his learning difficulties and shady past (his father is in prison for the murder of his mother). Maxwell's language is rife with slang that tends to ostracize Kevin further, defining him as alien and strange. He is "the weirdo robot boy" (p4) who was seen "scowling [from] one of those cripple vans" (p3). He is also the "crippled-up yellow-haired midget kid" (p7) who "scuttles" (p131) when he moves. Kevin relishes his unavoidable role as an otherworldly creature. Pretending to be an extraterrestrial, he approaches Maxwell demanding "identify yourself, earthling" (p9). During a Fourth of July celebration, Maxwell lifts Kevin to his shoulders so he can view the fireworks. Soon after, Kevin christens their alliance "Freak the Mighty", a combination of both boys' compensatory abilities. They learn to act as one entity, with Maxwell as the "brawn" and Kevin as the "brain". In their adventures around town and in school, where arrangements are made for Maxwell to accompany Kevin as an assistant, Maxwell carries Kevin on his shoulders.

At the end of the novel, Kevin meets a traditional fate. He dies because "his heart just got too big for his body" (p157). This happens just after his thirteenth birthday, and echoes the 'kill or cure' ethos of classic children's fiction. Thus the character never has to face his teenage years, let alone adulthood. Maxwell finds that he has been forever changed by his experiences with Kevin. Furthermore, he has even learned to 'overcome' his learning difficulties. Instead of continuing to languish in a special education class for the learning disabled, Maxwell has developed academic skills by accompanying Kevin in the regular class. Prior to his death, Kevin asks Maxwell to record their adventures and Maxwell discovers writing skills he never dreamed he had, becoming the author of *Freak the Mighty* itself as he reflects on how much he learned from Kevin.

Through the vivid narrative voice of Maxwell, *Freak the Mighty* becomes a fantasy. Commonplace details are stretched out of all proportion when masked by Maxwell's colourful and creative language. All of the characters, including Kevin's mother and Maxwell's grandparents, are caricatures. In this respect, Kevin and Maxwell are part of the general atmosphere. Continuing this tendency, Kevin uses his imagination to mythologize his life even further. Although he knows his impairment may lead to his death, Kevin tells Maxwell that he will receive a bionic or robotic replacement body in order to conceal the truth and spare his feelings. He calls his mother the "Fair Gwen of Air" (p13) after Queen Gwynevere of Arthurian lore. He describes his adventures with Maxwell in similar terms. Maxwell joins in the spirit, recording that together they were engaged in "slaying dragons and fools and walking high above the world" (p40).

There is no doubt that Maxwell and Kevin emerge as fascinating individuals; they are anything but boring. However, certain aspects of Kevin's life as a physically disabled person are simply not possible. For example, Maxwell is allowed to carry Freak on his shoulders all day in school. This would never be allowed by any public school in America, and certainly is not a feasible solution to providing accessibility in educational settings. Furthermore, Kevin is almost completely defined by stereotypes. His story leaves the reader with the impression that every impairment is counterbalanced by an amazing, almost mystic power. Although some conditions may cause an early death, Kevin's poignant death, conveniently before he reaches adulthood, is a modern version of an old cliché. Last but not least, the book perpetuates the stereotype that disabled people do not (or cannot?) live in the real world. Like Kevin, they must create a life of fantasy to escape those realities which the authors may not consider an appropriate or tasteful subject for fiction.

THE NECESSITY FOR FANTASY

The necessity of having a fantastic imagination to compensate for the realities of being a disabled person is the sole theme of *Mind's Eye* (Fleishman, 1999). The story is told in the form of a play. Before the action takes place, Courtney, aged sixteen, has become paralyzed from the waist down after a riding accident. Her parents are dead. She has no other relatives to adopt her, and her friends are allegedly repelled by her disability. She has been abandoned by her stepfather in a nursing home. Her roommate is Elva, an 88-year-old former English teacher. Elva insists that Courtney read aloud from a 1910 *Baedecker Guide to Italy*, since the print is too small for her. Thus springs the theme of the book — Courtney must experience the world through her "mind's eye".

Courtney is sullen and embittered by her impairments and the book offers no prospects for her outside of escapism. Courtney protests against the stereotype of compensatory ability, ranting that:

"I don't need to hear about some quadriplegic girl in the paper who's getting straight As in college and is engaged to get married and can probably play the freaking violin with the bow in her mouth and is so incredibly cheerful all the time." (Fleishman, p69)

Elva, her mentor, insists that these extraordinary abilities will be undeniable in Courtney's future life as a disabled person, replying, "Courtney, dear, that girl is you. You just don't know it yet." (p69) Apparently, disabled people cannot be ordinary. It is inevitable that an extraordinary ability counterbalances a disability.

Elva promises that reading from the Baedecker will "take us worlds away from North Dakota and winter and *wheelchairs* [the emphasis is mine]" (p12). Elva advises Courtney that "you'll need to spend hours on your mind, not your hair." (p10) Intellectual growth and the cultivation of creativity are worthy goals for anyone, but the implication in this book is that Courtney cannot do anything else. She must compensate for her disability by developing a keen imagination. Because she cannot live in the real world, she must envision travels and friends. Even at the story's end, Courtney, culturally enlightened by Elva's guidance, does not leave the nursing home to continue with her life. Elva mentions that she could do so if she had the desire, because "determination can make the miraculous possible." (p70) Nevertheless, the reader last glimpses Courtney resting in her nursing home bed, conjuring an imaginary trip and an imaginary boyfriend for hours on end.

CHALLENGING STEREOTYPES

A far more insightful exploration of compensatory ability is found in Elizabeth Feuer's *Paper Doll* (1990), a novel which to some extent challenges compensatory ability as a necessary and defining aspect of a disabled person. In this novel, Leslie Marx is a 17-year-old whose lower legs are amputated. Using prostheses, she can walk and climb stairs, although she experiences fatigue and problems with balance. Since the story is told through Leslie's perspective, there is increased insight into her character that is not achieved elsewhere. Leslie is an individual whose motivations, fear, and desires are understandable, human, and real. She is not perfect, flat, or fake, a mass of the usual stereotypes with a twist or two. At times she is foolish and confused. Refreshingly, the story is not about her disability but about her relationships with her family and friends.

Leslie does have a compensatory ability. She is a talented violinist training for Juilliard. However, she is an introvert, shy and insecure, and is an outsider among her classmates. At lunchtime she usually declines to sit in the cafeteria, preferring to go to the basement to practice her instrument alone. Leslie's timidity is detrimental to her musical career, as she is reluctant to perform in public and have people stare at her. Leslie's low self-confidence could be due to many factors, including her artistic interests that set her apart from others.

There is a second disabled character in the novel, Leslie's boyfriend, Jeff, who has cerebral palsy. For a teenage boy, Jeff seems almost too good to be true. He is perfectly wise, kind, sensitive, and understanding. His role is simply to be Leslie's boyfriend. This, however, does not significantly detract from the story, which is Leslie's relationship with her father and her relationship with the violin. These aspects of her life intertwine with each other and intertwine with her disability. The stereotype of the compensatory ability takes on new dimensions as the story progresses.

Soon after her legs were amputated after a car accident, Leslie began playing her brother's violin. Recognizing her skill, her father encourages her to develop her talent to the exclusion of all other activities. He disapproves of her relationship with Jeff because it distracts her from violin lessons. Claiming that no one thought Leslie would "amount to anything" after her accident (p117), he forces her to pursue music at any cost because he associates her talent as defining the sole purpose for her existence. Her father wants music to "shield" Leslie from being hurt (p180), revealing that he does not think she can have a 'normal' life. Painfully realizing this, Leslie considers renouncing the violin, but ultimately she does not. She recognizes that she does not need to internalize the repressive attitudes of her father, realizing that she is "not a freak, or a saint"(p112).

Paper Doll presents a challenge to the stereotype of compensatory ability. Leslie's talent is not that of a robotic prodigy. She is not a superhuman genius and often struggles with her art. Rather than embracing her musical gift as part of her identity, her father felt that it was a divine redemption for being disabled. At the book's bittersweet conclusion, Leslie breaks free from the stereotype that made her talent a constrictive force.

DISABLING ACCIDENTS

Numerous books in this period deal with the experiences of a formerly non-disabled girl who is injured in an accident. Examples are Cynthia Voigt's *Izzy, Willy-Nilly* (1986), Wendy Orr's *Peeling the Onion* (1996), Rowena Edlin-White's *Clo and the Albatross* (1996), Paul Fleishman's *Mind's Eye* (1999), and Harriet Sirof's *Because She's My Friend* (1993). These books are practically presented as horror stories, labeling disability as the worst thing that could possibly happen to the protagonist. Impairments cause the characters to experience a nightmare world where friends and family turn against them. The general impression imparted in these books is that life with disability is heartbreaking and without hope.

Characters in these stories indicate strongly that they fear disability more than death. In *Because She's My Friend*, Teresa observes Valerie in her hospital bed after her injury and thinks, "it gave me the shivers just to imagine being paralyzed and never running or walking again. If a horrible thing like that happened to me, I'd curl up and die." (p7) Beth in *Clo and the Albatross* says that she "didn't think there was anything worth living for [if she could not] run and swim and all those things" (p158). On the whole, these negative attitudes are unchallenged — such words come from the mouths of characters that the reader is supposed to sympathize with. Accordingly, these books do little to lessen the idea that being disabled is the ultimate catastrophe, and that disability erases a person's individuality and all of life's possibilities.

A common device in most of these stories is that, prior to their injuries, the characters are athletic, popular, or both. I can only assume this is to heighten the tragedy by imposing a greater contrast with their disabled state. The assumption is that being disabled excludes all those possibilities, making the characters helpless and rejected. In *Izzy, Willy-Nilly*, Izzy is a popular cheerleader who dated an upper-classman. In *Peeling the Onion*, Anna is a karate champion. Valerie in *Because She's My Friend* is a sophisticated globe-trotter. Courtney in *Mind's Eye* is popular and pretty. Beth in *Clo and the Albatross* is talented in gymnastics.

Once Izzy loses a leg, Courtney becomes a paraplegic, Anna experiences injuries to her neck and brain, Beth has a reversible brain injury and Valerie has a paralyzed leg, their formerly wonderful lives go downhill. Relationships with other people deteriorate. Izzy's brothers are ill at ease when they speak to her, and her popular friends are uncomfortable around Izzy and are averse to talking about subjects that they used to discuss freely. Her sister Francie is jealous of all the attention that she gets. Courtney's stepfather prefers that she live in a nursing home than stay with him. Valerie finds that everyone at school has changed. Anna's relationship with her love interest, Hayden, becomes tense and strained. Beth becomes completely passive, without any personality at all. As a consequence, these stories cheapen the value of friendship and families, presenting these relationships as shallow and easily ruined.

Courtney in *Mind's Eye*, trapped in a nursing home, is perhaps the most desolate portrayal of a disabled character among the 'injury stories'. She is so embarrassed by her state that she prefers to study independently than to go back to school. No one counsels her or encourages her to do otherwise. Courtney terrifies her friend Denise by bitterly recounting the degradations she has experienced from bedsores, laxative medications and catheters. According to this book, life as a disabled person is, by definition, limiting and degrading. The viewpoint dramatized in the film *Million Dollar Baby* lurks in the background. Few books could be further from the Social Model of Disability[1].

To be sure, there are differences when one becomes disabled. There are various adjustments that need to be made, personal and social. There are many new things to learn. Yet these books present the prospects of living with an impairment as being irrefutably grim. They send out the message that, if you become disabled, nothing will ever be the same. Your family will treat you differently; your friends will abandon you; your life will be without value or quality. Unless you experience a medical improvement, all is lost. This concept is presented not as a consequence of society's barriers, but as an inherent, unavoidable consequence of being disabled that no one can do anything about. In these stories, the disabled characters must endure their unrelenting humiliation and misery until their disabilities become less noticeable.

Such attitudes permeate the thoughts of the central characters. Due to their own disablist prejudices and misconceptions, their impairments fill them with self-loathing and cause them to turn against themselves. They feel that their very identity has changed for the worse. One thing is certain — they do not want to be considered impaired or disabled. The very words are hateful; in the minds of the characters, this classification banishes them from who they are and the lives they want to live.

Izzy thinks, "the words hammered down on the back of my neck. Crippled. Amputated. 'Not me,' I answered each one of them. Handicapped. 'No, not me.'" (Voigt, *Izzy, Willy-Nilly*, p50). She describes herself as "a thing, a messed-up body" (p52) and thinks that "everything was not going to be what I wanted, ever again" (p88). Anna in *Peeling the Onion* states that "impaired's an ugly word" (Orr, *Peeling the Onion*, p114) and asks, "Am I disabled? How could I be? I'm still the same person — just can't do a few things." (p114) When a doctor recommends that Anna use a cane, her reaction is that she has become "a freak teenager with a stick" (p70), and that a "stick makes me look disabled — spastic" (p70).

When Valerie returns to school on crutches, she comments:

> People who used to run to catch up with me no longer noticed me. Because I wasn't a person anymore; I was a crippled thing on crutches. In spite of all my scheming to fit in, everyone else moved in a different world — a world where the light was brighter, the bells rang louder, the chalk dust was more pungent. A world that was closed to me forever. (Sirof, p133)

The disabled girls cannot envisage disabled people, including themselves, as other than "things." They feel that becoming disabled will entirely exclude them from the 'real' world. According to these books, it apparently does.

The opinions of these characters could ostensibly be a stage in the exploration of living with an impairment. However, the issue is resolved by offering partial cures or recoveries. Anna, Valerie, and Beth can walk, and Izzy's prosthetic leg will soon be disguised and hidden away. Izzy is triumphant when Marco, who was responsible for the original car accident, calls her a "bitch" (Voight, p261). This pleases Izzy, who thinks that he would not have said that if he "dismissed her as crippled" (p261). Thus, greater questions are left unanswered. How would it be for these characters if they were not cured and they continued to use those crutches or wheelchairs? Would they still be themselves? Could they still live a normal life? This subject and its possibilities remain unexplored.

The development of character varie, as the central topic of these books is the emotional struggles of the characters and the supposed consequences of being disabled. While Izzy and Courtney are merely typical and popular girls, Valerie and Annie have especially strong qualities. Valerie is brash, irreverent, and feisty, while Anna is angry and intense, a fighter. Perhaps Valerie and Anna are given these characteristics as part of the 'overcomer' paradigm, particularly illustrated in the case of Valerie. In her temper tantrum at being pushed in a wheelchair, she tries to kick an aide and is able to budge her paralyzed leg for the first time.

The narration of *Izzy, Willy-Nilly*, *Peeling the Onion* and *Because She's My Friend* are in the first person. There is only dialogue in *Mind's Eye*. While this creates a sense of immediacy, it also makes it more difficult to remove the prejudiced opinions that the characters entertain about being disabled. In *Clo and the Albatross*, Beth is seen solely through the perspective of her sister, distancing us from an already distant character. As bad as the 'injury' stories were, this presentation is even worse. From Clo's perspective, Beth is presented as a horror. Clo is so embarrassed to be seen with Beth that she denies Beth is her sister, pretending that she is taking "some inmate from the local home out for a walk" (Edlin-White, p71). To Clo, Beth is a "deadweight" (p85). Clo hears Beth breathing at night and feels "repulsed" because "it was like sharing a bedroom with someone she didn't know and couldn't escape" (p22). Beth "remains a stranger, wearing Beth's clothes and sleeping in Beth's bed" (p39). It is only with difficulty that Clo realizes that she is "not an enemy alien" (p85). Beth remains a stranger to the reader as well. Even the descriptions of Beth dehumanize her; she cries "in a rusty, creaky sort of way" (p29) when she sees gymnastics on television and recalls the sport in which she used to excel. Even towards the end of the book, when Beth is afforded more dialogue, her personality remains a complete blank.

A DIFFERENT APPROACH

Fortunately, Lois Keith's *A Different Life* (1997) takes this storyline and the stereotype of disability as being the worst thing that can happen and reverses it completely. Libby experiences paralysis in her legs due to an unexplained illness, possibly contracted in the sea. Not only does she still use a wheelchair at the story's conclusion, but she finds that her life is not over after all. She is still the same person. Her identity and her world have not crumbled. Her friends and family have not changed and abandoned her. After her accident, certain aspects of her life may be altered forever, but her life is certainly not worse.

Unlike the other protagonists, Libby is not particularly popular or athletic before her accident. The reasons for this are not entirely explained; she is simply 'normal'. She becomes more well-liked after her accident than before it, as she matures into a well-rounded teenager. Rather than experiencing isolation and abandonment in the hospital, Libby meets new friends. Her old classmates do not shy away. They rally behind her cause to allow her to remain in the same school in spite of the discrimination of the administrators. Jesse, the boy who may have indirectly caused her viral infection by giving her a playful shove into the sea, volunteers to help modify her house. Towards the end of the story, a romantic relationship begins between the two.

A Different Life does not indicate that there is anything tragic or utterly devastating about Libby's impairment. Instead, this novel presents the Social Model of Disability[1]. In a memorable sequence, Libby's father invites reporters to interview the family as a way of exposing the pollution problem that potentially caused Libby's illness. When the news programme is aired, Libby is humiliated and enraged at the portrayal of her as a helpless victim. This moment shows how biased attitudes persist in the structure of society as a whole — Libby is far more upset by the condescending portrayal of her in the local media than by her need to use a wheelchair. When trying to return to school, she is more hindered by society's prejudices than by the paralysis in her lower legs. Even if Libby does not experience a recovery, the disablist prejudices of society can be 'overcome' and Libby can live a full life. At the novel's end, she is planning her career and looking forward to her future with confidence.

A Different Life is innovative in its attitude and encouraging to readers with and without impairments. The book very clearly sends a message against the grain of the other 'injury' stories. The author did not feel compelled to provide even a partial rehabilitation to assuage the stereotype that a disability is worse than anything else. To some extent, however, having experienced high school in the US around the same time as Libby experienced it in the UK, Libby's increased popularity after her accident does not strike me as being entirely plausible. Because of deep-rooted stereotypes, being disabled did make a difference in how my peers perceived me as a person. I have also confronted prejudices in the academic world and employment situations that none of my non-disabled peers fully understood. This, fortunately, has not been the dominant trend. If more books like *A Different Life* are written, the stereotype of disability as tragedy, as well as many other stereotypes, may be dispelled. Crucially, Lois Keith is disabled herself.

CONCLUSION

Every young adult reader hopes to sympathize with the protagonists of a book and to understand, and perhaps share, their feelings. However, many of these books were obviously not written with the consideration that a young adult with impairments might read them. While the stereotypes of compensatory abilities and determined 'overcomers' are silly and formulaic, characters in the 'injury' stories voice the opinion that life for disabled people is demeaning and worthless. This is perhaps the most harmful stereotype of all. Many misconceptions and prejudices remain unacknowledged and unchallenged.

For example, in *Because She's My Friend*, Valerie meets other disabled people on a bus. She learns that they became disabled from various accidents and thinks, "I thought they were born disabled, that they'd had a lifetime to get used to being half human" (Sirof, p58). As a person who was born with an impairment, I would not be able to enjoy this book after this moment. Similar attitudes of revulsion toward disabled people are found when Anna and Izzy are sickened to be considered "one of them". As a disabled reader, it is discouraging to consider that statement as a representation of how 'normal' people think of me.

It is disappointing when the author ascribes these thoughts to a character who is otherwise dynamic and engaging, and whose fate and circumstances could prove this statement to be entirely false. Even if the authors are personally more enlightened, they apparently assume that most young adult readers would be complicit with this attitude. These statements set the tone for the continued prevalence of stereotypes when portraying disabled characters of all ages. While negative attitudes toward disabled people are often expressed in the portrayal of adolescents, a stereotype on the other extreme is used to represent adult characters such as Annie. While contradicting that a person with an impairment is "half human", the author creates an over-achieving superhuman.

It is obvious that many of these books do not present a genuine picture of life with a disability. Neither do they begin to explore the range of impairments and access needs that exist in real life. There is a marked preference trend toward impairments that are relatively mild, thus conveniently enabling the characters to walk, albeit with difficulty. This is the case for Leslie in *Paper Doll* and Jessie in *The Ghost of Grania O'Malley*. With the exception of Maxwell's learning difficulties, there were no 'invisible' impairments in my survey: I found no blind, epileptic, autistic or Deaf characters.

I also found no characters with severe physical impairments. There are obviously many possibilities here, such as various forms of muscular dystrophy, spina bifida or cerebral palsy. Unsurprisingly, my impairment, osteogenesis imperfecta, is absent. Perhaps the authors did not know enough about these conditions, or were unwilling to portray impairments that may be considered obscure or unpalatable. Perhaps they assumed that most readers could not relate to such characters. However, including such characters in fiction may help tear down social barriers and clouds of mystery surrounding people with these impairments. Readers would learn to relate to them as individuals, rather than as unknown, otherworldly inspirations.

There is a marked tendency to portray impairments that have some sort of visual aid to accompany them, whether it is a wheelchair, prosthesis, or crutches. One can only surmise that the authors were more comfortable where there is something tangible to describe, thus indicating a predisposition to portray impairment on an external rather than internal level. In *Phoning a Dead Man*, for example, Annie's wheelchair is mentioned repeatedly, sometimes as a substitute for Annie herself. In a sequence when Annie answers the phone, a detail is added that Annie "kept her phone in a little pocket on the arm of her chair" (Cross, p4). Later on, Annie is "facing them with her wheelchair squeezed in between the armchair and the fireplace" (p18). The moment when John's mother criticizes Annie for causing John to go to Russia, she charges "towards the wheelchair" (p19). Why not "towards Annie"? The mere presence of Annie's wheelchair takes precedence over Annie as a character, making her more of a "thing" than a person.

Wheelchairs, canes, and crutches are overly emphasized in the 'injury' stories as well, but as symbols that ostracize their users from society and 'normal lives'. They are described as embarrassing and nasty. When Beth in *Clo and the Albatross* sits at the table (I assume this hides the wheelchair), she looks "quite normal," like the "real Beth" and as if nothing had "ever happened to change her" (Edlin-White, p79). When Courtney begins her mental journey to Italy, she refuses even to consider a wheelchair. She remarks:

> there's no way I'm going to be in a wheelchair and have people staring at me all over Italy and crossing themselves when they see me coming. So forget the wheelchair by my bed. ... I walk to the window. Just like anybody." (Fleischman, p37)

Valerie, in *Because She's My Friend*, says that the doctors "gave me a cane, but I refused to look like an old lady. I dropped the cane down the incinerator; it made a satisfying clatter as it fell" (Sirof, p182). There are similar comments in *Peeling the Onion* and *Izzy, Willy-Nilly*. Where does this leave those who are unable to be mobile without these objects?

In *Freak the Mighty*, the fantastic story of exaggeration and adventure, opinions are different. Maxwell is fascinated by Kevin's crutches and braces. Nevertheless, I am wary of the continued use of stereotypes in this novel, starting with

Kevin's astounding genius and Maxwell's unbelievable stature. Also, why must Kevin be called "Freak"? Nicknames can be fun among friends and I do not want to mask the world under the bland shades of political correctness, but why must Kevin be something other than human? Why must disabled characters be so supernaturally brave, smart and good that they seem closer to action figures, cartoon superheroes or hallucinations than real people? As entertaining as this story is, it sends a distorted message.

For a book that does not present the 'injury' scenario, only *Paper Doll* presents a disabled person as a believable and multifaceted human being with both strengths and weaknesses. Other books, such as *The Ghost of Grania O'Malley*, typecast disabled characters and present them using conventional formulas. With their impairments that disappear under the right circumstances, they remain unrealistic and almost ridiculous. To their credit, the 'injury' stories have a greater adherence to medical authenticity. The characters experience stays in hospitals and physical rehabilitation, just as, for many disabled people, increased visits to the medical world are unavoidable.

Another factor is absent or only weakly rendered in the depiction of these disabled characters — ethnicity. Although it is mentioned that Leslie in *Paper Doll* has a Jewish background and Jessie in *The Ghost of Grania O'Malley* is Irish, no portrayals went beyond this. In this respect, the portrayal of disabled characters is incomplete and superficial. I can only conjecture that because having an impairment places a character in one of society's so-called 'minority groups', the authors felt little incentive to add additional context or tackle multiple levels of personal background. Reality is not like this. In our diverse and multicultural society, numerous factors overlap. The treatment of this theme remains grossly incomplete.

There is no definite trend of progress over the years. While *A Different Life* was a great advance in the depiction of the lives of disabled people, *Mind's Eye* was published two years after this. Ultimately, most disabled characters are treated differently than other characters. In many cases they are manipulated for effect, or leveraged as devices to send various messages. These messages are not necessarily related to disabilities. Katie in *Willow King* is used to show the power of inspiration and determination; *Izzy, Willy-Nilly* reveals the consequences of drunk driving; Courtney in *Mind's Eye* and Kevin in *Freak the Mighty* develop the theme of the power of the imagination. The situations of the characters are used for a didactic purpose, and their impairments are present for a particular contrast or for stronger pathos. Unlike much other young adult literature, these books are not written simply to amuse readers with adventures, enchant them with intricate plots or challenge them with thorny moral issues. Even Libby in *A Different Life* is used to send a message about being disabled, although a very laudable and positive one.

Due to the frequent recourse to stereotypes, disabled characters are rarely life-like. Few books portray a disabled person as living a dynamic existence in a typical environment. It would be refreshing to read about a disabled girl or boy who runs for class president or who has a humorous experience at summer camp. Disabled characters should have adventures and solve mysteries without any extraordinary superpowers or sentimental moments of overwhelming determination.

Behind all the formulas used to present these

fictional characters is the overarching stereotype that having an impairment unavoidably and completely defines a person. Disability is seen to predominate over all other identifying aspects of an individual, producing particular temperaments and talents. Therefore, many authors find a dependable technique before them: once they decide to depict a disabled character, they can select from an array of prearranged consequences. Although the resulting character may not be fully believable as a human being, the character will still be familiar to readers in light of the stereotypes which prevail in literature and the media.

Nevertheless, I refuse to believe it is easier to exploit stereotypes than to present a disabled character as a real person. Once stereotypes are recognized, conventional formulas can be avoided with foresight and imagination. Otherwise, all that is needed is to establish a complete character and plot, insert the presence of a disability with appropriate details and descriptions, and take a look at the results. This might be closer to reality.

NOTES

1) The Social Model of Disability emphasizes dignity, independence, choice and privacy. Furthermore, it perceives the individual holistically rather than labeling them with medical terms. One of the key concepts of the Social Model is that society disables people, and that this occurs when a person is excluded because of their access needs from something that other people in society take for granted. For example, using the Social Model, a wheelchair user who is unable to use a bus or enter the cinema is disabled because the bus does not have a lowered floor and the cinema a ramp, and not because of their impairment. The medical terminology of the Medical Model is paternalistic and exclusive, thus putting barriers in the way of the person with an impairment; it has a 'cannot do' labeling which pigeon-holes the individual, while the Social Model adopts the 'can do' approach to impairment, looking for streamlined ways around any difficulties, including the individual at every opportunity.

REFERENCES

Cross, Gillian, *Phoning a Dead Man*, Holiday House, New York, 2002 (UK title: *Calling A Dead Man*, Oxford University Press, 2001).

Edlin-White, Rowena, *Clo and the Albatross*, Lion Publishing Ltd, London, 1996.

Feuer, Elizabeth, *Paper Doll*, Farrar, Straus, and Giroux, New York, 1990.

Fleischman, Paul, *Mind's Eye*, Henry Holt and Company, New York, 1999.

Keith, Lois, *A Different Life*, The Women's Press, London, 1997.

Morpurgo, Michael, *The Ghost of Grania O'Malley*, Viking, New York, 1996.

Orr, Wendy, *Peeling the Onion*, Holiday House, New York, 1996.

Philbrick, W, Rodman, *Freak the Mighty*, The Blue Sky Press, New York, 1993.

Platt, Chris, *Willow King*, Random House, New York, 1998.

Sirof, Harriet, *Because She's My Friend*, Atheneum, New York, 1993.

Voigt, Cynthia, *Izzy, Willy-Nilly*, Ballantine Books, New York, 1986.

ROLE MODELS

EARLY PERIOD

IV. NOT ALWAYS CURED OR KILLED: DISABILITY IN EARLY 20TH-CENTURY GIRLS' SCHOOL STORIES

HELEN A. AVELING

IN this chapter, I shall be focusing on the early girls' school-story writers and their portrayal of physical impairment in a selection of school stories originally published before the Second World War. The books that I shall be discussing in detail are Dorita Fairlie Bruce's three-book 'St Brides' series and her six-book 'Springdale' series; two stand-alone books by Dorothea Moore; and one of May Wynne's stand-alone titles. I will look at the extent to which the portrayal of disability within girls' fiction of this type was accurate, and how the depiction of disabled characters altered through the first thirty-nine years of the last century. I will also look at the extent to which disabled characters can be considered to be role models, whether or not a modern reader would regard these as being positive or negative, and whether or not this was intentional on the part of the author. I am, perforce, using broad definitions in my definitions of impairment in this chapter, and I am dealing solely with characters with poor or no vision or limited mobility, since these are the only impairments to feature.

When I was younger, I realised that it was very rare to find a positive portrayal of a physically disabled person in the fiction written at any point during the twentieth century, but even more so for the fiction written in the early years of the century. Further, the disabled child characters that I knew about were passive, 'too-good-to-be-true' children, as if impairment, passivity and moral superiority were inextricably bound together. It was only when, as a confirmed adult book collector, I stumbled across Dorita Fairlie Bruce's 'St Brides' and 'Springdale' books that I realised this may not be a fair assessment of the genre of girls' school stories.

This made me want to look more deeply into the portrayal of disability in children's fiction at the beginning of the twentieth century, and more specifically within girl's school stories, for two reasons. First — and quite apart from the fact that I collect girls' school stories as a hobby — once one reaches the turn of the nineteenth–twentieth century it is a definable genre, one specifically created for girls to read. The genre has a clear reading age range of between eight and fifteen years old; is presented in a definable format; and has a clear 'history'.

(The genre is commonly associated with Angela Brazil, whose first school story, *The Fortunes of Philippa*, was published in 1905 and is generally taken to be the prototype for the modern girls' school story. Despite this, Brazil is not being included in this study, because of the invisibility of disability within her better-known stories. She is also half a generation older than the authors included in this chapter.)

The second main reason for focusing on early girls' school stories is that they show us a microworld where girls and women function almost exclusively without male input and influence. Often the adult males are in the role of a token male teacher who clearly has his fair share of feminine qualities, or men have 'walk-on' parts with minimum influence on this cocoon of femaleness.

This feminine world is one which is breaking away from the Victorian models of girlhood and the imposition of standards which they had to meet to conform to the model of the "sweet little woman or girl" (Gill Frith, ' "The Time of your Life": the meaning of the school story', quoted in Rosemary Auchmuty, *A World of Girls*, p27, Bettany Press, 2004). The breaking away from role models imposed on girls by men offered an opportune vehicle to shed the more usually held perception of disability, yet few writers took up that challenge. However, in the context of the invisibility of disabled characters elsewhere in girls' fiction, their representation is still significant.

A LIFE ON WHEELS

The school-story writer Dorita Fairlie Bruce, best known for her 'Dimsie' books, created an absolutely memorable character in Winifred Arrowsmith when she wrote *Girls of St Bride's* (1923). In addition, the other two 'St Bride's' books show Winifred as an adult with a valid and purposeful role within the school community; not only is she allowed to grow up, but as with non-disabled characters, she is able to work.

Descriptions in children's books (and elsewhere) of individuals who lack some kind of physical ability (they do not need to be disabled, they can often just be 'ill') are nearly always linked to the person's temperament, and that temperament is universally either 'warped' or extremely 'saintly'. Although the language used by Bruce to describe Winifred is very much of the era in which the book was written and published — the word "cripple" features heavily — the characterisation is better and more life-like than some books that were written and published in the

1970s or 1980s. In breaking away from the 'classic' response to disability — although Bruce does touch on the 'warped' aspect at the beginning — she does something that none of her contemporaries do; she creates a believable girl who could transfer out of the book and into a modern lightweight wheelchair. The twenty-first century reader can definitely engage with Winifred and the girls and staff around her, and the school community is believable to the extent that it draws one into the story.

I first encountered Winifred when we were both adults, she in the small school community where she was an "honorary secretary" in Dorita Fairlie Bruce's *Nancy at St Bride's* (p16), and I in my book-collecting life. In spite of this, I did not register that I had found a wheelchair-using character who was *not* longing for a miracle cure to set her free until I bought a copy of *Girls of St Bride's* (1923) in the first three months of 1994. It was only then that I realised Winifred, one of the main protagonists in the book, used a wheelchair! The reason I can narrow my discovery of Winifred down to such a precise point was that I attended a centenary celebration for one of Dorita Fairlie Bruce's contemporaries, Elinor M Brent-Dyer, in Hereford in April of that year, and vividly remember sharing my excitement with other book collectors.

With hindsight, I cannot work out why I missed the (admittedly few) references to Winifred's chair in the other two 'St Bride's' books. It might have been because in the later books she is a member of staff, or because I read the books too fast, even on re-reads. However, I *did* miss the references at first, but that weekend in Hereford I was able to share my excitement with people who did not think me odd to be getting excited about a fictional character, even one who, if she had been alive, would by then have been in her early nineties. Why was this character getting me excited, and what made her different from her fictional peers?

Crucially, Winifred is not cured during the course of the books, and neither does she die before the end of the series. As a late teen in *Girls of St Bride's*, she would be at least in her mid-twenties in the third book, *Nancy Returns to St Bride's* (1938), where she is in flourishing good health and is happy and content even though she uses a wheelchair. This combination of adult life and health in itself remains unusual even today, though it is true that CM Yonge's heroines did sometimes survive their disabling event to become a valued member of the family (Dowker, 2004).[2] However, Yonge's stories revolve around family life, and were written as much for their mothers as for older girls and young women. In the context of the girls' school story, Winifred is rare, to put it mildly. Although these stories portrayed a female community where girls could achieve, on a fictional level, the same type of goals as their male cousins or brothers (Auchmuty, p15), it was nonetheless a community where girls learnt how to conform to real-life expectations. This in turn meant the acceptance of whatever came their way, and in terms of impairment, this involved needing (or wanting) to conform or be cured.

By the end of the three-book 'St Bride's' series, Winifred is an adult with an impairment that hampers her mobility, an individual who is not hankering for the ability to walk, but most importantly, one who is treated in the same way as any other member of staff. Why is this important? It is critical because it portrays a positive picture of impairment at a time when anyone who was impaired was frequently shut away from 'normal' life, either by their family shutting them off in their own home or through living in an institution (Borsay, 2005).[3]

At the beginning of *Girls of St Bride's*, Winifred is an established pupil who, as with the others, is from a middle-class background (her father is said to be a publisher). St Bride's is a boarding school on a remote Hebridean island off the coast of Scotland (in later books the island changes location and becomes less isolated). It has been founded for girls who are poor (though still middle class), or 'delicate', or both. Winifred is portrayed as having isolated herself by her acid tongue and unwelcoming manner, and as having traded on her inability to walk to get away with this behaviour without comment, the proverbial 'Cat That Walked Alone'. Within the world of the girls' school story, none of these attributes are specific to a character in a wheelchair, although the wheelchair does act as a magnifying glass in this instance — and, of course, there is some resonation with modern stereotypes of the 'crip with a chip' [on their shoulder].

This all changes with the arrival at the school of two sisters, Morag and Christine Maclean. Morag is placed in the Sixth Form with Winifred, while Christine joins the traditionally exuberant Fourth Form. In the first encounter between the two girls, Winifred is described as being 'peevish' — not a good example to anyone — but Morag stands firm and it is Winifred who gives way, perhaps for the first time in many years. Morag is the one who teaches Winifred to be a more amiable person and to be less prickly, rather than the saintly invalid teaching the lessons of patience to the non-disabled. This makes Winifred truer to life and more believable than her literary predecessors.

It is probably inevitable that it is the intervention of a non-disabled girl that allows Winifred to become part of schoolgirl society, rather than Winifred achieving this herself without help. However, the friendship and interaction between Winifred and Morag is the direct reverse of Beth March's interaction with her sisters, which prior to this had been the overwhelming literary model of female disability. It is also important to situate the characters' interaction within the wider conventions of the genre. In the world of the girls' school story, a common theme is the girl who learns to fit into the school community; often the girl is new to the school; but on occasion she is already an established pupil, in this case, Winifred. Another common theme is the girl whose family has lost their money and whose family home has become a school; this is Morag, who is therefore part of the story in her own right rather than functioning only to help Winifred.

When the girls first meet, Winifred automatically uses the disparaging approach that she expects Morag to respond to, saying:

> "Nobody ever does expect it [to see someone using a wheelchair] at a boarding-school — they *feel* St. Bride's shouldn't be used as a sanatorium even though they may be too polite to say it. But unfortunately, you see, I've got to be educated." (p41)

It is worth noting here that Bruce never questions Winifred's need of and right to education, despite the fact that disabled girls would not normally be regarded as 'having' to be educated, let alone alongside their peers.

Winifred has been so accustomed to manipulating people that, although she wants to be independent, she is at the same time, quite content to play the 'cripple' if it suits her (p217) — not to ask other people to do things for her, but to get away with being rude to them. (Perhaps this habit began partly to avoid rejection by getting in first.) However, later on in their friendship, Winifred realises that here:

> was a girl who treated her as an equal rather than a poor invalid to be indulged and humoured, and yielded all the homage of pity. It was a new sensation, and [she] came to the conclusion that it was a pleasant one. (p49)

Bruce does not shy away from the fact that Winifred has previously been isolated from the rest of her community, and instead tackles the issue of the differential treatment that she has come to expect head-on.

> "I wonder if you can have any idea, Morag, how hateful it is to be pitied all the time? Oh, I don't mean openly! but I can feel it, all the same, and it makes me want to assert myself somehow. That's why I give myself airs, as you think."
> Morag also grew grave. ...
> "Of course, you *have* to assert yourself," she said slowly. "But there are heaps of better ways. I think — I think people who pitied you anyhow would do it all the more if you bristled up..." (pp96-7)

The first encounter between Morag and Winifred sets the tone for the rest of the friendship. New girl Morag meets "a pale dark haired girl, whose eyes seemed too large for the rest of her face" when she runs into "an invalid carriage which was being propelled rapidly housewards by its occupant" (p40). The fact that Bruce has Winifred actively propelling her own wheelchair rather than being pushed is interesting in itself, as I am unaware of any other fictitious wheelchair user of the period pushing themselves anywhere. The plausibility of the action is another matter, as wheelchairs were sturdily built and the probability that a girl in her mid-teens could propel one at any speed is unlikely, particularly as the girls are on a path that goes past some shrubbery.

I find it intriguing, too, that not only does Bruce suggest, if by default, that the school buildings were extremely wheelchair-friendly — Winifred sleeps on the same floor as the rest of her peers — but also that the grounds were too. However, a remark from a short story published in an annual from the early 1930s suggests that Winifred did occasionally have some assistance at school (*Victoria Victrix*, p60). This revision may have resulted from Bruce's belated realisation that schools were not, by and large, accessible without difficulty — which, of course, is still true today. Normally, though, Winifred is referred to as wheeling herself about, both as a schoolgirl and later as an adult.

Leaving aside this practical aspect, which I will return to later, Winifred is introduced to the reader when she is actively doing something, just as any other girl in the school would be. This is also an indicator that here is a disabled character who is atypical when it comes to their portrayal. Gone is the 'pale but interesting' and 'brave' invalid. Gone, too, is the fleetingly disabled girl learning to conform to society's norm for a woman-to-be before making a full 'recovery'. Even in the supposedly enlightened twenty-first century, the media frequently uses the image of a 'brave and courageous' person who 'suffers' from a disability, as if every impairment is an illness requiring the individual to 'endure' life as the a 'poor, sweet, courageous' but fragile person. At no point in *Girls of St Bride's* does Winifred conform to the norms of the day, even though the school nurse feels the compulsion to apply them! Admittedly the two illustrations of Winifred show her well-wrapped up, but on a purely practical level, sitting in a wheelchair is not always very warm so the illustrator, H. Coller, may possibly be acknowledging this.

In spite of not playing games with her fellows, Winifred would have had to have remarkable physical stamina — as much, in a very different way, as the most athletic person in the school. Winifred must have had incredible strength in her arms and back to push herself around in her 'invalid carriage'. As far as my personal experience of British wheelchairs goes, as late as the early 1970s wheelchairs had heavy steel frames, not the nice, lightweight aluminium alloys used now. Looking at the illustrations in the 'St Bride's' books, it would have needed quite a lot of muscle power to propel a steel-and-wood 'invalid carriage' which was common from the 1930s up to the 1950s, especially being as well wrapped up as she is always shown.

The Railway Museum in York has a display of the type of things that were transported by rail and it includes a few wood-and-wicker wheelchairs with large front wheels, the style of chair that Coller draws Winifred sitting in. Although these wood-framed chairs would not be as heavy to manoeuvre as the wood-and-steel ones, they are no less cumbersome. For a non-disabled person pushing such wheelchairs, the ones that have the larger wheels at the front and the caster wheels at the back are far harder to push than the ones with the large wheels at the back. Therefore, Winifred would have had to push herself all day, every day, or at least provide a guiding hand when someone else pushed her.

Winifred is a three-dimensional person. She has both good and bad points. She does care about people, yet she rubs them up the wrong way by her prickly nature. She is interested in school activities, but feigns indifference rather than allow people to get close to her. No one who reads the book could describe Winifred as a paragon of virtue, to be held up as an example of goodness for non-disabled girls to emulate like Beth March or Cousin Helen. Instead, Winifred was the 'odd one out' at school, watching games rather than taking part in them (*Victoria Victrix*, 1930, p62).

Critically, nor is Winifred's character irretrievably 'warped' by her impairment. Rather, her inclination to manipulate those around her by playing on the fact that she is, in her words, "a cripple", is shown as a reaction to her past treatment. A fellow Sixth former tells Morag that they have been "so sorry for her that we give in to her right and left. She rides roughshod over every one, even the mistresses except, of course, the Head." (p287) This only adds to her believability — it would take a saint not to get fed up at being stereotyped, excluded and pitied — and can be attributed to Bruce's skill at characterisation.

I can only think of one character in the more widely accessible children's classics who is as manipulative as Winifred, and that is Colin Craven in Frances Hodgson Burnett's *The Secret Garden*. Both have been permitted to get into the habit of throwing tantrums or to be allowed to ride roughshod over every one in sight. Both resemble Katy Carr before Cousin Helen's visit, with the individual feeling sorry for themselves and determined to use that to achieve whatever they want — although Winifred pities herself because of her different social treatment, and not because of her impairment. Both have been unjustly treated in the past, and both have been denied the experience of normal childhood treatment because of adults' perceptions of them. Even the headmistress — a woman who normally has no difficulty in dealing with girls of all types — finds Winifred difficult to understand because she treats her as being different, and "had always been baffled by Winifred, and hardly knew how to tackle her but it had to be done." (p216)

Following Morag's lead, the Sixth Form begin to treat Winifred in a less pitying way, and gradually the girl is drawn into the form on an equal footing. This leads to a conversation in which Winifred explains why she allowed another Sixth Former to take the blame for reporting a group of the Sixth for breaking bounds. The conversation sees Winifred expressing resentment for *not* being considered capable of reporting her peers. A non-disabled girl would have been subject to the schoolgirl code of honour as outlined by Auchmuty[3], but she has been deemed exempt from being judged by that same code because her peers have consistently just dismissed her behaviour as "being 'just Winifred' "— an unaccountable person whose ways were not to be judged by ordinary standards." (p256)

This treatment continues when she has confessed.

> "I haven't explained," she retorted. "There isn't any explanation. And if it was anyone but me, you'd have a great deal more to say about it!"
> "Of all the weird creatures!" exclaimed Rhoda Harrington, the first to break it. "She didn't seem a bit grateful to Elizabeth for letting her down so lightly!" (p256)

Winifred goes on to admit aloud that she had "such

a hateful, detestable, jealous, malicious nature" (p255) for not confessing earlier, but while she is reflecting a stereotype of disability here, her actions show her nature to be far different to this. Overall, is she anything other than an ordinary girl? No, and this is part of her appeal.

In the climax to *The Girls of St Brides*, Winifred's friends set out to rescue her after she has been seen wheeling herself towards a building that is in danger of being swept away by the sea in a storm. They are afraid that, at the least, the wheels of her chair will have become trapped in the mud. In fact, Winifred has returned safely and competently on her own by another route, and it is her friends who need rescuing when they are swept out to sea by the flood. This is a complete reversal of the usual stereotype of the invalid who needs rescuing by non-disabled people.

At one telling point, though, Bruce does echo more common descriptions in her portrayal of Winifred. It comes when, ashamed by what she is about to say, Winifred looks "down at her wheels" (p254), as if the chair was a part of her body. Up to this point, Winifred's chair has been a subsidiary element in Bruce's description and, as we have seen, denotes her athleticism and independence. At this point, though, the girl and the wheelchair combine to form one entity, Borg-like, and it jars on me.

In both *Nancy at St Bride's* (1933) and *Nancy Returns to St Bride's* (1938), the adult Winifred fulfils the role of a staff member who can act unofficially without the headmistress or other staff having to become involved in a situation. This role is a familiar one to readers of the genre, that of an 'Old Girl' returning as to school as Matron or, as here, School Secretary and acting as the girls' confidante. Indeed, Winifred plays counter-point to the locum headmistress Miss Warren in *Nancy Returns to St Bride's* whenever Nancy (or others) have direct dealings with her. Her wordless understanding of the feelings that Miss Warren creates in the pupils reassures them they are understood, and she even steps in to encourage a junior to continue to tell her story when Miss Warren seems too stunned by what she is hearing (p227). Winifred represents here the coolly competent 'old' member of staff who upholds the school's values when a stranger is temporarily in charge, a plot device familiar to the genre's readers and which elsewhere is used prominently by Elinor M. Brent-Dyer in particular.

As a girl, though, even when Winifred has become part of schoolgirl society, Bruce does not shy away from portraying the reality of life in a disabling world. In the short story, *Victoria Victrix* (published in *Every Girls' Story Book*, 1930), we get a brief glimpse of the 'new' Winifred, the one who is far more an equal member of the Sixth Form, when the girls are discussing a scholarship exam that will take one of them to university.

> "… Who else is trying for the Fearney? You and I, and Morag Maclean, and Rhoda — is that all? Winifred isn't down, is she?"
>
> "Oh, no! Poor old Win! She couldn't very well go to College, even if she got the Schol. Life there would be quite different from St. Bride's, you know, and she'd be up against a dozen different difficulties every day."…
>
> "It's all right, Rhoda. Don't look so embarrassed. What Margaret said was perfectly true. Life at the 'Varsity would be a little beyond my limitations." (*Victoria Victrix*, p60)

Here Winifred is acknowledging the fact that she

knows life would be physically more demanding outside the safe confines of school, but is she hinting at a masked desire to try at the same time? Fellow schoolgirl Elizabeth Hawthorn comments of Winifred that she "always had such a good business head that one felt that she would have done well in a profession if she hadn't been a cripple, poor soul!" (*Nancy at St Bride's*, p16) The fact that Winifred returns to the school in *Nancy at St Bride's* (1933) as an honorary secretary begs the question for me of *why* she returned. I have never been sure that Winifred was a Scot, but assuming that she was, the island where the school is based is far enough away for any family in either Glasgow or Edinburgh to feel 'comfortable' in off-loading a social embarrassment. It would be even more attractive a solution if Winifred were from an English family.

> "Her father died ... and Winifred hasn't any near relations, so she wrote and asked the Head to take her on as sort of honorary secretary — which, of course, saves one salary, so it's a help to the school." (*Nancy at St Bride's*, p16)

Leaving aside the issue of why Winifred does not deserve to have a salary — is it because she has a private income and as a 'lady' should not take paid employment, or because she is disabled and therefore not worth a proper wage? — Dorita Fairlie Bruce here seems to have forgotten what she had written in a previous book, in this case in *Girls of St Bride's* where Winifred had said "... I may be handicapped in other ways, but, thank goodness! I've got both my parents, and liberty to have as many friends as I can make — as many as will consent to stand me, that is!" (p287) At this point Winifred's family background is indistinguishable from that of her peers. So, what has happened to her mother? Perhaps she is also dead. Or one may surmise, possibly, that following the death of Mr Arrowsmith, Winifred's mother washed her hands of this family embarrassment and burden, actively encouraging her daughter to write to her old headmistress.

From the school-story reader's point of view, though, Winifred's return to the school can be viewed quite differently. In the world of the girls' school story, returning to school as an adult to work was generally an indicator that a character was to be admired, with teaching, or any other post in the school, portrayed as being a fulfilling life choice in itself and not merely as a prelude to marriage. Winifred's "business head" provided her with a reason to return without having first to attend the inaccesssible "'Varsity", and the death of her father provided the excuse. In becoming a permanent part of the world of the school, Winifred was granted the ultimate accolade.

The adult Winifred is described by Nancy, at the beginning of *Nancy Returns to St Bride's*, as:

> "rather a marvel, for she has been a cripple all her life, and works herself about the place in a wheeled chair; but she's tremendously keen on St. Bride's, and when I was there she was very popular with all the girls. You see, she is a species of mistress, with all the advantages of having been one of the girls, which makes her a very understanding person."
>
> "Then you won't mind her being there still, even though she does know all about your murky past?"
>
> "Oh, dear, no! Winifred is different. Besides, she was always very decent to me, and she would be sure to understand." (p15)

Bruce does not make Winifred's disability invisible, but instead describes her as "wheeling" or as having a board across the arms of her chair on which she either wrote by hand or used her "little typewriter" (*Nancy Returns to St Bride's*, p180). Bruce creates an image of action and independence, thus stressing that Winifred is both disabled and the equal of anyone. During the climax of *Nancy at St Bride's*, Bruce writes of Winifred that she

> went off to take charge of the Juniors, and so release Mademoiselle (who was on duty) for more active service. The cripple was very popular with the Lower School, whose wildest spirits were far too chivalrous to take advantage of her infirmity, and indeed, she could keep order better than any other member of the staff except the Head herself. (p175)

This, then, is no weakling, no self-obsessed invalid who thinks the world owes them a raft of favours. Rather, Winifred is a competent adult who functions well within the perameters of the school story.

Why did Dorita Fairlie Bruce create a girl with a nebulous impairment without the seemingly obligatory death or miracle cure built into the storyline? Why was she able, rightly, to ascribe Winifred's resentment to her treatment by her peers and not to her impairment? Why was she able to show Winifred's character as ultimately being unaffected by her impairment, either for good or for bad? We do not know, but in doing so, Bruce created a memorable character for me. As an adult, book-collecting disabled woman, I am fascinated by the snapshot glimpses of Winifred. She is both able to do anything and nothing at the same time.

AN AMAZING AMERICAN

Dorothea Moore also bucked the trend when she created a blind girl, American Sadie Vanhessel, in *The Only Day-Girl* (1923). Sadie is pragmatic about her lack of sight, and is more three-dimensional than some other characters with a disability. Yet, in our first meeting with Sadie, Moore presents us with a totally dependent girl, sitting on wet grass among some trees. This Sadie is the sadly usual early twentieth-century disabled character, passively waiting to be rescued or helped. The principal character, Anne Jacobina Severn (AJ) asks Sadie:

> "You know the grass is dampish. Should you mind my going to your door with you? Colds are such hateful things, aren't they?"
> "That's kind," said the girl, a shade less flatly. "If it isn't a trouble to you, I'd be real glad. Ellen's young man passes this way from work, and I guess she's met him."
> She spoke with a weary matter-of-factness, as though she were well used to things of that kind happening to her. (p38)

Although AJ is puzzled to find anyone sitting on damp grass under the trees, her mind picks up on Sadie's speech; we are not told what AJ actually thinks it is. The description of a "flat voice" may equally refer to Sadie's boredom or to her American accent, which is typically contrasted with the clipped English upper- and middle-class diction as being flat and lacking the expected tonal qualities. Elinor Brent-Dyer employs the same writer's shorthand when introducing the American Cornelia Flower to the Chalet School readers in *Head Girl of the Chalet School* (1928). It is her nationality, as much as her blindness, that makes Sadie different.

Following their first meeting, AJ is inspired to attempt to experience what it is like to not have sight. The girl stands perfectly still, having decided to try to stand, with her eyes tightly shut for as long as it takes her to count to a thousand. As she does so, she ruminates that it:

> must be too awful to be blind and dependent on an Ellen. ... Other senses seemed curiously awake. There was a queer, acrid smell in the air, which she had not noticed ... now she wondered that she could have missed it, or not noticed it more when her eyes were open. (pp50-1).

This, I suspect, is what most non-visually impaired children would try if they got to know someone with sight problems, but Dorothea Moore falls back on clichés in this passage: the imagined compensatory workings of the other senses, so her voice seems louder and her sense of smell better. In fact, what AJ smells is the beginning of the gorse fire, which traps Sadie, and nothing supernatural! This, the first of three accidents, shows Sadie's total dependence on others.

> The flames were already surrounding the blind girl on two sides and half the third, and they were spreading with fearful rapidity. ... The poor child had her hands held out as though she were trying to feel in which direction the flames were.(pp53-4)

The equally compulsory rescue follows, with AJ braving the flames to lead the helpless Sadie to safety (and to her absentee father's arms). AJ takes control, while the hapless Ellen is having hysterics with Mr Vanhessel dismissing her on the spot. The frontispiece from the first edition of the book (here reproduced on p17) shows AJ dragging Sadie by the hand through the gorse, with a total lack of awareness of the difficulties for Sadie! The book's illustrator, GW Goss, portrays Sadie stumbling along behind her rescuer with AJ firmly grasping one of her hands, and I have a sense of her being reduced to the status of a small child for the purpose of the image, a feeling which is born out by the text.

This episode is the spur to Sadie's enrolment as a day pupil at AJ's school. Deputy headmistress, Miss Loring, having taken the plunge by agreeing to take Sadie as a pupil, quickly locates a writing system described only as a "special writing-pad with raised lines" (p186) and a mistress teaches the blind girl to write. Although AJ is the girl who is mainly responsible for shepherding Sadie around the school, she is not burdened with it. Other girls include Sadie in the social life between lessons, although as both AJ and Sadie are day pupils at a boarding school, this is limited.

However, on her first afternoon at school Sadie is the target of a prank in the swimming pool by two girls who think she needs taking down a few pegs for showing them up in an oral history test that morning. It is only as AJ rescues her that they learn that Sadie is blind, for Moore tells the reader that: "Sadie [had] walked so steadily, even in these unaccustomed surroundings that not one among the other girls upon that flurried morning guessed that she could not see." (p68)

There is only one irritant for me with the characterisation of Sadie, and it is Moore's bestowing upon her of a phenomenal memory and learning abilities. I have to admit to wondering whether Sadie had even known the alphabet prior to starting at the school; her progress is so startlingly exceptional! Sadie's classmates express their amazement as she hadn't even had stories read to her before she started at the school, although Sadie does qualify her statement when she tells the girls that occasionally Ellen would read "bits of the daily paper serial" to her.

> ... AJ, not for the first time, felt proud of her friend, as Sadie answered cheerfully: "Well, I guess everybody has got to have a beginning." (p187)

Mr Vanhessel had told AJ that Sadie was intelligent, and yet unlike Winifred's parents he had not done anything towards meeting his daughter's educational needs, preferring to leave her to the mercies of locally based servants. It was only after he saw the standard of care that she was receiving from them (and through being impressed by AJ's rescue of her) that he did anything about providing Sadie with an education.

Interestingly, Sadie is not averse to contributing to some playful misinformation when she and others are asked to show a visitor around the school, and this replaces the passivity of her portrayal in the early parts of the book. Sadie, too, is instrumental in bringing about the rescue of AJ's parents, although this comes about from her writing to her father and asking him to see to it. Clearly at that point Sadie had more belief in her father's ability to get things done than he had shown in hers.

For me, then, the treatment of Sadie is both positive in that she is not quite a two-dimensional character — her sense of adventure and mischief are indicators of that — but at the same time Moore does not wholly manage to break free of the conventions regarding the characterisation of a visually impaired character.

ANGEL CHILDREN

Dorita Fairlie Bruce created another character who experiences some physical limitations in Nicola Carter, younger sister of autocratic Sydney Carter in *The New House-Captain* (1934). When Anne Willoughby and Primula Mary Beton first meet Nicola in the garden of the house Sydney had rented, she is described as being "... frail and delicate, with a cloud of fluffy golden hair round her small white face" (p17). However, Nicola does the usual thing and becomes well enough to go through the rest of the Springdale series as an ordinary girl at school.

Compare the description of Nicola with the first description of Winifred in *The Girls of St Bride's*, pushing herself towards St Bride's when Morag bumps into her "... a pale dark haired girl, whose eyes seemed too large for the rest of her face" (p40). Nicola is clearly pretty, while, reading this, my instant impression of Winifred is that she is very plain. Winifred is almost plainer than the twelve-year-old Joey Bettany in *The School at the Chalet* (1925), with her "cropped black hair [that] was so straight as almost to be described as lank, her big black eyes made the intense whiteness of her face even more startling than it need have been, and her cheeks and temples were hollow with continual ill-health" (p40).

Nicola's appearance in the second book of the series, *The Best House in the School*, manages to combine the 'interesting invalid' description with that of a classic schoolgirl minx. It is also the only time that she is described in this book. Described in

The Best House in the School as "a fairy-looking child with blue eyes and golden hair ... nursing [her cat, and having] gentle, dreamy tones that matched her face" (pp37-8), she is a hybrid of the butter-wouldn't-melt-in-her-mouth character and a frail child. Full of mischief, she personifies the female version of the innocent looking choirboy, and yet she is consistently described almost as if she was a frail and delicate child.

Some of the descriptions of Nicola are on a par with those of Brent-Dyer's Robin Humphries, a child with potential tendencies for tuberculosis, or indeed LM Montgomery's Emily. Despite — or in spite of — her air of fragility, Nicola is in the thick of any mischief, but she resented "her fairy-tale beauty, which she regarded with secret shame" (*The New House at Springdale*, p140). A prefect who had "learnt to suspect Nicola most when she appeared most cherubic" (*Captain of Springdale*, p193) highlights this ambiguity in Bruce's depictions of Nicola. This is certainly not the norm for a delicate character! The Nicola for the next two books is far more of a tomboy than an interesting invalid, and is hardly described at all. I found it interesting, however, to see a virtually identical description of Nicola in the opening chapter of *Captain Anne*, the final book in the Springdale series, to when Bruce first introduces her in *The New House-Captain*. The description seems to signal a decline in Nicola's health. I think it is telling that, when Nicola returns to school for the final two chapters, Bruce does not describe her at all, save for "[Nicola] turned round, revealing a rose-tinted face and a pair of seraphic violet eyes" (*Captain of Springdale*, p276). It is almost as if Bruce finds Nicola less interesting as a character once she has regained her health.

In contrast to Bruce, little Bernadine (Dina)

Willoughby in Elinor Brent-Dyer's *Seven Scamps* (1927), part of a seven-book series that flows into the Chalet School series, is described in extravagant terms, having a "mane of redgold hair which hung loosely over Dina's shoulders, making a mantle of glory in the sunlight" (pp17-18). Dina not only possesses a conscience appropriate for a budding angel, but she sees herself only in terms of her physical impairment, calling herself a hunchback and hating herself for it. Dina needs — and receives — surgery before she is cured.

Following this major and life-saving surgery, Dina goes with the rest of her family to Guernsey for the summer and gained "strength every day. The sun and the sea breezes had tanned her cheeks and the rich Guernsey milk and the happy life were filling up the hollows in her face. Her eyes were bright, and the bitter lines had vanished from her mouth" (p271). This is a huge contrast to the girl who was obsessed by the fact that "one shoulder was higher than the other", calling herself "deformed" and saying that she would "always go humpbacked" (pp17-18). Here, the stereotypes go unchallenged throughout. Dina can only be happy once she is no longer disabled, and in the mean time her character is embittered.

SWEET INVALIDS

In *Septima, Schoolgirl* (1915) Dorothea Moore created Septima Compton, the seventh child in a motherless and massive thirteen-child family, who is sent to school at the age of thirteen through her great-aunt's intervention in her nephew's family. Unused to school life, Septima unintentionally breaks a rule on her first afternoon there when she leaves the school grounds without permission. In her haste to try to find her way back, she bumps into a "spinal carriage" in which lay a girl who had "a little wedge of face that looked all eyes, and a perfectly charming smile" (p36).

According to the Beamish Collection's website, a spinal carriage is a flat basket on wheels that may or may not have a canopy.[5] The description gives a length of 207cm (6ft 1 inch) and a height of 84cm (2ft 9ins) with a width of 64cm (2ft), which makes it a rather cumbersome piece of mobility equipment! It is small wonder that Septima bumped into it as it was being wheeled along a pavement.

Following this meeting Septima sees the girl on a few occasions, although each time Moore references the invalid carriage as the means by which Septima identifies the young woman in it. The woman, whose name is withheld until the last few pages of the story, is passive and always cheerful, though Moore does not make this feature of her characterisation the dominant one. Rather, it is her physical attractiveness that Moore seems to linger on. When I collated the descriptions, I found that there was very little substance behind them.

In the seven occasions in which the occupant of the spinal carriage is described, four of them depict her having eyes which are far-seeing, two mention her "little face", two others make reference to her having a "very merry sort of laugh" with a "low voice" and the seventh simply describes her as a "strange grown-up girl, who was so wonderfully easy to talk to".

The book culminates in the inevitable rescue of the young woman in the spinal carriage by Septima, although a literal reading of those pages suggests that the schoolgirl was rescuing the carriage, not its occupant!

> Then she was up with the spinal carriage just as it touched the shaky fencing at the cliff edge, bursting through it.
>
> Septima did not try to seize the handle of the spinal carriage, instead she grabbed the springs beneath the basket and tried desperately to stop the carriage rolling off the edge.
>
> Above the roaring in her ears she heard a voice that came from the spinal carriage, and seemed oddly familiar — a voice that cried: "Septima, let go!"
>
> But she held on! (pp233-4)

It is only at the end of the book that the reader, through Septima, learns the character's name, and she turns out to be the "well-known novelist" Morwen Hey Seton. Rather than being entirely passive, this character has a successful career. However, the withholding of her name for the bulk of the book reflects a common thread in literature and results in almost nullifying the 'invalid's' persona, giving their characters the same invisibility factor and insignificance that I still experience when *not* being accosted in the street by people doing surveys. Morwen is used very obliquely to represent a goal of goodness and patience that Septima should strive for, but Septima regards her much more as a friend rather than an example along the lines of Cousin Helen or Beth March. The closest Morwen comes to being employed as an 'example' is at the end of the main encounter with Septima, when the schoolgirl wonders:

> whether having to lie all day in a spinal carriage made this girl's path a very uphill one. It would have seemed almost too steep to climb if she had been in her place. (p167)

Here are faint echoes for me of both Katy and her cousin, and, bizarrely, Pollyanna, with the outward-looking approach of the invalid, but Dorothea Moore then changes tack abruptly with the arrival of one of the other schoolgirls, who seems not to notice either the carriage or its occupant! We are not told whether Septima continues to wonder about what her friend's life was like, or if it slipped her mind.

FEMINISED BOYS

Another author of girls' school stories, May Wynne, introduces the schoolgirl reader of *Peggy's First Term* (1922) to a six-year-old boy who is variously described as having a "humped" or "twisted" back and who is "delicate". Tom McGregor, nephew of the headmistress, is befriended by Canadian new girl Peggy Winways. Interestingly, he is described as a very young child who can be amused with feminine pursuits such as being sung to, told fairy tales, making daisy chains or picking flowers.

> A woman in grey cloak and bonnet was pushing a light bath-chair in which was seated a small, dark-haired boy of about six. His brown eyes seemed too large for his small face and held a look of suffering. (p14)

Peggy and another girl, Daisy, stop to talk to the little boy, and although their words are not patronising, it is easy to feel that they are talking down to the boy, increasing the sense that Wynne has 'babyfied' the young boy.

> "Will you give me one of your bluebells?" [Peggy] asked, with a bright smile. "I've never seen one before."

Tom was delighted. He gave all his bluebells, and was immensely interested in hearing that the new friend came from over the seas. (p14)

Once again the description follows the formulaic way of representing a character with an impairment, but Wynne resists the temptation to kill him off when he succumbs to measles shortly before his seventh birthday.

The illustration of Tom and Peggy sitting in a clearing in the woods is interesting because the boy is *not* wrapped up so much that one only sees his face, shoulders and arms (facing p144). Illustrator J Dewar Mills has drawn the boy in short trousers and shirt, tie, and shows him to be thin but not angular or gawky, and certainly as not having "brown eyes seemed too large for his small face".

In feminising Tom, Wynne renders him even more of a helpless child who needs looking after and protecting from the world. Tom does not hanker to go to school with his two elder brothers, nor does he show any interest in the school's game of cricket, the quintessential boy's game, preferring Peggy to tell him fairy stories. He is reluctant to go outside because he feels self-conscious about his body, and responds in a girl-like way to the end of a fairy tale invented by Peggy.

> Then [the Fairy] touched his eyes and smiled.
> "I've given you magic wings," said she, "and folded them inside your back. No one will guess what they are, but when you sleep at night you will be able to unfold them and fly away from here to Fairy-land. Now, good-bye." ... Tom gave a gasp of ecstasy.
> "Oh, Peggy, what a lovely story! It almost seems true, ... and I can feel where Fairy Queen

folded my wings. I won't mind now if I have rarver a humpy back, I'll say to myself, 'No one knows but Peggy, that they're really my magic wings.' " (p145)

The feminising of Tom renders him a baby who is unable to make any decisions apart from very simple ones. Even six-year-old Robin Humphries does not lisp or speak in such a babyish manner when she first appears in *Jo of the Chalet School* (1926), the second book of the 'Chalet School' series by Elinor Brent-Dyer. Delicate Robin is described in a sentimentalised way up until the second half of the fourteenth hardback title, *The Chalet School in Exile* (1940) (as discussed further in Ju Gosling's chapter), but even she is never portrayed as being as infantile as Tom is. It is quite possible that Tom will never grow up at all, despite Wynne allowing him to recover from measles and to receive a present of a kitten from Peggy at the end of the book. The reasoning for giving a feminine pet is because the dog his mother owns is "too big and clumsy to be a chum when [he] is not well" (p188). Tom will need to grow out of his femininity, just as Colin Craven does, as well as become healthy if he is to be a true boy, interested in boyish things such as sport, but there is no indicator that this will happen.

CONCLUSION

The characters discussed here are important as role models (positive or negative) because they are representatives of the society in which their creators lived, and were used to teach readers lessons in how to behave. When I review the school stories, I see an ebb and flow in the way that disability is handled. Initially one has realistic characters like Sadie and

Winifred alongside the childish portrayal of Tom McGregor, but once the latter part of the 1920s approaches, Dorita Fairlie Bruce's characterisation of schoolgirl Nicola Carter becomes increasingly stylised.

The characterisations of Winifred, Sadie, Morwen, Nicola, Dina and Tom are at the same time similar but also distinctly different. The characters are the same (or at least similar) because they are set apart from their peers, with the resulting air of being 'special'. Two of the six, Morwen and Dina, will regain full health in time, while Nicola already has done so by the end of *Captain Anne*, thus following the 'cure' model. There is no certainty that little Tom McGregor will attain adulthood at all, but if he does, he seems likely to be a permanent invalid; he will not take part in wider society and will continue to fit more closely into a passive feminine role than that of an active male.

It is only Winifred and Sadie who remain as they are when we meet them, and who will continue to live and work alongside their peers. In neither case does the girl express a longing to be relieved of the 'burden' of a disabling condition. Neither is a classically drawn disabled person: Winifred holds grudges but is not irretrievably warped in character, while Sadie is sufficiently endowed with mischief to be a part of the tricks played on a visiting school-story writer. Both want to be able to take part in school life as an equal, and within the parameters of their physical limitations they succeed in doing so.

There are, however, certain facets that I feel draw on the archetypal images of a wheelchair user or a visually impaired person which affect the believability of their portrayals. Winifred has boundless energy and the strength to whiz around the school grounds, whilst Sadie has an audio version of a photographic memory. However, in the context of other fictional portrayals of disabled people, including those of the twenty-first century, this is perhaps inevitable.

The fact none of these characters are not moralising, pious characters goes a long way towards making them believable, for both their original audience and the early twenty-first century readership. Neither Tom nor Dina, prime candidates for moralising, do so — to their creator's credit — although they are the weakest drawn characters of the group of six. They rely on authorial shorthand for the fleshing out of their characterisation — I would far rather meet Sadie or Winifred, both of whom could step out of their books into the twenty-first century. I would like to get to know them as *people* not characters from books. This, then, is my personal acid test: who would I like to get to know? I think that Morwen and Dina would irritate me with their patient enduring, while there is not much which appeals to me in the characterisation of Nicola or Tom.

As a late twentieth-century/early twenty-first century adult, I wonder how much Winifred hankered after the life she saw her contemporaries embarking upon, and how much she simply accepted the received wisdom that there was no point in considering any ambitions outside of the world of the school because she was disabled. In my late teens I went unquestioningly along with the received wisdom that what those around me had decided was right, and so went from special school to a residential centre-cum-college. It is moot, at this remove, to speculate whether, in the final analysis, that decision (made on my behalf) was right for me as an individual, but I still wonder where my life would have taken me if I had questioned those options at the time. Would the adult Winifred have understood my passive decision? I suspect she may have done.

AUTHOR DATES

May Wynne 1875-1949

Dorothea Moore 1880-1933

Elinor Brent-Dyer 1894-1969

Dorita Fairlie Bruce 1885-1970

NOTES

1) Helen Aveling, 2D or 3D characters, *Disability Studies Quarterly*, Winter 2004, www.dsq-sds.org/_articles_html/ 2004/winter/dsq_w04_aveling.html

2) Ann Dowker, 'The Treatment of Disability in 19th and Early 20th Century Children's Literature', *Disability Studies Quarterly*, Winter 2004, www.dsq-sds.org/ _articles_html/2004/winter/dsq_w04_dowker.html

3) Borsay, Anne, *Disability and Social Policy in Britain Since 1750*, Palgrave Macmillan, London, 2005.

4) Auchmuty, Rosemary, *A World of Girls*, The Woman's Press, London, 1992 (Bettany Press 2004), p68.

5) Photo of a spinal carriage, Photo Number 95351 at www.beamishcollections.com

REFERENCES

Auchmuty, Rosemary, *A World of Girls*, The Woman's Press, London, 1992 (Bettany Press 2004).

Aveling, Helen, 2D or 3D characters, *Disability Studies Quarterly*, Winter 2004, www.dsq-sds.org/_articles_html/2004/winter/dsq_w04_aveling.html

Brent-Dyer, Elinor M, *The School at the Chalet*, W. & M. Chambers, Edinburgh, 1925.

Brent-Dyer, Elinor M, *Seven Scamps*, W. & M. Chambers, Edinburgh, 1927.

Brent-Dyer, Elinor M, *Head Girl of Chalet School*, W. & M. Chambers, Edinburgh, 1928.

Bruce, Dorita Fairlie, *The Girls of St. Bride's*, Oxford University Press, London, 1923.

Bruce, Dorita Fairlie, *The New House-Captain*, Oxford University Press, London, 1928.

Bruce, Dorita Fairlie, *Victoria Victrix* in *Every Girl's Story Book*, Dean & Son, London, c.1930.

Bruce, Dorita Fairlie, *The Best House in the School*, Oxford University Press, London, 1930.

Bruce, Dorita Fairlie, *The New House at Springdale*, Oxford University Press, London, 1934.

Bruce, Dorita Fairlie, *Prefects at Springdale*, Oxford University Press, London, 1936.

Bruce, Dorita Fairlie, *Captain Anne*, Oxford University Press, London, 1939.

Bruce, Dorita Fairlie, *Nancy Returns to St. Bride's*, Oxford University Press, London, 1938.

Bruce, Dorita Fairlie, *Nancy at St. Bride's*, Oxford University Press, London, 1939.

Dowker, Ann, 'The Treatment of Disability in 19th and Early 20th Century Children's Literature', *Disability Studies Quarterly*, Winter 2004, www.dsq-sds.org/_articles_html/2004/winter/dsq_w04_dowker.html

Keith, Lois, *Take Up Thy Bed And Walk*, Women's Press, London, 2001.

Moore, Dorothea, *Septima, Schoolgirl*, Cassell, London, 1915.

Moore, Dorothea, *The Only Day-Girl*, Nisbet, London & Edinburgh, 1923.

www.beamishcollections.com

Wynne, May, *Peggy's First Term*, Ward Lock, London, 1922.

MIDDLE PERIOD

V. A CHOICE OF VIRTUES

DEBORAH KENT

For me, as a blind child growing up in the 1950s, books were scarce and precious commodities. I lived in a quiet New Jersey suburb where nothing exciting ever seemed to happen, and reading opened the door to the life of adventure that I craved. I loved the Nancy Drew books, in which a fearless, clever young woman solved baffling mysteries; and Enid Bagnold's *National Velvet* (1935), the tale of a girl who stuns the world by riding her horse to victory in the Grand National. In my favourite books young heroes (and, better yet, heroines) explored the wilderness, championed the oppressed and battled daunting enemies. I longed to live in such stories myself. Time and place melted away as I joined each exploring party and rescue mission.

Yet one sliver of reality never completely disappeared. All of the adventurers I so admired could see. Didn't blind people ever have adventures? Weren't they interesting enough to be portrayed in fiction? For a number of formative years, the only blind character that I encountered in my reading was Mary Ingalls in Laura Ingalls Wilder's 'Little House' series. To my mind, Mary embodied the worst possible image of a blind girl. While her sister Laura scrambles through life finding adventures, Mary sits in her rocking chair. She is protected and loved, but most of the time she remains so passive that she barely exists at all. I felt that the world expected blind girls to be much like Mary Ingalls. We were supposed to stay out of the way, to sit on the sidelines and to leave real life to others.

Then, when I was eleven, I discovered a very different blind character, Susan Oldknow in LM Boston's novel *Treasure [Chimneys* in the UK] *of Green Knowe* (1958). The novel is a fantasy in which a modern boy meets his 18th-century ancestors, Susan among them. Susan's mother sees her daughter as being a burden and a family disgrace and tries to keep her out of sight, but Susan does not let her mother's attitude define her. She seizes every opportunity to stretch toward independence and engagement with the world. Susan has plenty of spirit, and she is not always sweet. In fact, sometimes she is even angry over the way that her family treats her.

Unlike Mary, Susan is never passive and resigned. When adventures come her way, she springs into action. Both the negative stereotype reflected in Mary Ingalls, and the positive, self-directed image of Susan Oldknow, played important roles in shaping my identity. Mary Ingalls showed me what I might become if I yielded to the fears and beliefs of others. Susan demonstrated that I was not alone in imagining that a blind girl could be bold and adventurous — somehow, an English author named LM Boston had conceived of the same idea.

MARY INGALLS IN THE 'LITTLE HOUSE' BOOKS

In the 'Little House' series, first published between 1932 and 1943, Laura Ingalls Wilder tells the fictionalised story of her childhood and adolescence on the American frontier of the late nineteenth century. Throughout these books, beloved by generations of readers in the US and overseas, Laura's family is shown to be caring, courageous and boundlessly resourceful. Laura, the main character, is the second of the four Ingalls girls. Her older sister Mary appears in nearly all of the books and plays an important supporting role. In the first three volumes — *Little House in the Big Woods* (1932), *Little House on the Prairie* (1935) and *On the Banks of Plum Creek* (1937)— Mary is fully sighted. In the first chapter of the next book in the series, *By the Shores of Silver Lake* (1939), we learn that Mary has just lost her sight due to scarlet fever. Mary then appears as a blind character in four of Wilder's books — *By the Shores of Silver Lake*, *The Long Winter* (1940), *Little Town on the Prairie* (1941) and *These Happy Golden Years* (1943).

From the beginning, Wilder establishes the fact that Laura and Mary possess very different personalities. Laura is adventurous by nature, while Mary is retiring and domestic. Mary is happy to stay inside helping Ma, while Laura hungers to play and explore outdoors. Laura firmly believes that her older sister is prettier, more capable, and in general a better person than she is herself. For the most part she holds Mary in great admiration, but on rare occasions she reveals a flash of resentment. In a scene toward the end of *Little House in the Big Woods*, Laura accidentally tears the pocket of her dress and reflects that Mary would never be so careless. She goes on to observe that:

> Mary was a good little girl who always kept her dress neat and minded her manners. ... Mary looked very good and sweet, unrumpled and clean, sitting on the board [seat] beside Laura. Laura did not think it was fair. (pp174-75)

When Mary becomes blind at the age of thirteen, her response is totally in character. Wilder describes Mary's convalescence after the scarlet fever attack:

> She was able to sit up now, wrapped in quilts in Ma's old hickory rocking chair. All that long time, week after week, when she could still see a little, but less every day, she had never cried. Now she could not see even the brightest light any more. She was still patient and brave. (*By the Shores of Silver Lake*, p2)

By the time that Mary recovers, the rocking chair is no longer Ma's, but her's. It is her refuge of comfort and safety. Whenever the family moves to a new location, Mary's rocking chair is one of the first pieces of furniture to be put in place. Once it is set up, Mary sits patiently while the rest of the family unpacks and sets the new house in order.

Even before Mary lost her sight, Laura perceived her as patient and good. Her blindness only accentuates these traits, which were already strongly embedded in her character. In one regard, however, Mary's blindness brings about a radical change. As a sighted child, she kept busy helping with endless household chores, but her blindness renders her nearly incapable of playing a useful domestic role. This shift is apparent in an incident which occurs early on in *By the Shores of Silver Lake*. Pa plans a trip to Kansas, a journey that will require him to be away from the family for two months. Ma assures him that she will have no problems managing the household in his absence, since Laura and Carrie will be there to help her. In this statement she discounts any possible help from Grace, her youngest daughter, who is only a toddler. Her comment also dismisses any thought that Mary, once her mainstay, can be of help any longer. Now that Mary is blind, she and her baby sister share the same status.

Over time, Mary resumes some family responsibilities. She learns to sew, to make beds and to wash dishes. She helps to care for little Grace, rocking her for hours in her lap and telling her stories. In *The Long Winter*, when the Ingalls family is besieged for months by one blizzard after another, both Mary and Laura perform tasks essential for everyone's survival. They spend back-breaking hours each day grinding wheat into flour in Ma's coffee mill and twisting hay to make "kindling sticks" to keep the kitchen fire alive. But when Ma takes in a stream of boarders, it is Laura who helps with the mountains of cooking and cleaning. Mary never lends a hand, staying upstairs with the younger children.

Not only is Mary shut out of opportunities to be useful at home after she becomes blind, she is also excluded from a variety of recreational activities. In *The Long Winter* Pa makes a checkerboard and checkers out of wood. The family fills the winter evenings with lively games — everyone, that is, except Mary. It never occurs to anyone that Pa could make a board with raised squares so that Mary would be able to join in the fun. In another scene in the same novel Pa plays the fiddle, and encourages Laura and Carrie to learn the waltz. He exclaims proudly that both of them are going to be fine dancers some day. Mary, meanwhile, sits by the stove, listening quietly to the music, her hands folded on her lap. No one suggests that Mary, too, could learn to dance, and Mary never asks for a lesson. Mary's exclusion from the dancing lesson implies a far deeper exclusion — as a young woman who is blind, she is no longer seen as a sexual being.

In *By the Shores of Silver Lake*, Pa tells Laura

and Carrie to stay away from a nearby railroad camp, where rough men use vulgar language. Laura and Carrie receive further admonitions from Ma, who cautions them not to walk where the men might see them. No such warnings are extended to Mary; there is no likelihood that she might venture near the camp or become a temptation to the workers. Both the pleasures and the dangers of sexual expression are outside Mary's sphere.

Mary's patient acceptance of exclusion is completely in keeping with the role that she is given by her family and the community after she becomes blind — that of moral example. A conversation between Ma and Reverend Alden, a visiting preacher, reveals their belief that blindness has made Mary especially virtuous. Ma tells the preacher that Mary is a great comfort to her, and marvels that Mary has never once repined. Reverend Alden replies that Mary is a lesson to all of them. He goes on to say that "a brave spirit will turn all our afflictions to good." (p217) Thus he implies that Mary's patient acceptance of her disability will help to build character in those around her.

Just as Reverend Alden suggests, Mary's blindness furnishes Laura with the opportunity to learn self-sacrifice. In *By the Shores of Silver Lake*, the Ingalls family sets off by wagon to a new home in Dakota Territory. The children spend long hours each day confined to the jolting wagon. Laura yearns to get down and walk beside the wagon for a while, but she does not express her wish out loud. She is certain that Mary would not be able to walk fast enough to keep up with the wagon; therefore Mary does not have the option to get down and walk, and because Mary cannot get down, Laura feels it would not be right for her to do so herself.

Silently she endures her discomfort and continues to keep her older sister company.

Mary's blindness presents Laura with a far greater challenge: a shift in the family's expectations about her future. Until Mary lost her sight, her parents had hoped that she would become a teacher. However, a teaching career is out of the question for her as a blind girl. Laura, the next daughter in line, is therefore expected to become a teacher in Mary's place. Laura has no innate gift for teaching, and no wish to spend her life inside a classroom. Nonetheless she accepts her fate with fortitude; uncomplaining, she studies for her teaching certificate.

By the standards of her family, Laura has a rebellious spirit that must be brought under control. With uneven success, Laura strives to emulate Mary's goodness. In *Little Town on the Prairie* (1941) she confides to Mary that she wants to be just like her. She laments that she can never come close to the example that Mary sets every day. Mary modestly denies that she is as good as Laura thinks she is, and admits that she sometimes has angry thoughts. However, she nearly always manages to keep these thoughts to herself, safely hidden away.

The reader is never told what triggers Mary's secret angry thoughts. One possibility might be her exclusion from school upon the loss of her sight. Before the scarlet fever, Mary was an eager and diligent student. Blindness automatically interrupts her formal education. Each night Mary listens intently as Laura and Carrie do their homework. With their help and encouragement, she learns their lessons beside them, but no one considers that Mary could go with her sisters to the school in town and learn orally with the sighted pupils. Though Mary's mind is as agile as ever, her blindness somehow precludes her from sitting in a one-room schoolhouse. The whole family is thrilled when Reverend Alden describes a special "college" in Iowa for blind students. When Ma asks the reverend about the cost, Laura thinks her voice sounds "choked and hungry." (pp217-8) In one scene Mary sheds her usual stoic decorum and bursts forth with a torrent of enthusiasm. She exclaims:

> "Oh, I do care about [going to school]. I want it more than anything. There's so much to learn, I always wanted to go studying on and on. And to think that I can, if we can save the money, even now that I'm blind. Isn't it wonderful?" (*The Long Winter*, p117)

The Ingalls family works with single-minded focus to save for Mary's education. Laura redoubles her commitment to teaching, knowing that her salary will help Mary fulfil her dream. Of the four sisters, Mary is the only one to go away from home to study. Homebody though she is, she is willing to leave her family (and the ubiquitous rocking chair) and venture into the unknown.

Mary leaves for the school in Vinton, Iowa, midway through *Little Town on the Prairie*. At this point she largely drops out of the narrative, though there are occasional references to her weekly letters. These letters — though never quoted directly — assure the family that Mary is making excellent progress. Mary reports that she has learned to run a sewing machine, and sends home samples of her fancy beadwork. She is even studying the organ. Thrilled, Pa buys an organ and has it shipped to the Ingalls' Dakota homestead as a surprise for Mary when she comes for a visit.

Mary is away for three years, only once returning

to spend a summer with her family. During this visit Laura and Carrie are struck by their sister's increased independence. When Carrie asks Mary if she had been afraid, riding home alone on the train, Mary replies:

> "Oh no, I had no trouble. We like to do things by ourselves, at college. It is part of our education."
> (*These Happy Golden Years*, p124)

The family observes that Mary seems much more sure of herself, moving freely around the house instead of sitting quietly. When Pa brings in her trunk, Mary unlocks it "quite as if she saw it" (p126).

After Mary hands out presents to her parents and sisters Laura reflects:

> Mary had often smiled, but it was a long time since they had heard her laugh out, as she used to when she was a little girl. All that it had cost to send Mary to college was more than repaid by seeing her so gay and confident. (p126)

Despite Mary's accomplishments, however, Ma and Pa foresee a bleak future for their eldest daughter. At the end of Mary's visit Ma shares her thoughts with Laura. She points out that Mary will return home to stay when she finishes the programme at school, and that she might never again have the chance to travel. She tells Laura that it is nice for Mary to have these wonderful experiences and the opportunity to make new friends. Ma concludes: "She will have it to remember" (p180). Mary's education is not seen as a springboard into a future of productive work or one of marriage and children. Instead, it is a gift of sweet memories to help buoy

Mary through the empty years that inevitably stretch ahead.

At the end of *These Happy Golden Years* (1943), Laura prepares to marry her sweetheart, Almanzo Wilder. *The First Four Years* (1971), based on a manuscript left unfinished at Laura Ingalls Wilder's death, chronicles the early years of Laura's marriage and the birth of her daughter Rose. Mary's name appears only once in this final volume of the Little House series — in a passing reference to her rocking chair.

SUSAN OLDKNOW IN TREASURE OF GREEN KNOWE

LM Boston published six novels in the 'Green Knowe' series, of which *Treasure of Green Knowe* (1958, first published in the UK as *The Chimneys of Green Knowe* in the same year) is the second. Green Knowe is an ancient house in the English countryside, alive with memories of its past inhabitants. In *The Children of Green Knowe*, seven-year-old Tolly visits his great-grandmother, Mrs Oldknow, at Green Knowe during his school holidays, and she tells him stories about the children who lived in the house long ago. In *Treasure of Green Knowe*, Tolly returns on his spring holiday and hears another set of stories. This time the central figure in Mrs Oldknow's tales is Susan Oldknow, who grew up at the end of the eighteenth century. Susan also makes brief appearances in *An Enemy at Green Knowe* (1964) and *The Stones of Green Knowe* (1976), but *Treasure of Green Knowe* is the only book in the series in which she plays a major role.

Tolly first hears of Susan when he asks about the patchwork quilt on his bed. He learns that it was made for Susan by her grandmother. Tolly's great-grandmother goes on to tell a short story about the quilt. She explains that Susan's grandmother loved quilting, and made a patchwork quilt for Susan's mother, Maria. However, Maria had refused to have a patchwork quilt for her bed, preferring satin or lace. Offended, the grandmother declared that Susan could have the quilt some day when she married. On hearing this suggestion,

> Maria said Susan was hardly likely to get an offer of marriage, but if Granny liked to go on making patchworks, Susan could have them in bundles of a dozen. Susan wouldn't mind how old-fashioned anything was. (LM Boston, *Treasure of Green Knowe*, pp15-16)

For some reason which Mrs Oldknow does not yet reveal, Susan's mother does not hold Susan in high regard.

Soon Tolly gathers other clues about Susan's history. He opens a chest in his great-grandmother's room and discovers a box filled with exotic sea shells and polished stones. At the bottom of the chest he finds the model of a sailing ship, the *Woodpecker*. Mrs Oldknow explains that these were gifts to Susan from her father, a sea captain who was often away from home for a year at a time. Susan cherished all of her father's presents, especially the *Woodpecker*, a model of his own ship.

Finally Tolly comes face to face with Susan's spirit in the doorway to the music room (Mrs Oldknow refuses to use the word "ghost" to describe the ethereal children who share the house with her). When he tells Mrs Oldknow about this brief meeting, he comments that Susan is somehow different from the other spirit-children he has met. He feels that she looked at him as if he wasn't there.

At this point Mrs Oldknow explains that Susan was blind from birth, and goes on to tell more stories about her childhood long ago. She begins her first story about Susan with a clear statement that sets the tone for everything which follows:

> "What is really hard to believe is that her mother and old Nanny Softly did everything they possibly could to keep Susan from learning to find her way about." (p28)

The reactions of each member of the household, upon learning that baby Susan is blind, reveal both character and social milieu. Maria, Susan's mother, laments:

> "Whatever shall I do with a blind daughter — I can't take her into society — she'll never be married — there will be no pleasure in dressing her — she won't even be able to dress herself and we'll have her for always." (p28)

According to the grandmother, "it was a judgment on Maria for her flighty life, and though the child would be little more than an idiot, she would try to see that it was at least a Christian one" (p28). Sefton, Susan's spoiled older brother, is secretly delighted to learn that Susan is blind, sure that she will never compete with him for money and favours. Caxton, the butler, "would pinch her cheek and talk baby talk" when Susan's father or mother were present," but "when only Nanny Softly was there, he would say, 'It should have been drowned like a kitten.' " (p33) Old Mrs Softly, the children's nanny, is the person who spends the most time with Susan and has the most devastating impact on her life.

Nanny Softly rocked and wept and clasped the child to her featherbed bosom and said at least the poor little thing wouldn't be without someone to love her. What bumps her poor dear little head was going to get! But she would watch her day and night and never let her out of her sight. Her old Nanny Softly would always be with her. (p29)

Wisely, Mrs Oldknow points out to Tolly that Nanny's relentless coddling was far worse for Susan than her mother's indifference, "because though it was good for her to be loved, it was dreadful never to be allowed to try to do anything herself." (p29).

True to her word, Nanny hovers over Susan constantly, with an endless litany of warnings and reassurances. Nanny fetches Susan's toys, buttons her shoes and ties her hair ribbons. She even feeds Susan at the table, so that she never learns to use a knife and fork. Nanny does her best to convince Susan that the world is a very dangerous place, which Susan cannot possibly negotiate on her own.

In all the busy household of family and servants, only Susan's father, Captain Oldknow, believes in her innate abilities and understands her need to explore. He recognizes that Nanny and Maria are mishandling Susan grievously, forcing her to be helpless when in fact she is full of eagerness and curiosity. Each time he returns home from one of his ocean voyages, he is pained to see that nothing has changed. The situation makes him feel helpless himself. He longs to make life better for his daughter, but does not know what to do for her.

LM Boston, in the voice of Mrs Oldknow, places the attitudes of Susan's family within their historical context. Mrs Oldknow tells Tolly that in those days Braille and schools for the blind were not available. If a blind person was poor, she or he had to live as a beggar. Blind people from wealthy families were "prisoners with servants." (p36) The captain, for all his good intentions, has no guidance, no positive example to follow. He is entirely on his own. Boston is remarkably insightful in her descriptions of Susan's early life. She recognizes the critical need for a blind child to explore through touch, and conveys a poignant sense of Susan's deprivation.

To prevent Susan from falling or breaking things, Nanny Softly keeps her strapped in a chair most of the time. Her only toy is a large wooden doll, which is also tied to the chair. Mrs Oldknow points out that no one wants a toy that is tied to her. With mischievous approval she adds, "it was a wooden doll, and [Susan] could hit out nicely with it, and once Nanny Softly caught a good rap over the head" (p31). Susan is only liberated from the chair when someone leads her through the house by the hand.

> In leading her they were impatient, because their idea was to get her quickly where they were going, while Susan's idea was to feel everything possible on the way there. Everything was to her most mysterious, because she only felt a bit of it as she was dragged past, a ledge or a knob, a fold of curtain, or perhaps she felt nothing, but there was a different smell or a hollower sound. She had no idea how big things were or what shape. They stuck out of space like icebergs out of the sea. For this reason she enjoyed the continuous pleasantly shaped stair rail and liked to draw her fingers along the banisters as she went up and down, pushed and pulled by Nanny Softly. (p30)

Captain Oldknow encourages Nanny to let Susan touch things, but meets with solid resistance from her. Nanny is determined to break Susan of her incorrigible habit of "fingering" everything within reach. If Susan had her way, Nanny insists, everything in the house would be lost or broken. Susan's hands and clothing would always be dirty, and Susan would be sure to injure herself. The captain appeals to Maria, urging her to teach Susan to do things for herself. Maria retorts that teaching Susan would require an angel's patience — patience which Maria lacks in abundance. Maria reminds the captain that Susan's grandmother teaches her about religion, and that is the only education she will need.

Despite their best efforts, Maria and Nanny Softly are powerless to quench Susan's natural curiosity. Mrs Oldknow tells Tolly:

> [S]he wanted to catch everything in the act of being real. She even put her finger in the candle flame to see what being burned was like. (p102)

Because her experience has been so severely limited, Susan has large gaps in her knowledge about the world around her. When she hears frogs croaking in the moat, she pictures them as little men dressed in suits of wet leather. When Captain Oldknow tries to tell Susan about his life at sea, he is aghast to discover that she does not understand what a river is, or what he means when he uses the word "float". To help Susan understand what a boat is and how it floats on the waves, Captain Oldknow gives her a model of the *Woodpecker* which she can play with in her bath. However, he is painfully aware that she needs far more than a few toys to nourish her ravenous mind.

When Susan is seven years old, Captain Oldknow hires Jonathan, the seventeen-year-old son of a neighboring pastor, to be her tutor. At first

Jonathan is doubtful that he can teach Susan anything. The captain urges him to teach her orally and to use his imagination. Above all, he tells Jonathan to answer Susan's questions and to make sure she understands his answers. Despite Sefton's mockery and his own misgivings, Jonathan finds Susan to be an apt pupil. Taking the captain's advice, he answers her questions and reads her stories out loud. Susan delights in his reading of *Robinson Crusoe* and other tales of adventure.

Even so, the captain longs to widen Susan's world still further. The following year, during a stop at Barbados, he strikes upon an unconventional solution. He buys Jacob, an eight-year-old slave recently brought to the Caribbean from Africa. The captain promises Jacob his freedom if he will be a companion to his blind daughter in faraway England. Thus Jacob comes to Green Knowe and transforms Susan's life forever. Like Susan, Jacob possesses immense curiosity and a vivid imagination. The children take to one another at once, and instantly become fast friends. At their first meeting Captain Oldknow sends them to play in the garden together. When he looks out the window he sees them marching along the paths playing a newly-invented game. He exclaims to Maria that this is the best thing he has seen in years, and that Susan is playing like any other child at last. Conveniently, Nanny Softly falls ill soon after Jacob's arrival, and the children are left to their own devices.

With Jacob as her mentor, Susan's education truly begins. The contrast with her earlier life is dramatic. Mrs Oldknow tells Tolly: "Susan had always been taught to walk as carefully as if it were the most difficult thing in life not to fall, in a world beset with water, fire, staircases, high windows, open doors, and pits." (p86) Jacob has no such apprehensions. With his liberating guidance, Susan explores her surroundings and learns to walk freely through the house and garden. She gets her dress muddy as she turns somersaults on the lawn. She learns to climb to the top of the tallest beech tree at Green Knowe, pretending that she is perched in the rigging of the *Woodpecker*. In response to Susan's eager questions, Jacob captures frogs, birds, hedgehogs and other creatures to show her. Jonathan, the tutor, is inspired to teach Susan her letters, shaping them with bread dough.

Confident and independent, Susan becomes a full-fledged player in the dramas of the household. Sefton has seized every opportunity to humiliate Jacob. Susan helps Jacob to retaliate through a series of nettling pranks. Sefton never thinks to suspect her. He does suspect Jacob, however, though he can prove nothing against him. The tension between Sefton and Jacob continues to build. When Sefton forces Jacob to climb into the chimney like a chimney sweep, Susan rushes to her friend's defense. She flies at Sefton and kicks him squarely in the shins. Finally, Susan and Jacob work together to rescue their friend Fred, the gardener's son. Thirteen-year-old Fred has been caught poaching rabbits, and will be hanged or sold to a press gang for service in His Majesty's Navy. The children hide Fred in an underground chamber and smuggle food to him until he can make a safe escape.

As Tolly's visit draws to a close, he asks his great-grandmother what happened to Susan and Jacob when they grew up. Mrs Oldknow tells him that Jacob became a groom at Green Knowe, caring for the horses and driving Susan in her carriage. On a trip to Barbados with the captain, he married a woman of African heritage and brought her back to England with him. Susan married Jonathan, her former tutor, and "and had lots of children who could all see." (p214) Jacob's wife served as their nanny. Susan and Jacob remained the best of friends all their lives.

Unlike Mary Ingalls, Susan is granted a "happily ever after" ending, complete with marriage and family. She grows up and takes on the responsibilities of motherhood, with the help of a nanny as befits her era and social class. The statement that all of Susan's children could see hints that the ending would have been less happy if any of Susan's children had been blind, and that blindness is not entirely acceptable, even for the enlightened Mrs Oldknow. Within its context, however, the comment seems intended as further assurance that Susan led a fulfilling life and made a positive contribution to the family.

A CHOICE OF VIRTUES

The 'Little House' series and *Treasure of Green Knowe* are books by twentieth-century authors that portray children of earlier times. Mary Ingalls and Susan Oldknow are shaped by the eras in which they lived, when opportunities for blind people were severely restricted. Yet the girls grow up in very different environments, within very different philosophical frameworks.

On the American frontier, the Ingalls family lives by the Protestant ethic of hard work and fortitude under adversity. For the most part Mary's blindness exempts her from hard work; she is no longer expected to be an active, contributing member of the family unit. But Mary is cast in a new role — she is a model of patience. For the Ingalls family, and apparently for Wilder herself, patient acceptance is one of the highest possible virtues.

The patient acceptance of physical frailty was exalted in the literature and ideology of Europe and the United States during the nineteenth century. In the 1830s Laura Bridgman, a deaf-blind child educated at the Perkins Institution for the Blind in Massachusetts, became an international celebrity. School records indicate that Bridgman was a feisty little girl who sometimes flared up in violent fits of temper. Nevertheless, accounts by reporters and visitors overflow with praise for Bridgman's sweetness, goodness and uncomplaining acceptance of her afflictions. The public turned Bridgman into the idealized figure of patient suffering that it wished her to be, and served her up as a moral example to a generation of children.

Popular literature of the Victorian era provides numerous examples in a similar vein — girls who rise to heights of goodness through their patient acceptance of illness or disability. Little Nell in Charles Dickens' *Old Curiosity Shop* and Beth March in Louisa May Alcott's *Little Women* are unremittingly sweet, selfless and gentle as they fade toward death. Clara, the invalid in Johanna Spyri's *Heidi*, is the embodiment of goodness. Clara accepts her limitations without protest, and by her example teaches Heidi to endure her own hardships with patience.

Mary Ingalls is not destined for an untimely death like Little Nell or Beth March, and she is not confined to her couch like Clara. But her blindness becomes a form of confinement and a kind of death. Blindness means the death of Mary's plans to become a teacher, and the end to any possibility of romance, marriage, and children. It destroys her capacity to make a full contribution to the family and community, and thus to be regarded as a responsible adult. Except for her experience at the school for the blind, Mary's blindness confines her to her home and her rocking chair. Like Little Nell, Beth March and Clara, Mary bears her losses with patience. Wilder refers frequently to Mary's patience and goodness, as though these traits are almost synonymous. Mary's willingness to sit on the sidelines in her rocking chair is never portrayed as laziness. Rather, Wilder conveys her admiration for Mary's graceful acceptance of her fate.

As a blind child reading the 'Little House' series, I was appalled by Wilder's depiction of Mary. Mary's silent acceptance of limitations and exclusion collided with everything that I aspired to achieve in my own life. To me, her uncomplaining patience was not a sign of goodness, but of an infuriating passivity. What on earth was so enthralling about that rocking chair of hers? How could she be so content to sit on the outskirts of life? Why did she relinquish her right to play an active part in the world? Why didn't she seize every opportunity to prove that she could still be useful and active, whether or not she could see?

Almost as distressing to me as Mary herself was the attitude of her family. Mary's parents and sisters love her deeply. Yet no one in the family challenges the assumption that blindness has put an end to Mary's active participation in life. When it comes to including Mary in the full range of family and community activities, the Ingalls family shows a profound lack of will and creativity. This is ironic, since their very survival on the frontier depends on their ability to find solutions to unexpected problems. The Ingalls family is endlessly resourceful when it comes to building shelters, gathering food, traveling where there are no roads, and having fun in spite of extreme hardships. Somehow, though, this can-do spirit founders before

Mary's blindness. Instead of tackling the challenge of blindness with pioneering resilience, the Ingalls family falls back on time-honored beliefs, equating blindness with helplessness. To their credit, they never treat Mary as if she is a burden, and are never ashamed of her or embarrassed by her presence. But their gentle, almost reverent treatment of her only helps to ensure her isolation. When they see her patience as admirable, a manifestation of goodness, they quietly justify keeping her in a special place apart.

At first I thought that Mary's experience at school would transform her perspective on life, and would awaken her family to new and endless possibilities. In fact, Mary makes dramatic changes, even travelling hundreds of miles alone on the train. This is an amazing feat for a girl who previously would not rise from her rocking chair to unpack a trunk. However, to my vast disappointment, Wilder strongly hints that Mary's school years are an aberration. When she completes the program she will return home, where sweet memories of friendships and adventures will help her bear with patience the empty years before her.

When I was growing up I knew that, despite their relative newness, the 'Little House' books were considered to be 'classics.' People had already been reading about sweet, passive Mary Ingalls for years, and they would go on reading about her for countless years to come. It dismayed me to realize that the majority of these readers probably accepted the author's view of Mary without question. They would carry away the image of patient Mary in her rocking chair, glowing with goodness. I feared that the image of Mary Ingalls would reinforce some of the worst stereotypes about people who are blind.

Even as a child I was keenly aware of such stereotypes and their oppressive effects. It seemed that whenever I wanted to venture into untried territory — to start babysitting, to learn to ride horseback, to attend my neighborhood school instead of a special class for blind children — I had to fight past the objections of doubters and detractors. I knew that the nay-sayers would have been greatly relieved if I had been willing to sit patiently and accept whatever crumbs of experience were offered to me by others. To my very core I rebelled against such a passive stance. I did not want experience to be filtered and selected for me by other people. I wanted to make my own choices and gather firsthand experience of the world.

In Susan Oldknow, I felt that I had found a kindred spirit. Susan is an explorer, stretching out her hands to discover her surroundings despite the reproofs of Nanny and her mother. It is not her blindness that holds Susan back, but the stifling behavior of the people around her. Susan's experience resonated deeply with my own. I, too, had heard endless warnings about stairways, fire, sharp objects and myriad other components of daily life. Like Susan, I had learned not to take most of these warnings as truth, but to test reality for myself. Fortunately, like her, I had significant people in my life who believed in me and who made sure that I had the opportunities I needed.

In striking contrast to Mary's life on the frontier, Susan is a child of Regency England, growing up amid servants and luxury. Her father sees Susan's blindness as a difference that need not define or hamper her. He does not expect or want her to sit patiently with folded hands; instead, he seeks to help her engage with the world. As he points out to Jonathan, her tutor, it is only a matter of finding creative approaches to her education.

The approaches to blindness in *Treasure of Green Knowe* and the 'Little House' books represent two distinct philosophical views of humanity. The Protestant ethic which rules the Ingalls family regards human nature as being intrinsically bad, although humans can be saved from evil by resisting temptation. Mary Ingalls could easily be tempted to anger and self-pity (clearly regarded by Wilder as negative emotions to be overcome), but she rises above such impulses and holds to higher ground. Captain Oldknow is guided by the philosophy of Rousseau and other Enlightenment thinkers of the eighteenth century. Rousseau and his followers saw human nature as being essentially good, and believed that organized society had a corrupting impact on the child's innate purity. Susan Oldknow is an innocent, a pure child of nature, untainted by the materialism of her mother and brother; she embraces life with eagerness and joy. Her father delights in her spontaneity and encourages her spirit of adventure, in defiance of the strict rules that govern the behavior of proper little girls of her era.

Jacob, Susan's invaluable teacher (Boston's version of Helen Keller's Annie Sullivan), is a child of nature himself. Jacob spent his early years in Africa, among the lions and elephants, and he still carries a host of animistic beliefs. When Susan and Jacob are at play, the garden at Green Knowe bears a passing resemblance to Eden. Captain Oldknow selects Jacob to be Susan's mentor because he is a free spirit, full of playfulness and imagination. Despite the hardships of slavery, Jacob is morally and emotionally intact. His nature has not been twisted by the constraints of uppercrust English society. As an outsider to that world, he is able to appreciate Susan for who she is and to meet her with intuitive understanding. Although Susan is very different from Mary Ingalls, she, too, shines with a kind of goodness. She is loving and loyal. She has not learned affectations, and judges others on their merits rather than their social status. Her lifelong friendship with Jacob is a case in point. Susan is free from racism, and is outraged when others treat Jacob insolently. Perhaps, if she were sighted, Susan would have been as arrogant and self-absorbed as her brother Sefton. Her blindness allows her to follow a very different path.

In a sense both Boston and Wilder idealize their blind characters, investing them with virtues that stem from their disabilities. Yet as a blind girl, trying to find friends and heroines in books, I found Mary Ingalls cloying, and rejoiced upon meeting Susan. I cheered when Susan kicked Sefton, and celebrated when she climbed to the top of the giant beech tree. I thrilled as she discovered that her life brimmed with possibilities. Susan was learning exactly what I myself wanted to believe, and wanted the rest of the world to know.

REFERENCES

Alcott, Louisa May, *Little Women* (first published 1868), Dell, New York, 1987.

Boston, LM, *Treasure of Green Knowe* (first published in US 1958), Harcourt Brace, San Diego, New York, 1986. (UK title, *The Chimneys of Green Knowe*, Faber, London, 1958.)

Dickens, Charles, *The Old Curiosity Shop* (first published 1841), Everyman's, New York, 1995.

Freedman, Ernest, *The Education of Laura Bridgman, the first Deaf and Blind Person to Learn Language*, Harvard University Press, Cambridge, MA, 2001.

Gitter, Elisabeth, *The Imprisoned Guest*: Samuel Howe and *Laura Bridgman, the Original Deaf-Blind Girl*, Farrar Straus and Giroux, New York, 2001.

Spyri, Johanna, *Heidi* (first published 1880), World, Cleveland and New York, 1946.

Wilder, Laura Ingalls, *By the Shores of Silver Lake* (first published 1939), Harper and Brothers, New York, 1953.

Wilder, Laura Ingalls, *The First Four Years*, Harper and Row, New York, 1971.

Wilder, Laura Ingalls, *Little House in the Big Woods* (first published 1932), Harper & Row, 1959.

Wilder, Laura Ingalls, *Little Town on the Prairie* (first published 1941), HarperCollins, New York, 1969.

Wilder, Laura Ingalls, *The Long Winter* (first published 1940), HarperTrophy, New York, 1968.

Wilder, Laura Ingalls, *These Happy Golden Years* (first published 1943), Scholastic, New York, 1953.

LATE PERIOD

VI. "I DON'T WANT TO BE DIFFERENT": DIABETES IN CONTEMPORARY YOUNG ADULT FICTION

MEREDITH GUTHRIE

WHEN characters within traditional children's literature are ill or disabled, there are two possible outcomes. The child is either cured — usually miraculously — or dies. As other chapters from this collection demonstrate, examples abound in classic children's stories, from Beth in *Little Women*, who dies, to Pollyanna, who is cured. Lois Keith, author of *Take up Thy Bed and Walk: Death, Disability, and Cure in Classic Fiction for Girls* (2001), believes that this teaches readers to believe that: "there is nothing good about being disabled" (p7); and that periods of disability must be got through as quickly as possible and by any means possible. What happens when this doesn't occur, though? How can children's and young adult fiction deal with chronic and potentially disabling, but manageable, illness?

Medical advances have made it possible for chronically ill and disabled people to live full lives without being cured. There are currently millions of people in the US, Canada, and the UK living with diabetes[1], including hundreds of thousands of children and teenagers[2], and young adult literature is changing to reflect these current realities. In this chapter, I will examine how chronic illness is depicted in contemporary young adult novels, focusing on three young adult novels that feature diabetic protagonists: *Sugar isn't Everything* (1987); *Living with a Secret* (2001); and *Sweetblood* (2003).

As Joanne Brown and Nancy St. Clair note in their book *Declarations of Independence: Empowered Girls in Young Adult Literature 1990-2001* (2001), young adult literature tends to focus on stories that tell "a rite-of-passage story that moves its protagonist from innocence to experience" (p26). Keith adds that, when the protagonist develops an illness or disability, the rite of passage involves the often difficult process of learning to "reach some kind of accommodation to their new situation" (p221). The girls at the centre of each of the books in this study go through just such a process to learn how to manage their diabetes. In the process, the narrative explores themes such as "changed self-image, loss of self-esteem, relationships with family and friends, sex and romance" (ibid), and adjusting life to the demands of her illness.

SUGAR ISN'T EVERYTHING

Willo Davis Roberts wrote *Sugar isn't Everything* in 1987, soon after she was diagnosed with diabetes herself. Subtitled *A Support Book, in Fiction Form, for the Young Diabetic*, Davis Roberts intended to include trustworthy information about diabetes within a fictional narrative with which her readers could identify. This would provide all of the knowledge of a pamphlet or textbook in an entertaining matrix that children and adolescents were more likely to read and retain. Furthermore, readers were meant to try to emulate the protagonist's journey in her gradual acceptance of her status as a diabetic. In fact, I was given this book by my grandmother when I was about twelve to teach me about my family's genetic history and predisposition to diabetes. I read it many times, both because I enjoyed the story and because my grandmother was anxious that I should learn what the book had to teach.

Twelve-year-old Amy, the protagonist, is trying to enjoy the summer before seventh grade. Amy lives with her parents, her wonderful big brother and her annoying little sister. Amy begins exhibiting many of the symptoms of untreated diabetes, including great and unsatisfied hunger and thirst, frequent urination (including, at one point, wetting her bed in her sleep), and fatigue. Amy is also moody and quick to anger, something that her family chalks up to normal adolescent mood swings. When Amy collapses with a high fever, however, her parents take her to the hospital where she is diagnosed as a Type I, or insulin dependent, diabetic. Amy spends the rest of the summer trying to come to terms with her new identity as a diabetic with the help of Ed (a nurse at the hospital and the leader of a diabetes education and support group for kids), her family, her best friend Pudge and her new friends from the support group.

In the other books in this study, the protagonists are both a little older than Amy and have been living with their diabetes for years. However, neither has come to terms with her diabetes, and both would like to forget their illness and its demands altogether. These girls rightly feel that they should not have to make diabetes the central or sole defining characteristic of their identities. However, they sometimes get confused between being defined first and foremost by their illness and allowing space within their identities to take care of their bodies' needs.

LIVING WITH A SECRET

Deborah Kent's *Living with a Secret* (2001) was published as the second volume in a series titled 'Why Me?', about teen girls living with various illnesses and disabilities. Kent (the author of the previous chapter) has written extensively about the intersections of disability and adolescence in both fictional and non-fictional formats.[3] In *Living with a Secret*, Cassie Mullins, who is fifteen, has been diabetic for two years. Although her diabetes is not always completely under control, she resents the constant surveillance of her mother and father and wishes they would let her grow up (p10). Cassie is dreading the upcoming summer before high school, because she fears she will have to "live and breathe diabetes" under her mother's constant supervision (p145). When her aunt offers her the chance to work at a camp for diabetic kids as a junior counselor, Cassie jumps at the chance to get away.

The camp will provide the perfect opportunity for Cassie, she thinks, because while her aunt believes that she will "be a fantastic role model for all those kids" (p48) and her parents are happy about the constant medical supervision at the camp, Cassie sees being away from home as a perfect opportunity to escape from her identity as a diabetic. Cassie decides that she will not tell anyone at the camp, except for the on-site nurse, that she has diabetes, believing that keeping this secret will allow her to fit in better with her fellow counselors.

At first, Cassie does well, getting along with her campers and making friends among the counselors. Without the constant supervision of her mother, and because her new responsibilities make her feel "grown up," Cassie keeps her diabetes under control by eating well, secretly monitoring her blood sugar and giving herself injections of insulin in the bathroom. When her aunt and mother unexpectedly visit the camp and 'out' her as a diabetic, though, Cassie rebels by eating sweets and falsifying her blood sugar in her records. Her relationship with her fellow counselors, especially with the "cute" Jason, begins to sour.

Finally, Cassie's blood sugar gets completely out of control and she has to be rescued by the camp nurse and Jason. Cassie spends the rest of the book working out how she can both control her diabetes and shape a comfortable identity. Like Amy, readers are meant to want Cassie to find a workable relationship with her diabetes, and any diabetic readers are supposed to want to emulate Cassie's final state as a healthy diabetic, rather than her early state as an out-of-control one.

SWEETBLOOD

Pete Hautman published *Sweetblood* in 2003, nearly twenty years after he was diagnosed as a Type I diabetic.[4] In *Sweetblood*, sixteen-year-old Lucy Szabo has been diabetic for ten years. Unlike Amy and Cassie, who want to fit in with the popular crowd, Lucy goes out of her way to be an outsider. She drapes herself in black clothes and makeup, dyes her long hair black and does everything she can to avoid looking 'normal'.

Like Cassie, Lucy has trouble keeping her diabetes under control. In fact, she openly rebels against the restrictions of her illness and chooses to ignore her parents' worries. Where Cassie learned that it was generally normal to have one or two episodes a week where her blood sugar got too low (Kent, p33), Lucy has six or seven episodes a week (Hautman, p14), which is meant as an indication that she is not taking good care of herself.

Lucy's life is out of control in other arenas as well. She has trouble making or keeping friends (p6); has stopped caring about her schoolwork (although she used to be what American schools call an 'honor student': a student who always earns good grades); and chooses to spend hours a day online rather than spending time with people in 'real life'. While I do not necessarily believe that spending a lot of time online is pathological, Hautman seems to connect Lucy's time online with a refusal to connect to 'real' people. This is particularly evident when Lucy's return to health is connected with her rejection of some of the people that she met online.

Lucy spends most of her time online at "the Transylvania Room", a chat room full of self-described "vampires". She believes that she belongs in this group because of her diabetes. In Lucy's words: "Diabetics were the original, the real vampires. They weren't evil or superpowerful or immortal. They were just sick. Like me." (p42) Before the advent of modern medicine, diabetics inevitably died, but before they did so they exhibited many characteristics, such as constant thirst and photophobia, which were traditionally attributed to vampires. People feared diabetics because they did not understand the biological forces at work, and they attributed supernatural forces to what they could not quantify.

Lucy goes so far as to name everyone who has been kept alive through modern medicine as a member of the "undead" (p3), a group that includes both Lucy and her father (her father has had his appendix removed). When Lucy writes an essay explaining her theory and turns it in at school, she gets into trouble. Her parents take away her computer because they fear the amount of time she spends online; and they make her go to a therapist.

Lucy reacts to this by rebelling further, lying to her therapist and spending time with Draco, one of the "vampires" from the chat room. Draco is attracted to Lucy, he says, because of her theory about vampires, but he is actually an adult man who surrounds himself with teenaged "goth kids", throwing parties at his house and buying the teens alcohol. Lucy sneaks out on Halloween night to attend a party at Draco's. When her ride gets too drunk to drive her home, Lucy, who has eaten a lot of candy and drunk a lot of wine, decides to walk home during a snowstorm. Part-way home Lucy passes out and goes into a diabetic coma in the back yard of a childhood friend, the mild and "normal" Mark. Mark rescues her, and she wakes up later in the hospital. Like Cassie, Lucy has to figure out why she acts out in self-destructive ways and learn to construct a new identity that allows her both to be true to herself and to control her diabetes.

FEELING LIKE AN OUTSIDER

Amy, Cassie, and Lucy all come from relatively privileged, white, intact families. Their parents can afford to give their daughters the best medical care, as well as pay for various other things such as horseback riding (Cassie) and computers (Lucy). All of the girls can afford to go out with friends with a little spending money in their pockets, and except for their diabetes are healthy and non-disabled. Despite all of these privileges, each girl feels that her diabetes keeps her irrevocably separated from her peers.

Why do Amy, Cassie and Lucy feel like outsiders? At the most basic level, of course, young adolescents can feel that anything different about them places them outside of their peer group. Brown and St Clair point out that girls are traditionally placed outside of dominant culture simply by virtue of their gender, but "such factors as race, ethnicity, class, and sexual orientation can further magnify a girl's outsider status, increasing her distance from the norm" (p87), and making it that much harder to find a sense of self and group acceptance. I believe that illness plays much the same role in these books. Amy, Cassie, and Lucy believe that having diabetes makes them different — or at least makes *feel* different — from their peers, and they want to be able to forget about this difference. Each girl defines difference as being inherently bad, even deliberate outsider Lucy.

For at least part of the narrative, then, the girls at the centre of these novels feel like outsiders. Keith notes that the outsider is a potent figure in contemporary young adult literature, because it allows readers to explore the complexities of how those who cannot fit in with the norm come to some level of self-acceptance (p208). Stories told from the outsider's point of view have such potency because most adolescents feel like outsiders at one time or another, and they identify with the protagonist's position. For this to work, however, Keith points out that the outsider must be the protagonist of the story, and her viewpoint must be "seen as valid" (ibid). Keith worries that this does not usually happen with characters who are disabled or who have a chronic illness, because such characters are usually denied full subjectivity. This can leave disabled characters doubly outside of mainstream adolescent experience, because they are not allowed the voice to tell their story.

This is one reason why it is important that these girls are the protagonists of their stories. While each girl feels like an outsider, each is also taken seriously enough by the narrative to be able to tell her own story, rather than having her story told from the viewpoint of others (such as a friend or parent) or playing a peripheral role in someone else's story. Perhaps most importantly, readers are asked to identify with the girls, whether or not readers are disabled themselves.

The protagonists' fears of being different can be fed internally as well as externally. As Susan Wendell states:

> The disciplines of normality, like those of femininity, are not only enforced by others but internalized. For many of us, our proximity to the standards of normality is an important part of our identity and our sense of social acceptability, an aspect of our self-respect. We are unlikely to notice this until our ability to meet the standards is threatened in some way. (Susan Wendell, *The Rejected Body: Feminist Philosophical Reflections on Disability*, 1996, p88)

The diagnosis of diabetes shakes each girl's sense of self, and the ways that they rebuild this forms their narratives. Each girl must come to terms with her illness while still shaping an identity as a capable, maturing person, whether this means coming to terms with her status as an outsider, or realizing that being diabetic does not keep her from being, for the most part, 'normal'. Of course, this is not an easy or unproblematic process, but one that entails a great deal of effort, pain, anger and many missteps along the way.

The necessity for daily insulin shots; to check their blood sugar often; and the inability to participate in communal "pig outs" with friends; all make young diabetics different, and they may fear that this will make them socially unpopular. In *Sugar isn't Everything*, Amy is afraid that her new medical alert bracelet will "be like branding her forehead [...] telling everyone she had diabetes. That she was different." (p114) Several times Amy describes feeling like a "freak", and "different"[5], which to her is synonymous with "bad" or "weird". Like Amy, Cassie didn't like her medic-alert bracelet because it "was one more thing to set me apart from my friends" and keep her from being "ordinary" (Kent, p34). Lucy reacts differently to her perceived differences. Because Lucy believes that her diabetes has already irrevocably separated her from normality, she goes out of her way to go the other way, stating "they want weird, I'll give 'em weird" (Hautman, p55).

On a deeper level, though, what Wendell terms society's "strong ideals of bodily perfection" (p63) causes a deep-rooted fear of illness, where society equates any form of disability or chronic illness with the "failure to control the body, and everyone's vulnerability to weakness, pain, and death" (p60). Anyone who cannot live up to the ideal (a group that obviously includes more than just people with chronic illnesses) is in danger of becoming the rejected Other, kept from 'normal' life because she reminds society how fragile our bodies really are. Because of this, the girls' fears of being viewed by their peers as "weird" are not unrealistic, unfortunately. Their peers sometimes do reject them because of their diabetes.

Soon after she was diagnosed, Cassie wasn't invited to a good friend's sleepover because that girl's mother said it was "too much responsibility for her" (p35). At school, other girls refuse to drink after her because they're afraid they'll "catch" diabetes, and they accuse her of being a drug addict when they see the needle marks on her body when she changes for gym class (p35). Once she's at camp, Cassie is glad she has chosen not to reveal her diabetes to her fellow counselors, because she feels that: "a chasm yawned between counselors and campers, between us and them." (p62)

This chasm places the care-givers, or non-diabetics, on one side and the cared-for, or diabetics, on the other. Jason, the boy she likes, admits that he feels badly for his campers because "they have to go through their whole lives" being diabetic (p64). Cassie doesn't want him to classify her as an object of pity. Furthermore, she feels like "the counselors were taking their first steps toward becoming a group, and [she] wanted to be part of it." (ibid) If they thought they would have to take care of her, the other counselors would not view her as an equal or a peer.

In *Sweetblood*, Lucy and her mother's rocky relationship revolves around Lucy's diabetes. Lucy believes that her mother both fears her and defines Lucy as fragile or breakable. Her mother has previously admitted that she and her father stopped having children because they were afraid that future children would also be diabetic, leading Lucy to believe that her parents think she is defective and disappointing (Hautman, p100). Lucy tries to avoid telling new people about her diabetes because, she says: "I get so bored with being Diabetes Girl, it's nice to have friends who don't think of me as a diseased cripple." (p130) The girls always feel in danger of being pitied, of being defined as helpless, because this is how their relationships with their parents — the primary relationships in their lives — are structured. They worry about being seen not as individuals, but as a "responsibility" or something to be cared for, because they believe this is how their parents define them and so they worry that others will define them in this way as well.

While Amy, Cassie, and Lucy feel different from their 'normal' peers, they also feel excluded from a larger community of people with illnesses or disabilities. Because they are dealing with a chronic illness that leaves very few visual markers on their bodies, and that marks them as, at this point, only potentially impaired, diabetic children and adults are often not defined as being either completely healthy or ill, and must exist at the margins of both groups. In many ways, they feel that they are completely alone. However, perceptions of illness and disability are beginning to change. As Susan Wendell states in her book, *The Rejected Body*:

> If we consider that many more people in North America are disabled by arthritis, heart or respiratory disease, or diabetes than by blindness or paraplegia, we are compelled to adopt very different paradigms of disability." (p20)

This paradigm shift is at least two-fold. First, as I said above, this means that people with disabilities are not always easy to spot. People with many chronic illnesses such as diabetes, chronic fatigue or cardiovascular disease carry few outward signifiers of their condition, and can often appear no different from people without these conditions. For Amy and Cassie, the only outward sign of their condition is their medic-alert bracelets, which is why the girls place so much importance on them. This lack of visibility can have a double edge for people with chronic illness. On the one hand, they do not have to live with the social stigma of being obviously ill or disabled. On the other hand, they are not often given the emotional and physical support that they need to deal with their conditions. People may believe that they are being 'lazy', or are lying about their physical limitations. Even when others accept their condition, they do not realize the financial and emotional impact that the conditions can have.

Attending support groups provides one way for Amy and Cassie to combat their feelings of being outsiders and to find a sense of community with other people who have chronic illnesses and/or disabilities. Amy attends a support group led by Ed, a nurse, when she is first hospitalized. Amy's group is attended only by young diabetics, and is intended primarily to educate the members about how to meet the demands of their new condition. In her group, Amy learns how to check her blood sugar, inject herself with insulin, eat appropriately and keep her blood sugar within acceptable levels. However, Ed does offer some advice about how to cope with their emotions. He says:

> "We all want to go home, don't we, kids? We want to go home and be normal again. And it's normal to feel scared and resentful about what's happening to us." (Davis Roberts, p79)

Group members discuss their emotions about their new status as diabetics, and Ed offers them advice on how to cope with them. Once Amy goes home, her parents make no plans for her to keep attending a support group. However, she has made some friends from her group and remains in contact with them.

Cassie attends a support group led by a nurse named Midge, both during her intermittent hospitalizations and once a month as an outpatient. Cassie's group is attended by teenagers with a wide range of different illnesses and disabilities. While there are a couple of other diabetics in her group, there are also group members with cancer who are recovering from surgery, and others who have some level of paralysis. When Cassie was introduced to the support group soon after being diagnosed with diabetes, she was uncertain about whether she would fit in because "I felt oddly out of place. Without my IV pole, I carried no outward sign of my disease. I saw the others looking at me, taking my measure, as if they wondered what right I had to be there." (p30)

Because she lacked visual clues to help others identify her illness, Cassie worried that the other group members with more readily apparent conditions would reject her. Fortunately for Cassie, this does not occur. Cassie's group exists primarily to offer emotional support for its members. In the group they discuss their feelings about their physical conditions, and how this affects their relationships with parents and peers. Cassie enjoys attending her group, because it helps her realize that she:

> "was not alone with my illness. Some destiny had handed out injuries and diseases to each of us who sat in the lounge. We were each alone when we hurt, when we faced some painful test or procedure. But here in the group we were all together." (p7)

Because both Amy and Cassie have a group of peers who understand their physical condition, they feel that they are part of a community, no matter how small, that does not identify them as somehow different or deficient. Both receive helpful support. Lucy, however, has no such community. Furthermore, she resists the idea of joining one.

When her parents put her in therapy, Lucy actively resists working with her counselor. She refuses to answer his questions, or lies and tells him that everything is going well (Hautman, p176).

Lucy may not be entirely at fault here. While Amy and Cassie are surrounded by peers who can validate their feelings and experiences, Lucy is alone with her counselor. While one-on-one therapy can greatly benefit individuals, for this to occur the therapist and person in counselling must be able to develop a sympathetic relationship with each other, and Lucy and her counselor may have been ill-matched to each other. Granted, Lucy does little to assist this relationship. Because of her lack of support, Lucy feels that she is entirely alone, both from her 'normal' peers and from others with diabetes and other chronic illnesses.

The second paradigm shift in Wendell's new concept of disability requires us to realize that most disabled people (including people with blindness and paraplegia) are not "globally incapacitated" (ibid), but have varying ranges of ability. Amy, Cassie and Lucy can participate in most physical activities with the right planning and care. For example, Amy can jog with her brother or ride her bicycle with her friend Pudge, and Cassie can go horse-back riding, so long as both are careful to check their blood sugar beforehand and they bring along snacks in case their sugar levels get too low. Although they cannot participate in their favorite activities as carelessly as non-diabetics can, they can still participate. When the protagonists are not able to participate in some activity, or do poorly, the narrative makes it clear that the girls have not planned well enough in advance and are not taking care of themselves. For example, Lucy tries to take a long walk down some railroad tracks from the mall to her house. As her blood sugar drops, she starts to feel more and more incapacitated:

> "My head feels large. The wind fills my ears. My legs are like puppet limbs, loose-hinged and numb as wood. I am having some trouble staying centered on the tracks. I wish they were railings, waist high, something to hang on to.
> "I am moving very slowly now, as if time is coming to a stop. Something is very wrong. An internal voice says to me, 'Eat something'. I step off the tracks and walk a few yards to a patch of low grass, moving as if through water; the air is thick and hard to breathe. 'Eat,' says the voice."
> (Hautman, p65)

Lucy only begins to feel better when she forces herself to eat a granola bar, sit down and wait. Once she begins to feel better physically, she starts to berate herself emotionally, saying:

> "That was a bad one. I could have passed out. I almost did. I feel stupid. I am shivering. I should have eaten the granola bar before leaving the mall, but I was so busy feeling sorry for myself because I couldn't have any pizza that I forgot about the calories I'd need for the walk home."
> (Hautman, p66)

The fact that she must have a detailed plan of action for everything she does makes Lucy resent her diabetes even more. Although Lucy knows that her temporary inability to continue was brought on by her failure to plan for the walk correctly, it doesn't make her feel any happier about her situation, because she resents the fact that no one else she knows (other than the "perfect diabetic",

Sandy, at her school) has to worry about such circumstances. Again, Lucy believes that her difference defines her, and she is alone.

ANGER AS A RESPONSE TO DIFFERENCE

Being different makes Amy, Cassie, and Lucy feel a great deal of anger at their diabetes. Anger can be a difficult emotion for girls and women to express in socially acceptable ways, and this difficulty is compounded by illness or disability. As Keith states, traditional narratives of illness play:

> on the stereotypical idea that what ill or disabled people need most is the pity and kindness of others. But in order to deserve this treatment, they must not burden those around them with strong emotions such as rage or disappointment. (Keith, p55)

In these narratives, ill or disabled girls cannot be protagonists. Rather, "they must be self-effacing, leaving plenty of space for the non-disabled character to develop and learn" (ibid). In other words, characters with illnesses or impairments generally serve to teach the protagonist a lesson, rather than having a subjectivity of their own. Only when these characters are allowed to form the centre of the narrative — only when they are taken seriously, in other words — are they allowed to feel angry at their situation.

In *Sugar isn't Everything*, Amy is angry at nearly everyone. She's mad at her sister for playing music and for being messy when she wants to read. She's mad at her parents for being worried, and she's mad at her friends for eating candy when they think she isn't looking. The author seems to imply that neither of her friends should be eating the candy anyway. Pudge shouldn't eat it because she is overweight, while Natalie is a recovering bulimic. Amy's mother gives her a pamphlet called "Anger: A Message to the Adolescent with Diabetes"[6], which describes anger as a natural and understandable reaction to her diagnosis, and offers some healthy ways to express that anger such as talking to someone or exercising. Amy realizes that her family is also angry about her diagnosis. Her parents are angry because they're worried about Amy's health and how to pay for her medical needs, and her little sister is mad because she feels like Amy is always the centre of attention. The pamphlet, and a talk with her much beloved big brother, help Amy to realize how she and everyone else is feeling.

Cassie and Lucy both feel angry, but rather than viewing this as a healthy or understandable reaction to their situation, they try to deny and bury their anger. Early on in *Living with a Secret*, Cassie realizes that she was not really mad at her parents, but was instead "angry at diabetes itself. I wanted to rage against this disease that held me in its grip. It stifled my spontaneity, it sapped my freedom. It set me apart from everyone around me." (Kent, p12) Cassie doesn't want to feel angry. Instead, she wants to be like a girl in her support group, Moira, who has just gone away to college. To Cassie, Moira "was the perfect diabetic, cheerfully following all the rules. How had she learned to live so fearlessly and confidently? I wished I knew her secret."(p31) Instead, she feels disappointed in herself because "I wasn't Moira Kent. For me life with diabetes was a constant struggle." (p36)

Although Lucy denies to her therapist that she's angry[7], her actions betray her. When she gets ready to leave the house, her makeup consists of "lots of black around the eyes because I'm in a black mood. I go with the purple lipstick and I add a spot of red to the tips of my black nails. They want weird, I'll give 'em weird." (Hautman, pp54-55) Lucy's anger and lack of a clear identity cause her deliberately to push others away, using her "weirdness" as a wall between herself and others. I do not believe that dressing or participating in goth always expresses emotional damage, nor do I believe that goth is an inherently damaging subculture. However, in Lucy's case I believe that Hautman has Lucy use the goth look as an expression of her own personal anger and alienation.

Like Cassie, Lucy compares herself to another, more "perfect" diabetic. She states that:

> "Sandy just got diabetes last year and to talk to her you'd think that God reached down and gave it to her as a gift. She was insufferably cheerful and disciplined and friendly before she got sick, but instead of calming her down, the diabetes made her even more unbearable. Now she's like the diabetes ambassador." (Hautman, p27)

Although she seems to make fun of Sandy, Lucy reveals a certain wistfulness when she thinks that:

> "I should just do what they tell me to do. Go to school. Be good. Do my homework. Be nice. Dress dorky. Eat meat. Act my age. I could be an actress. Is that what Little Miss Perfect Diabetic Sandy Steiner does? Is she onstage 24/7? Maybe inside she's just as messed up as me." (p168)

Lucy struggles with how to react to her situation, knowing that her current rebellious ways are not working for her, but fighting the urge to lose herself in conformity. Where Amy seems immediately to learn ways to express her anger in healthy, socially acceptable ways, Cassie and Lucy tend to act out in self-destructive ways, turning their anger against themselves.

While the narratives in young adult novels tend to define becoming empowered as some "rejection or rebellion against the status quo" that helps characters grow and mature (Brown and St Clair, p28), this rejection can be dangerous if the protagonist equates the 'status quo' with the need to manage her diabetes. The pamphlet that Amy's mother gives her warns against just such a course of action, telling her not to take her anger out on her own body. This is exactly what both Cassie and Lucy do in the midst of their anger. Both refuse to eat well or check their blood sugar, and when their blood sugar runs too high they ignore the fact. Only when their health spirals almost completely out of control do Lucy and Cassie admit that their anger is only hurting themselves.

This self-destructive behavior may arise for a couple of reasons. Narratives in young adult literature tend to focus on the protagonist's movement towards maturity, and when the protagonist has a chronic illness this process can be more difficult because she can feel infantilized by her parents' and relatives' constant surveillance and control. As Martha Westwater states in her book *Giant Despair Meets Hopeful* (2000), "most of the despair characteristic of modern adolescent fiction stems from a rebellion against the prolonged state of subservience, a subservience for which parents are usually castigated." (p9) When the protagonist has a chronic illness or impairment, this period of subservience can be lengthened. Cassie and Lucy feel this pressure more deeply than Amy, probably because they are a few years older and their desire for independence is greater. In fact, Cassie and Lucy's stories can be viewed as one way that Amy's story could be told a couple of years down the line, if she has still not fully learned to accept her new identity as a diabetic.

Cassie feels that her mother is constantly watching her, worried that she'll make a mistake. She feels that diabetes (in the guise of her mother) "fenced me in with its rules and regulations" (Kent, p11). Cassie's mother does not want her to continue her hobby of horseback riding, even though her doctors and nurses encourage her to keep riding (p25). Her parents tell all of her friends and teachers at school about her diabetes and encourage them to watch her in case of problems, which embarrasses Cassie (p33). When Cassie gets out of the hospital after her "crisis", her mother re-doubles her efforts at watching her daughter, prompting Cassie to wonder why she can't "make mistakes and move on, like other kids did in their lives? Would I ever be allowed to grow up?" (p37). She feels that her parents have labeled her as "an emergency waiting to happen", when she wants them to acknowledge her as "me, their daughter, Cassie Mullins!" (p53) As long as her parents constantly watch and control her, Cassie feels that she cannot grow up. Furthermore, she has no incentive to grow up. As she says to her mother, "Why should I take care of myself? You come spying on me no matter what!" (p112)

In *Sweetblood*, Lucy's parents seem to identify their daughter completely by her illness. Her mother never calls her by her name, but by endearments like Honey, Sweetie, or Sugar, which are all tied to her diabetic "sweetness". By contrast, her father calls her Sport or Tiger, nicknames left over from when she was very small. Both parents ignore the fact that their daughter is neither very sweet nor athletic, choosing to define her as they want her to be rather than as she is. All of this impacts on the way Lucy sees herself. When she paints an "honest" self-portrait in art class, she paints a picture of someone who is "blonde and stupid and grinning and thoughtless" (Hautman, p16), which doesn't describe her any better than her parents' nicknames. Neither Lucy nor her parents have a true conception of who she is.

Lucy has lived under her mother and father's worry and control for so long that she has managed both to internalize and ignore it. Lucy feels that her glucometer[8] "judges me mercilessly. I've been good or I've been bad. Perfect or flawed. Virtuous or wicked." (p96) When her glucometer tells Lucy that her blood sugar levels are too high, her internal monologue tells her that she is "Too high! Bad girl! Bad, bad, evil, wicked girl!" (p21) Just as quickly, however, she turns off these thoughts in favor of "Ho-hum" (ibid). Because her parents do not allow her to have responsibility for her own body, Lucy believes that she will always be in the wrong, her diabetes will never be under her conscious control, and it is not worth her time to feel too badly about it. Worry, disapproval and disappointment have become such background noise to Lucy that when her parents or school administrators lecture her about her health or performance in school, she merely hears "BLAH BLAH BLAH" (p72).

Both Cassie and Lucy feel that their parents are keeping them from maturing at the rate they desire, and think this is one more way that they are unfairly being kept from growing up like other kids their age. So long as their parents insist on treating Cassie and Lucy like children, the girls rebel against being made to feel different from their peers by acting out in potentially self-destructive ways. And because they rebel, their parents redouble their efforts to control them. Throughout their stories, Cassie and Lucy must work out how to break this cycle. The parents of all three girls worry about their daughters, and this worry is not without justification. The girls do have a potentially life-threatening illness, and Cassie and Lucy are not acting in healthy ways. At the same time, however, their parents need to realize that refusing to allow their daughters some independence may be exacerbating rather than helping the situation.

Cassie and Lucy's lack of self-care could also arise out of a desire to forget their diabetes by ignoring the body. Wendell points out that "the body as corpse, not the body as lived experience, is at the heart of Western medicine" (p120). This view alienates both the doctor and the patient from the patient's body, because it refuses to take into account how the person feels. At some level, it refuses to acknowledge the body as a necessary part of a person's identity. This can be very difficult, because our Judeo-Christian influenced society connects the mind with the intellect, the spiritual, the masculine and the higher functions of our identities, while simultaneously connecting the body to the appetite, the earthy, the feminine, and the (necessary evil) of base bodily functions. The mind is glorified while the body is demonized, meaning that we understandably try to avoid having identities tied to the body.

This makes controlling diabetes harder than it needs to be, because it requires people to identify with their bodies and acknowledge their needs in a society that equates any connection to the body with weakness or difference. Diabetic girls are doubly embodied, because they live in a culture that defines both illness and femininity with this devalued embodiment, and Amy, Cassie, and Lucy all resent being forced into this type of identity. Before they can maintain a healthy state, Cassie and Lucy have to find a way to overcome this resentment, and learn how to value their bodies enough to take care of them.

HETEROSEXUALITY AS A MARKER OF NORMALCY

Within each of these books, a normal or 'successful' teen life is measured for the girls, at least in part, by them having a boyfriend. All three girls worry that diabetes keeps them outside of their peer group, and separated from normative femininity — especially from romantic relationships with boys. Each of the girls is not only unproblematically heterosexual, but also actively seeks boyfriends. This is encouraged by the narrative, which explicitly includes finding a boyfriend as part of the journey of acquiring a more mature and healthy identity. Although having a boyfriend does not signal that the protagonist is completely healthy, it does imply that she is well on her way to being so.

For Amy, liking boys and having a boy like her is a symbol of her return to normal life and her place within her peer group. Soon after leaving the hospital, Amy wonders if Danny, the boy she likes, will ever like her. She "was surprised again to realize that she was thinking something so normal. For a while, she'd wondered if she'd ever think anything normal again." (Davis Roberts, p88) Worrying about boys, then, is explicitly situated within normal life. Amy starts running with her big brother as a way to expel some anger and control her blood sugar, and Danny notices her as she runs, which pleases her because "to have a boy single her out for attention was a first in their group. A feather in Amy's cap, as Gram would have put it." (p140) Neither Natalie nor Pudge have got any attention from boys, and this attention signals Amy's possible superiority to them; in fact, Pudge speculates that boys don't like her because she's "too fat" (p105). At the end of the book Coby, a diabetic friend from the hospital who has just won the championship baseball game, calls her at home, and Amy can't wait to brag to her girlfriends (p186). With attention from not one but two cute and popular boys, Amy's place within the social hierarchy is assured.

Cassie also uses attention from boys to assure herself of her normality and popularity. She also bases a lot of her body image on the regard of boys. Before her status as a diabetic is revealed at camp, when the other counselors decide to eat a lot of ice cream and candy together Cassie declines, saying "I'm just not a big eater." Jason, the boy to whom Cassie is attracted, replies "I can tell," with an admiring look at her figure. Cassie's personality also falls within acceptably feminine parameters for Jason. He admits to Cassie that he went out with another counselor the summer before, but broke up with her because she was too bossy. He likes the fact that Cassie is "nicer" (Kent, p90). When Cassie is outed as a diabetic, Jason reassures her that he doesn't mind, and kisses her (pp156-7). Cassie is relieved that being diabetic doesn't make her unattractive, and her self-confidence grows from this point. She states that "With Jason, anything was possible. [...] Jason was the best. I couldn't figure out how I got so lucky." (p159) Cassie is not alone in using her boyfriend as a marker of her normal status. One of her campers, nine-year-old

Julia, now defines Cassie as her role model because she's 'normal'. She states, "You hang out with the other counselors. And Jason likes you." (p161) Having a boyfriend marks Cassie as normal, as an insider, to herself and to others, and erases the differences brought on by diabetes.

Although Lucy has less interest in being normal than Amy or Cassie she is equally interested in having a boyfriend, though she often looks for one in inappropriate places. When she meets an attractive goth boy named Dylan at school, Lucy wonders "if maybe he is the one who will complete me. I have always thought that I am only part of a person, and that there is someone out there who will fit to me the way a key fits a lock." (Hautman, p76) Without a boyfriend, Lucy believes she is incomplete, broken, or locked. When Dylan proves to be unsatisfying as a romantic partner by getting too drunk at a party to pay attention to her or drive her home, she is briefly distracted by the attentions of the adult Draco. She feels connected to him because she thinks he is not afraid of her, and he doesn't believe she's fragile (p224). When Draco makes a pass at her during his Halloween party, she realizes that Draco doesn't really care about her as a person or an intellectual equal. Neither Dylan nor Draco are appropriate boyfriends for Lucy, because neither really cares about her.

Lucy has the opportunity for a more appropriate partner in Mark, a boy who lives on Lucy's street. Throughout the book Lucy calls Mark her best friend, although the two seem rather awkward around each other. Mark and Lucy have known each other all of their lives, and Mark seems as baffled by Lucy's current darkness and self-destruction as her parents. Still, Mark offers Lucy stilted support, stopping to talk to her when she'll let him and lending her his beloved letter jacket[9] when she asks for it. When Lucy is caught in a snowstorm and passes out because her blood sugar is too high, it is Mark who saves her. At the end of the book, Mark also gives his approval of Lucy's appearance, which she has changed as a symbol of her decision to try to be healthier. Rejecting her long-standing goth look, Lucy strips the black dye from her naturally blonde hair. This leaves her long hair dry and unhealthy, so she shaves her head into a half-inch long burr. Mark asks if he can touch her hair, and admires the way it feels (p242). At the end of the novel, although the reader is unsure whether Lucy and Mark will end up linked romantically, the pair's friendship is strengthened.

The girls' desire — nay, need — for boyfriends can be seen as less than ideal from a feminist viewpoint. This is something that should not be ignored, particularly in Kent's book. Cassie and Lucy's lack of an identity without a boyfriend is troubling, as is the fact that both Cassie and Lucy must be rescued by boys. However, it is also important that these girls are allowed sexual identities, however stereotypical they might be, because sexuality is something that is often denied characters with chronic illnesses. Because forming an individual sexual identity is part of the maturation process for adolescents, this is one important way in which these books allow their protagonists to grow and form lively, healthy identities.

HAPPY ENDINGS

Although finding a boyfriend (or the possibility of one) is part of how the girls themselves define success, how does the narrative tend to define a happy ending? As Brown and St Clair point out, "because young adult fiction is essentially optimistic, the protagonist's journey usually concludes with his or her gaining some measure of maturity and independence." (p26) Within the three books included in this study, "maturity" is defined primarily by the ability of the protagonist to manage her diabetes, which entails eating well and keeping her blood sugar within acceptable levels, while still enjoying a full and enjoyable life. Maturity, then, requires that the girl rebuild her sense of identity to include the label of 'diabetic', something that each has fought against doing for much of the narrative.

Learning to control her diabetes allows each girl to become more independent from her parents, and to 'grow up' at a rate on a par with her non-diabetic peers. As she becomes more independent from her parents, however, each girl's relationship with them strengthens. Ironically, this concurrent split and re-attachment to parents is also a sign of maturity. As Brown and St Clair are careful to point out, in narratives with female protagonists, maturity does not entail the complete independence favored by traditional male protagonists. Instead, maturity requires that girls be able to form and maintain healthy relationships with others. Mature girls do not completely break or reject a relationship with their parents, but re-form that relationship to include more adult respect and affection. Under these relationships, parents do not act as agents of control and surveillance, but instead as agents of support and friendship.

Amy matures in a number of ways. First, Amy starts running with her big brother and riding her bike with Pudge so "I can eat more of what I want" (Davis Roberts, p137), and so she can deal with her emotions in a healthy way. Her bike rides remind her that "it was a good feeling to have energy again" (p163). Amy has also strengthened her relationships with her family and her best friend Pudge. Because Pudge has agreed to stop eating candy in solidarity with Amy, she loses weight. Amy and Pudge agree that, once seventh grade starts, they'll only let other people use Pudge's real first name, Sylvia (p163). Although Pudge and Amy had a rough time staying friends when Amy was first diagnosed as a diabetic (primarily because their friendship revolved mostly around eating food together), their friendship is now stronger than ever before.

Finally, Amy has learned that sometimes it's necessary and acceptable to act aggressively. In her support group, Ed tells Amy that "sometimes you'll have to speak out forcefully on your own behalf, when you know you're right. You're the diabetic, you know about your own condition and what's best for you to do." (p166) This advice comes into play when her friend Coby's blood sugar gets too low during a baseball game. While other onlookers speculate that Coby is drunk, Amy steps forward and demands that he get the proper help (p183). At the end of the book, Amy declares that: "I'm an ordinary healthy person. I just happen to have diabetes." (p185)

Cassie follows a similar trajectory. After she needs to be rescued by Jason and the camp nurse, she worries that "I'd made such a mess of things, no one would ever trust me again." (Kent, p150) After blaming her parents for her behaviour throughout most of the book, she finally recognizes that she is responsible for her own actions, and that no one will trust her to keep her diabetes under control until she proves that she *can* be trusted. At the end of the book, Cassie makes a statement similar to Amy's, saying that: "I could be so many things at once — weird and standard. Healthy and diabetic. Maybe they didn't really contradict each other." (p175)

Like Cassie, Lucy insists upon blaming everyone for her actions. She blames her parents for producing an imperfect daughter, and for their constant micro-management of her life. She blames Dylan for being a bad boyfriend, and she blames school administrators for only wanting normal, compliant students. She visits Antoinette, the local tattoo artist, who tells her that she has no one to blame but herself for her situation. Antoinette explains to Lucy that identities are not imposed upon one by others, but are fluid and self-defined. People can change their identities to be who they want or need to be rather than who they are at that moment, stating, "You don't like what you see? Change. You've done it before." (Hautman, p233)

With this revelation in mind, Lucy decides that the first step to changing her life is changing her appearance. With this accomplished, she begins to try and repair her distant relationships with her parents and friend Mark, and starts doing her schoolwork again. Most importantly, she begins to take care of her body. Stripping the funereal dye and paint from her body and ridding herself of her death-like pallor symbolizes Lucy's return to her life. No longer self-identifying as a member of the undead and denying her body's needs, Lucy is ready to accept and even enjoy her embodied state. At the same time, Lucy is not seeking an identity grounded in the normal or mainstream. She still identifies as different, but this is a difference that allows her healthy relationships with herself and others. As she states: "I'm still the same twisted individual. Just different." (p242)

Once Amy, Cassie, and Lucy have learned to manage their illness, they are allowed to be more independent. Their parents and medical caregivers exercise less control and surveillance over each girl, because they know they will control and monitor themselves. Although each book has an undeniably happy ending, the possibility remains that, in the future, the girls may continue to have problems. Their relationships with their boyfriends may end, as most relationships between teenagers do. The girls' parents may continue to have moments of being overprotective or over-controlling. Perhaps most importantly, the girls may continue to have problems managing their diabetes, and they may face diabetic-related health problems later in life.

In other words, there is no guarantee that these girls will live 'happily ever after'. However, by forming healthy identities, each girl has given herself a better chance at a happy life.

CONCLUSION

Amy, Cassie, and Lucy all felt like outsiders, kept separate from their friends and family because of the difference caused by their diabetes. Ultimately, though, Amy and Cassie both realized that they were not, in fact, outsiders. By the end of *Sugar isn't Everything* and *Living with a Secret*, both Amy and Cassie have found that their diabetes does not make them different enough to be excluded from their peer group or families. Both create strong relationships with others, and realize that they are 'normal' and 'healthy'. Evidence of their insider status comes in the form of attention from boys, and their ability to 'hang out' with friends and do everyday teenage activities. Amy can ride her bike, run and go to baseball games, while Cassie can ride horses, perform in a talent show and be a good camp counselor. Both girls define themselves as no different, or as little different, from their peers.

Lucy is another story in *Sweetblood*, because at the end of her book she still insists upon her difference from the mainstream. She still dresses in creative and unusual ways, and defines herself as "twisted" (which, in her vernacular, is a positive thing). However, Lucy no longer connects her difference to her diabetes. Instead, Lucy is different because she chooses to be, and not because of what her body can and cannot do. Furthermore, Lucy's new definition of difference need not build walls between herself and others. She no longer dresses differently to make others feel scared or uncomfortable, but simply because she enjoys the way she looks. Lucy does not need to push her parents and potential friends away consciously to assure them of her "weirdness", but can form and maintain relationships without losing herself in these.

Finally, Lucy no longer centres her identity around rejecting her body, but around accepting her embodiment. Throughout most of the book, keeping her blood sugar under control was a mystery to Lucy. She rejected her responsibility for keeping her body healthy, instead blaming others for her situation. From the moment Lucy leaves the hospital, though, she connects her own actions to the way she feels, choosing to do what it takes to remain healthy. Lucy learns that she can maintain her unique identity while still doing 'normal' things such as eating well, sitting in the sunshine and finishing her homework. Finally, Lucy has managed to separate being different from being wrong.

What Amy, Cassie, and Lucy have in common is that their narratives take their rites-of-passage seriously, allowing their stories to take centre stage. Where earlier young adult novels would have made the girls into supporting characters, and used their illnesses to teach the protagonist some lesson about life, these more contemporary novels take the girls seriously enough to allow them to learn their own lessons. Although the girls cannot be cured and will not die, this does not mean that they must remain immature, forever trapped in static identities.

Instead, each girl finds that she can change and mature. Rather than being defined completely by her diabetes, each protagonist is allowed to have a well-developed, complex identity. Diabetes becomes only one part of how each girl identifies herself. While each girl sometimes feels like an outsider, excluded from mainstream teenaged life, within the narrative she is the ultimate insider because it is her story, and no one else's, that is considered important enough to be told. Throughout, these girls' stories are held up as possible role models, both for diabetic readers hoping to work through their own issues with their bodies and identities, and for non-diabetic readers dealing with other forms of bodily difference. Readers are encouraged to identify with the protagonists' healthy acceptance of their bodies and their new, more mature, relationships with their peers and parents. By making this maturity part of the 'happy ending', readers learn to accept, rather than fight, bodily difference.

NOTES

1) There are nearly 21 million people with diabetes in the US, 176,500 of whom are under 20 ("Total Prevalence of Diabetes", American Diabetes Association, www.diabetes.org/diabetes-statistics/prevalence.jsp). As of 2004, there were about 1.8 million people with diabetes in the UK. Of these, about 14,000 were under the age of 15, and 261,000 fell between the ages of 15-44 ("Diabetes in the UK 2004", Diabetes UK, www.diabetes.org.uk/infocentre/reports/in_the_uk_2004.doc). Canada only provides statistics for diabetics over the age of 20, but the government estimates that as of the year 2000, about 5% of their population was affected ("Responding to the Challenge", National Diabetes Surveillance System, www.phac-aspc.gc.ca/ccdpc-cpcmc/ndsssnsd/english/pubs_reports/pdf/WEB_NDSS_English_Report-nocover.pdf).

2) Children and young adults tend to develop Type I (also called insulin dependent or juvenile) diabetes, while adults over 40 tend to develop Type II (non-insulin dependent) diabetes.

3) See, for example, *Why Me?* (New York: Apple Press, 1992); *The Disability Rights Movement* (New York: The Children's Press, 1996); *Too Soon to Say Goodbye* (New York: Apple Press, 1996).

4) Pete Hautman, "Sweetblood Essay", www.petehautman.com/sbloodessay.html

5) See, for example, Davis Roberts, p123 and p133.

6) This is an actual pamphlet that Davis Roberts quotes extensively from pp144-158.

7) Hautman, p176. Unlike the girls in the other two books, therapy does not help Lucy.

8) A glucometer is a device that reads a person's blood sugar levels. With modern glucometers, a person pricks their finger and places a drop of blood on a special disposable strip placed in the device. The glucometer reads the blood sugar levels in a few seconds and displays the results digitally. Diabetics are urged to check their blood sugar several times a day. Older methods of measuring blood sugar levels, described in *Sugar isn't Everything*, included special color changing strips that you could place in urine or (more recently) blood. The color of the strip was then compared to a chart which indicated different sugar levels. Modern digital glucometers are far more precise.

9) A 'letter jacket' is a short coat in the school's colours which usually has a wool body and leather or leatherette sleeves, with a prominently displayed letter on one breast that stands for the first letter of the school's name together with a symbol of what is has been achieved for. Students earn the jacket from their school for different types of achievement, usually sporting. Letter jackets are usually a marker of high social status.

REFERENCES

Brown, Joanne and St, Clair, Nancy, *Declarations of Independence: Empowered Girls in Young Adult Literature, 1990-2001*, The Scarecrow Press Inc, London, 2005.

Davis Roberts, Willo, *Sugar Isn't Everything: A Support Book, in Fiction Form, for the Young Diabetic*, Atheneum, New York, 1987.

Hautman, Pete, *Sweetblood*, Simon Pulse, New York, 2003.

Hautman, Pete, "Sweetblood Essay," www.petehautman.com/sbloodessay.html, 2004.

Keith, Lois, *Take Up Thy Bed and Walk: Death, Disability, and Cure in Classic Fiction for Girls*, Routledge, New York, 2001.

Kent, Deborah, *Living with a Secret*, Arch Paperback, New York, 2001.

Wendell, Susan, *The Rejected Body: Feminist Philosophical Reflections on Disability*, Routledge, New York, 1996.

Westwater, Martha, *Giant Despair Meets Hopeful: Kristevan Readings in Adolescent Literature*, The University of Alberta Press, Edmonton, 2000.

INCLUSION & SEGREGATION

EARLY PERIOD

VII. DOING NOT DREAMING: DISABILITY & MENTAL HEALTH IN ELSIE J OXENHAM'S BOOKS

JU GOSLING & JULIE NEWMAN

INTRODUCTION

TODAY, Elsie Jeanette Oxenham is probably the least well-known of the 'big five' authors of the 20th-century British genre of girls' school stories, the others being Angela Brazil (who wrote stand-alone novels), Elinor M Brent-Dyer (best known for her Chalet School series), Enid Blyton (best known for her St Clare's and Malory Towers series) and Dorita Fairlie Bruce (best known for her Dimsie and Nancy series). Unlike Brazil, Brent-Dyer and Blyton, Oxenham's books never made the transition into paperback in the 1960s — although some have been reprinted unabridged in paperback format by Girls Gone By in the 21st century — nor did they reappear in hardback in the 1980s as Bruce's books did. The few of Oxenham's titles that survived in Children's Press hardback editions into the early 1970s were heavily abridged, and in many cases were unrepresentative of her work as a whole.

However, in her day — from the First World War until the middle of the twentieth century — Oxenham and her 'Abbey Girls' were immensely popular with both schoolgirls and younger women, and she was regarded as being second only to Brazil in status. Oxenham wrote 38 novels in her Abbey series, published between 1914 and 1949, with many of her other novels loosely connecting in the sense that characters also appeared occasionally in the Abbey books. Oxenham was also the first to create an Alpine school linked to a Sanatorium, although Brent-Dyer's Chalet School remains better known today.

Superficially, Oxenham shared many of the characteristics of her better-known peers, all of whom were born in the late nineteenth century and whose own childhood experiences of school life were reflected in their books. She was born in 1880, the daughter of the journalist William Dunkerley, who became better-known under his pseudonym John Oxenham for his romance novels and poetry. She spent most of her girlhood in the London suburb of Ealing, and attended private schools there. Oxenham never married, but remained living with family members until her death in 1960. She was, though, an active member of the English Folk Dance movement, as well as being heavily involved in girls' organizations including the American-led Camp Fire movement.

After writing a number of romances for girls, Elsie J Oxenham's first school story, *Rosaly's New School,* was published in 1913, followed in 1914 by *The Girls of the Hamlet Club*. This story, set in a Buckinghamshire school where a division existed between the wealthier girls who lived in the town and the poorer girls who lived in the surrounding hamlets, marked the first of the series which was later to become known simply as 'The Abbey Girls' after the publication of the book of the same name in 1920. In contrast to Brazil, whose *The Fortunes of Philippa* (1906) is regarded as being the first modern girls' school story, representations of schooling are largely absent from Oxenham's books, even when the action supposedly takes place within school. Instead, the action revolves around the girls themselves and their leisure organisations, chiefly the Camp Fire movement, the Girl Guides and, centrally, folk dancing. The majority of the 'Abbey Girls' books, in fact, are set away from school, and many of them take place when the 'girls' are adults. Oxenham recognized that it was schoolgirl society, rather than school itself, that was central to readers' enjoyment of the books.

TEMPORARY INVALIDS

In terms of the representation of physical illness and disability in her books, Oxenham's overall approach is broadly similar to that of her peers: major characters are either cured; or they die. Disabled and sick characters are both mentioned and included within the community to a greater extent than with most other girls' books of the period, but this inclusion is presented as being strictly limited, and the limitation is seen as resulting inevitably from their illnesses or impairments rather than from society's responses to them.

Oxenham's first published book, *Goblin Island* (1907), features a girl, Marjory Lesley, who for unexplained reasons is the ward of heroine Jean and her writer father (themselves based loosely on Elsie and John Oxenham). Marjory has had an accident two years previously and must spend her time laying flat on her back as a result, but is expected to recover as she gets older. She spends most of her time in her room, but is included in the community to the extent of making friends with the younger members of the Colquhoun family. (Jean's romance with Donald Colquhoun is at the centre of the story.)

Another minor character who will recover in the long term is Malcolm Forsyth, who appears in *Expelled from School* (1919), Oxenham's first story set in a Swiss school. Malcolm is recovering from pneumonia and is staying in Switzerland with his nurse, Polly. He acts as a confidante for the two heroines, Retta — the girl who is expelled from school — and Pamela. He is seen as a character to be admired, since, like Marjory, he appears to be reconciled to his situation and has the self-discipline to co-operate with the regime that is necessary for his cure to take place. Similarly John Firth, who first appears in a short story that was later incorporated into *Peggy and the Brotherhood* (1936), while not forced to spend his time laying down, is reconciled to having his activities curtailed through the risk of his developing TB, although this is seen as being very bad luck on his part.

BETTER OFF DEAD

Child characters with more long-term impairments do make an appearance in Oxenham's earlier books, but are only really noticeable as being significant when contrasted to their almost complete absence in the works of her peers. For example, in *A Holiday Queen* (1910), a group of children form a 'Band' of friends and give themselves titles; the disabled Nigel Scott is made Marquis of Cove and is included in the Band so far as is possible.

Then, in 1919, 'Wriggles' was introduced as a character in Oxenham's 'Rocklands' books. He was particularly unusual because he was based on a real child, Reginald Willis Wilson or 'Ribbie'. Oxenham had corresponded with Ribbie from the time that he was eight years old, after learning from a woman friend how much Ribbie had enjoyed the friend reading Oxenham's books to him. Oxenham arranged for him to be a 'mascot' to her Camp Fire girls, who also wrote to him, and who along with Oxenham regularly sent him presents. Ribbie was apparently a highly intelligent and talented child, both musically and artistically, and he was skilled in a variety of craft activities (Godfrey, p85). He died in 1919 when he was ten and a half years old, of "tuberculosis of the spine, tubercular peritonitis and exhaustion" (Godfrey, p91). Oxenham later attempted to have a collection of their correspondence published, but this were rejected by her publisher as being aimed at too young an age-group, and as being too personal, to be commercially successful (Godfrey, p83).

Wriggles is first introduced in *A Go-Ahead Schoolgirl* (1919). He has been left very frail after an illness, and must spend his time laying flat in an invalid carriage (this is likely to have resembled a large, shallow 'pram'). Wriggles has two older brothers and an older sister, and lives with his nurse in a house on the Yorkshire moors that is owned by his aunt by marriage. Perhaps because of his real-life counterpart, Wriggles is not a wholly stereotypical 'suffering invalid'; he also plays a more important role in the life of the household than he might otherwise have done. The fact that he is the youngest sibling also, of course, sets him up as a character to be somewhat petted regardless of his disability.

Wriggles continues as a minor but very important character until his death, 'adopted' by the schoolgirls who spend each summer term in a wing of the house, in an echo of the way in which Ribbie became important to Oxenham's real-life Camp Fire girls. Inevitably Wriggles dies young too, but this can be seen as reflecting his real-life counterpart's early death rather than merely stereotyping. However, Oxenham does perpetuate the belief that his death is preferable to continuing disability, albeit that this perhaps comforted her in her own sense of personal loss about his death. In *Rosamund's Victory* (1933), one of the schoolgirls, Rena, who is now an adult, tells Rosamund of Wriggles:

> "He died when he was eleven. It was far better for him; he could never have been well. We tried to think he was getting better, but it never lasted long, and we came to see that it couldn't be a real improvement and that recovery and health were out of the question. So it was better for him to go. But we missed him terribly, and we miss him still."
>
> "But if he could never have been well, you can't be sorry," Rosamund exclaimed. "It would be dreadful to live an invalid life for years. And you say he was only eleven!"
>
> "I'm not sorry; I'm glad. He'd had years of it. We made him very happy, but as he grew older he'd have realized more and more how much he was missing. He was interested in everything, and I don't think he suffered much, either pain or from being shut out of things. But he'd have grudged being helpless if he'd lived."
>
> "It's much better to have a happy memory of him." (pp50-1)

Rosamund's Victory also introduces the character of Geoffrey Kane, later to be the Duke of Kentisbury and Rosamund's husband. Geoffrey is "a middle-aged man, with a thin, lined face and grey hair, sitting under the trees in an invalid chair." (p250) However, Rosamund does not marry him until she has found treatment for him that allows him to lead a virtually 'normal' life. Other adult male characters who are threatened with disability, usually after an accident, also make full recoveries, including the central character Jen's husband Ken. In this sense, Oxenham follows the 'kill or cure' treatment of disability in classic children's literature that has been identified by Lois Keith, where death is seen as being preferable by far to continuing disability (*Take Up Thy Bed and Walk, Death, Disability and Cure in Classic Fiction for Girls*, 2001).

Meanwhile, in *The Abbey Girls at Home* (1929), Betty is bereft because her twin has died of TB:

> Betty freely admitted that for Meg all was well; Meg was freed from the burden of weakness and ill-health which she had borne for years. But for herself, used through all her childhood and growing period to be one of two, the loneliness and sense of incompleteness were crushing. (p5)

By the end of the book, Rosamund's mother has died in the same Swiss sanatorium that Meg had died in. Rosamund later says:

> "It was so *much* better for her. She's well now, and she could never have been anything but ill here. I'd have done anything I could to make her well; the only way to do it was to let her go on to something better, so I can't be too sorry about it." (p274)

Similarly Nils, in *The Captain of the Fifth* (1922), has learning difficulties and is 'delicate', in particular being at risk of developing TB and dying from it as his mother did (in the same sanatorium that Meg and Rosamund's mother died in). Nils is a member of Oxenham's Swiss boys' school, St John's, so is included in the community despite his impairments. His twin sister Astrid explains:

> "He can do things with rules in them, like sums and algebra and exercises, and he can answer questions if they're fair ones, put plainly and properly, you know. Of course, problems or anything tricky catch him at once, but ordinary straightforward stuff he can do as well as anybody. And he can learn and remember all right, though it takes him a long time. But he doesn't have ideas of his own; they don't come, somehow. He can sit and stare at an empty page for an hour and not write a word; and I can scribble reams! ... He's always been delicate, and behind other boys." (pp82-83)

Perhaps inevitably, by the end of the book Nils has died after falling into an icy river by accident and becoming ill as a result.

> "It is far better for Nils, children, and really for Astrid too, though she cannot understand that at present. But he would have needed care all his life; he could never have been strong and normal. She would have delighted in giving her life to tend him, but it is better for them both it should not be required of her. Astrid has powers which, rightly used, will enable her to do great things. Nils, unhappily, would only have held her back, and knowing that, he would have had little pleasure in life." (p321)

Another character who dies young is Cicely Everett's youngest daughter (Cicely being the founder of the Hamlet Club). Originally it is her youngest son that is ill. "He has always been weakly, and has given her constant anxiety." (*An Abbey Champion*, 1946) Later, though:

> "The President [of the Hamlet Club] has lost her baby girl, little Shirley Rose. She's the first of us to lose a child. Shirley was never strong and she died last February." (p29)

What is noticeable here is that Cicely "is the first of us"; Oxenham grew up in a period where women accepted the possibility that their children might die in infancy or early childhood, and where this was, of course, much more likely to happen than it is today. By the mid-1940s infant mortality had dropped dramatically, but there was still a much greater acceptance of the fact that some children are born with life-limiting conditions than there is today, and again, in that sense Oxenham is merely reflecting reality rather than following stereotypes when her characters die young.

Oxenham's most clichéd treatment of disability comes in a short story, *Muffins and Crumpets*, that was published in 1926 but may have been written, and possibly published first, some years earlier. Crumpets is a disabled teenager from a very poor family whose short stature makes her appear much younger than she really is. She does not want to grow up because she is concerned that, as a small person, she will be stared at and mocked for her appearance. After realizing that taking part in 'drill' and becoming fitter cannot change who she is, she dies in a fall saving both her dog (the Muffins of the title) and the girl who leads the drill class from a fire. She survives just long enough to reassure the (inevitably middle-class, non-disabled) girl she has saved that she is glad she won't reach adulthood. Stella Waring and Sheila Ray conclude that here

Oxenham was writing in the style of the evangelical 'street arab' stories, that became popular in the late 19th century, but continued to be published to some extent until the 1930s (Waring and Ray, pp103-4).

ALTERNATIVE WAYS OF LIVING

This is not to say, though, that Oxenham wholeheartedly embraces the idea that death is preferable to disability. In contrast to Crumpets and Nils there is Claude, who also makes his first appearance in *The Captain of the Fifth* (1922):

> "He's tiny, but he'll never be any bigger," Greta said impressively. "He was born like that. But he's strong, you know — fearfully strong in the arms and legs, although his back is all curled up. And Pauline [his sister] thinks the world of him; he's older than she is, and she looks up to him, and thinks he's all that's wonderful." (p48)

Claude's mobility may be restricted when walking, but he is portrayed as being an excellent driver. Claude eventually marries one of Pauline's friends, Thora (*An Abbey Champion*, 1946), despite a probably realistic lack of support from some of her friends. Crucially, perhaps, Claude is middle-class and male; it is far easier for Claude to lead a full life when he can afford a car and has a wife to support him than it is for a working-class disabled woman like Crumpets would have become to form a family and find work.

Most strikingly, in *The Abbey Girls Go Back to School* (1922) when the central character Jen is badly hurt in a traffic accident, the friend responsible for causing the accident, Joy, wonders if Jen would be better off dead or in a coma than fully conscious if she is unable to walk again. Her friend 'Miss Newcastle' disagrees.

> "No, Joy! It wouldn't be more terrible; not for Jen. She'd still have something within her, something she could never lose. It would be very hard to have to live on memories, to look back all her life; but better that than never to have known such joy as Jen has had... And Jen would find other ways of happiness, if all she has had were taken away from her... How? I can't tell you. But she'd do it, because she's Jenny-Wren." (p281)

Later on, Oxenham's ballet star, Damaris Ellerton ('Mary Damayris'), has to find an alternative career when she is badly hurt in an accident on stage. Unlike Jen, she has no family money to fall back on, although her cousin Maidlin, of whom more later, is an heiress. Damaris is portrayed as struggling to accept her fate — which in itself is only realistic — but relatively quickly turns instead to a new career as a gardener.

> "She loves the garden, and she's happy in it. But she hasn't forgotten her life in town. She says she feels like someone who has lost a limb, or whose sight or hearing has gone. She's carrying on, but she misses her dancing all the time. With Damaris it's not a case of being entirely contented to be here, but of brave acceptance of a second-best." (*Guardians of the Abbey*, 1950, p211)

Damaris eventually, in a later book, regains the power to dance, but almost immediately retires from the stage to marry. Recovering the power to attract a husband and form a family is seen as being far more important than recovering the power to make art. Damaris really returns to the stage to prove that her marriage is not "a brave acceptance of second-best".

POVERTY AND DISABILITY

Aside from Wriggles, younger disabled child characters play only a peripheral role in Oxenham's books, and are usually working class — reflecting, of course, the real-life link between poverty and disability. They are, though, on occasions allowed to be much more active than Wriggles, Marjory et al, which is probably due to their class — families with working mothers are unable to afford paid carers, let alone to send their children to Switzerland.

In *The Abbey Girls Again* (1924), leading character Joy offers to take some disabled children from the East End of London (a very poor district) for a drive in the country. These children must have had their counterparts in reality, as 'the Pixie' — of whom also more later — who put Joy in contact with them was a real person who worked at a YMCA (Young Men's Christian Association) mission in Plaistow, East London. It seems unlikely that the children had been institutionalised rather than living with their families or Joy would not have been allowed to take them out in this free and easy way, but they must have come together for some kind of group activity.

The picture that Oxenham paints of the trip is worth quoting in depth, contrasting as it does not only with more passive descriptions of disabled children, but also with the lack of detail more usual when they are simply objects of charity.

> "The Pixie had them waiting when I called at the Club, five of them — poor little twisted things;

Jen, it's horrible! Tiny kids, and they'll never be any better! ... We packed them in and I whizzed them off into the country... they were off their heads with excitement... I'd only meant to give them a two or three hours' ride; but when I saw it was the great day of their lives, I couldn't bear to cut it short. I took them to the inn and gave them lunch in the garden — eggs and jam and cakes and milk, because I wasn't sure what they could eat. Then we went into a field and picked buttercups,— and if you'd heard the shrieks of excitement! They'd positively never done such a thing before. So then we went and bought a basket at a cottage — where, by the way, they saw white hens, and yellow hens, and a canary in a cage, and ducks, and a black and white cat. More wild excitement! And in the woods we filled the basket — it was a big one — with fir cones, which they thought perfectly wonderful, and with a heap of those lovely long yellow leaves of sweet chestnut that cover the ground in there; and they've taken them home, and heaps of wild flowers. We had tea — buns and cakes — on logs in the wood; they only had to walk a very few yards, and they were simply crazy to get out and kick about in the leaves." (pp47-8)

Joy, as an upper-class young woman with no professional training or experience in working with disabled children, seems to finds it easy to treat the children as normal children, rather than as a collection of medical conditions with special needs. As a result of her first experience, Joy buys a bigger car and takes a different group of disabled children for a drive every week. When she later marries and travels to Africa, she sends her secretary to take them out instead. Never again, though, are the children seen in such detail, although Joy describes further outings to Jen in *The Abbey Girls Again*.

Other working-class disabled characters are not so active. Rose, in the 'Rocklands' books, "has to lie in a long chair all the time" (*The Second Term at Rocklands*, 1930, p10), as does Jim in *The Abbey Girls on Trial* (1931), disabled in a motorbike accident. Like Wriggles, though, they both do handcrafts. Rose knits, although she has no sense of colour, while Jim carves beautiful wooden animals that Rosamund sells for him in her craft shop.

> "When I asked if he'd let me show a few and try to sell them for him, his mother broke down and cried. I nearly wept myself at the sight of his face. It's not so much the money, though they'll be glad of it; but he'll feel he's of some use to his people if he can sell his carvings. It was like new life to him" (p210)

This might seem to echo the 'basket-weaving' stereotype of disabled people, were it not for the fact that Oxenham's love of crafts is evident throughout the books. Rather, crafts are seen as being accessible to everyone, including disabled characters. Oxenham also recognizes that Jim, as with Damaris, can still work despite his impairment, and that exclusion from work is a major cause of his distress rather than impairment itself. This is not to say, though, that basket-weaving does not make a perhaps inevitable appearance in Oxenham's work in relation to visual impairment. In *The Crisis in Camp Keema* (1928), Phyllis has got her best friend Bel "a topping basket, made at the Blind Workshop; she loves anything of that sort-handwork, with some association with it." (p55) Sure enough, Bel has "been wanting one for ages" (p60). At least these baskets are seen to be highly desirable in themselves, and are not just purchased for charitable reasons as another author might have portrayed them.

NERVES VERSUS BREAKDOWNS

What really separates Oxenham from her peers is her treatment of mental and emotional health, a subject that rarely, if ever, appears in the rest of the genre. Mental health first features in the plot of *A School Camp Fire* (1917), although its handling is relatively crude when compared to later books. Fifteen-year-old Priscilla lives with her mother at an isolation hospital on the Yorkshire moors, where her mother is the housekeeper. Although from a middle-class background, the family has literally lost all of their money, since Priscilla's father has had some form of breakdown, become paranoid, and has hidden the family's capital in a place that he can't remember. Prior to his breakdown, caused by the death of his brother, he had:

> "held quite a good position in some business. But I fancy he has always been rather queer, given to fits of depression and morbid anxiety for the future." (p19)

Now:

> "All his brain-power seems to have gone. He's very gentle and quiet; you don't need to be afraid of him. Just speak to him if you meet him; he likes it. He does whatever they want, in a quiet way; but he isn't strong, and never goes far from home. Of course, we can't depend on him for anything, any kind of work, even gardening. He isn't

reliable; if you gave him directions he'd forget them and do the work all wrong, or wander away in the middle of it." (p21)

This is a very matter-of-fact explanation, and in particular Oxenham's underlining of the fact that his illness does not make him dangerous would still be welcome — and perhaps even more necessary — today. At the end of Book I — the story is in four parts — Priscilla finds the family's money buried near a distinctive rock formation, after her father has recovered slightly following a dose of flu and has provided her with a clue. She is then able to afford to join the friends who have helped her at their school, and the relief of finding their savings means that her father is expected to be able to recover enough to function to some extent in society again.

Oxenham also suggests that physical ill-health can have psychological causes. In *The Abbey Girls at Home* (1929), Jen is concerned that Joy should not be too protected after the death of her husband and the birth of her twin girls.

"You don't want her to turn into a whining invalid, pitying herself and expecting to be sympathized with and waited on, do you? She's nowhere near it yet; but haven't you seen it happen in people after some big shock or illness, when their kind friends were too kind and went on treating them like eggshell? They like it, and so they develop neuralgia, or nerves, or headaches, or rheumatism, so that people will keep on sympathizing and waiting on them. I'll save Joy from that, if I make her hate me for ever." (p51)

Of course, even in Oxenham's day the reality of life

for disabled people was highly unlikely to be as attractive as this. Rather, the description is a very stereotypical view of disabled women as exaggerating or making up their symptoms in order to attract attention, and needing to 'pull themselves together' rather than to be sympathized with. At the same time, though, in her following books Oxenham sensitively portrays the effects of Joy's grief and her related seclusion over a period of years before Joy eventually begins to socialize publicly again and remarries. Achieving full reintegration into society requires Jen's intervention to urge Joy to 'pull herself together' on more than one occasion.

DREAMERS

Overall, though, Oxenham adopts an approach to mental and emotional health that resonates with contemporary thinking by mental health system users/survivors today; in particular her belief that nature, exercise/occupation, colour and aesthetics and sympathetic and friendly support are what are most needed to alleviate symptoms. Even with Priscilla's father, it is the peace of the moors, rather than any more active or medicalised treatment, that is primary to his care management. Most often, though, Oxenham equates mental illness with stifled creativity, initially with the character Mary Dorothy, who first appears in *The Abbey Girls Again* (1924). Mary is a thirty-year-old London typist, living with her much younger sister Biddy in a small and shabby flat after the death of her parents and brothers. Disappointed in life, whenever possible Mary lapses into a romantic dream world.

"It had happened so simply. She had a vivid imagination, inherited from her father [a journalist]. She had tried to write down her dreams, but he had told her plainly she was on the wrong lines and was producing nothing that could be published. To change all her way of thought, and become practical in her imagining, had been too difficult and troublesome. She had kept the dreams, but had kept them for herself alone. Whenever the outer world was dull, or where problems were too hard, Mary lapsed into her dream world and was happy. She was much alone, with little to think about; the habit was a great comfort to her, and kept her placidly contented when she ought to have craved very much more. It was far easier to dream than to study and think, so she did not trouble to read much, though the library was not far away.

And, quite blind to what she was doing, she wondered that she could not cope with Biddy, or be a companion to her. (pp22-23)

The turning point for Mary comes when 'Abbey girl' Jen enters her life, and introduces her to country dancing. Even the thought of it stimulates her:

It was not so easy to lose herself in unreal romance after the new and very real happenings of the day ...

It was an unusual experience for Mary to have something fresh to think about; her life had been monotonous, with Biddy and work for its only interests. Work as a subject for meditation at home had been unsatisfying; Biddy had been a difficult problem. The way of escape from both had been all too easy. But this was different. Here was something pleasant to think over; something to look forward to which in its very novelty would be exciting. (p38)

Without understanding, Jen is determined to get Mary to dance, and in this she is supported by a character who stands for Oxenham herself, 'The Writing Person', who says to Mary:

> "I'd never done anything of the kind, either, 'till all this got hold of me, about three years ago. Not a thing; not gym, nor tennis, nor even cycling. I went long country walks, that was all. It was all new to me. I don't see why you shouldn't."
>
> She did not add, "I'm older than you. If I can do it, you can," but she implied it. (p97)

Mary duly begins to dance, and soon this starts to have an effect on her mental and emotional state.

> The dreams were part of her life. For years she had lived in them, unknown to her mother, unsuspected by Biddy, whose matter-of-fact temperament would have asked "What's the good of it?" The good of it, to Mary, was the unfailing way of escape she thus had from anything troublesome or difficult, any worrying problem. The unreal romance was real to her ... That there was a real and great danger to herself, and a serious wrong to Biddy, in this curious absorption of hers in an unseen world — that this contentment with things as they were, and this lack of all desire for outside friends, were unnatural and wrong and dangerous — Mary dimly suspected; but characteristically refused to face the thought.
>
> But tonight ... the feeling of discomfort was greater than usual. It almost amounted to a sense of guilt. It was so strong that she actually faced it for a few moments. (pp153-4)

Soon:

> She had a very definite feeling that to lapse into unhealthy secret ways would be treason to all those happy healthy people who had given her such enjoyment. (p165)

And:

> Without the slightest effort on her own part, she found herself dreaming less, because she simply had not the time for it. When she had time for thought, in bed, or while busy with dressmaking preparations for the following week, she was always trying to fit movements to tunes, to remember the difference between introductions and figures, which still seemed much alike to her, to disentangle the sequence of events in "Rufty," "Peascods," and "Sellenger's Round".
> [all being folk dances]

It is only when Mary visits the country, though, for a stay at Joy's home, that a real change is effected. Jen also begins to understand Mary better.

> "Well, if you were the beginnings of a poet, or a writer of some kind, and someone sat on you heavily and told you your work was no good, wouldn't you want to curl up and die? And if you couldn't quite do that — if you'd got a little sister to bring up, for instance — wouldn't you go on with your everyday work, but go all dead and hopeless inside?" (p220)

Soon Mary confirms this theory, and goes on to 'confess' to Joy and Jen about her habit of dreaming.

> Jen looked frankly puzzled. This was a thing unlike anything she had ever met.

Joy's face was troubled; she was older and had a little more experience of life to help her judgement.

"I never heard of any one doing it before," she said slowly, "but it seems to me it couldn't be quite right, Mary-Dorothy. It's unnatural, to begin with; not normal. That means it must be wrong. Didn't it unfit you for ordinary life? Didn't it make you — well, dreamy and half awake?"

Mary agrees, and goes on to explain:

"I'd tried and tried to give up those dreams and stories, you understand; but I'd always slipped back, till at last I had given up trying. It was just like taking a drink, or a drug. I couldn't live without it, I thought. I often used to think — when I thought about it at all — that I could never say things about drunkards, though I might be very sorry for them; for I was just as bad myself." (pp249-50)

Mary refuses to promise not to slip back into the habit, because she knows that she might not be able to keep her word. Oxenham never opts for an instant 'cure' for Mary, and instead traces her development over the course of the rest of the series, with Mary becoming one of her favourite characters.

In the short term, Joy tells Jen that they must continue to support Mary.

"Have you had time to think how it would have ended, if she'd gone on like that, living half the time in another world, inside her mind? ... I believe she'd have had a bad nervous breakdown. Don't you see how unhealthy it was? Seems to me she was living on her nerves and her imagination.

> It couldn't be right. I don't know where she would have landed herself, but it's somewhere she's never going to get if I can help it." (p262)

As it is, Mary is considerably less capable than the younger Jen and Joy as a result of her dreaming habit. When Joy's ward Maidlin is saved from drowning and Mary is left to help, the male rescuer concludes:

> This girl was older than the other two, but far less capable, and had far less command of her nerves ... He summed up Mary mentally, with a brief, "Nervy. No use. Going all to pieces. The other two had twice her grit. (pp275-6)

Mary, though, is self-aware enough to realize this, and to be determined to change.

PSYCHOLOGY AND THE PIXIE

Joy and Jen seek additional advice from 'the Pixie', a character first introduced in *The Abbey Girls Go Back to School* (1922). This book introduces a number of real-life characters from the English folk dance movement, thinly disguised by the use of nicknames. Among them is Daisy Caroline Daking, nicknamed 'the Pixie' in the 'Abbey' books because of her small stature, whose friendship with 'The Writing Person' must have been several years old by the time that Oxenham created Mary. It is likely that Daking, though younger than Oxenham, played a highly influential role in developing Oxenham's approach to mental health, and that characters who 'dream' may have been based on real-life cases that Daking described to her. Certainly the Pixie is always described with the utmost respect for her wisdom and knowledge, as well as for her integrity and talent. In her fictional persona as The Writing Person, Oxenham writes: "Everyone goes to her for comfort and advice. And she always has it to give. I know, for I go, too. She's one of the best!" (*The Abbey Girls in Town*, page 143)

Daking taught folk-dancing for the English Folk Dance Society and at various clubs, including the YMCA at Plaistow, as well as designing dresses for Liberty. (She is portrayed as doing all of these activities within the Abbey books that she appears in.) During the First World War Daking had been part of a concert party that worked with the troops in France, teaching them dancing as a means of escape from the violence. Alongside this she took a keen interest in psychology and was the author of two published books on the subject: *Feed My Sheep* and *Jungian Psychology and Modern Spiritual Thought* (Godfrey, p107). Aside from her authorship, which was not mentioned, real-life details of Daking's life were provided in the books in which she appears, all of which were published in the 1920s. In the book where she is first introduced, *The Abbey Girls Go Back to School* (1922), two whole chapters are devoted to her background and personality.

In reality, Daking — 'the Pixie' — committed suicide in 1942, at which time she was the superintendent of a girls' hostel in London (Oxenham sets a number of scenes in working girls' hostels in her Abbey 'connectors'). Despite a great deal of speculation by Oxenham fans, no motive has ever become apparent, although possibilities include the rejection by Daking's publishers of another psychology book, strained family relationships, and the failure of the authorities to let her return to working with the troops (Godfrey, pp106-8). It is quite possible, of course, that Daking's own interest in psychology was sparked by personal experience of mental illness, although there is no evidence available to support this theory, and it is equally possible that the depression which led to her suicide was her first. It is extremely poignant in the circumstances, though, to read the final lines of *Queen of the Abbey Girls*, where Pixie is talking to Mary. " 'You'll have problems, of course; but those are what makes life so exciting,' said the Pixie."

By the time Daking died she had already disappeared from the 'Abbey' books, folk dancing having faded in significance once the original 'girls' had married and had children of their own, although it continued as a minor theme until the end of the series. It seems that Oxenham and Daking were no longer close by the time that Daking died, and that possibly Daking even resented Oxenham's fictional portrayal of her. In the period between their leaving school and marrying, though, the 'Abbey girls' continually consulted 'the Pixie' on 'matters of psychology'. When Jen and Joy consult 'the Pixie' about Mary, she pronounces:

> "It's abnormal, and horribly dangerous. Children are different; they have to dream dreams and see visions! But for a grown woman to waste her life and energies so — no! It was very serious indeed. I can't tell you how it would have ended, but it would have been in something very unpleasant. You'd get complete dissociation eventually, I suppose; — but that's rather beyond us to discuss! But I'm certain your Mary couldn't go on living unnaturally, exciting her imagination without giving it any outlet, without paying very heavily for it... Her nerves would have given way, probably; she'd have become a neurasthenic invalid in a few years more; or it might have been

her brain... she'd have lived only in her dreams; happy enough, perhaps, but ruined for life, with no mind left to use." (p291)

The Pixie goes on to voice what becomes a mantra to Oxenham:

"... what Mary has been starving for, all along, has been an outlet. Her nature's been craving for it. As she couldn't have the natural one she had a right to, she had to create an unnatural unhealthy one. Of course, it was unconscious, but that's what it comes to... you've got to help her express that life. She must find her outlet; something worth living for. She must do things; that's what it comes to." (pp294-5)

As an immediate first step, The Pixie suggests that Mary take on a small class of beginners and passes on the dancing skills she is learning. Mary is thus seen from an early stage as being capable of giving as well as receiving, and of being able to take responsibility that will help her but also others. The Pixie is also clear that Mary must learn to be healthy in the city before Joy suggests a permanent move to the country; she is shown as being capable of becoming fully independent, not as being well only so long as she is being supported by others.

THE HELPED BECOME THE HELPERS

In a subsequent book, *Queen of the Abbey Girls* (1926), Mary does move to the country, having been persuaded to take up a position as Joy's secretary. This was actually a more responsible position than it might sound, as Joy marries at the same time and travels abroad for a year, leaving Mary in sole charge of her home, her dependants and her bits of social work, including taking the disabled children for weekly drives in the country. Mary's development is chronicled in some detail. First, she identifies another girl who has fallen into the 'dreaming habit', Nell Bell, who is staying at a holiday home that Joy has founded in an old farmhouse in the local village. Mary persuades Nell to confide in her, and learns that Nell's fiancé died of pneumonia, leaving her to work as a clerk and to live in a large girls' hostel in London. Nell has created a whole dream world where she lives with her husband and children, causing her to become too ill to work.

> "You won't go feeling bothered about me? I'm quite happy so long as I can have my castle in the air. I know it can't be real. But a day-dream is next best." (pp178-9)

Oxenham clearly believes that 'dreaming' is a common mental health problem among women. Jen, talking to Mary about Nell, says:

> "There are heaps of others. Their dreams won't be the same as yours, but the results will be the same; waste of time, no real interest in life, ill-health, and—you can't deny it—poor weak minds that can't decide things, and daren't tackle difficulties, and collapse before problems." (*Queen of the Abbey Girls*, p149)

Mary also talks to the Pixie about Nell, and reports back to Jen:

> "The Pixie's as sure as I am that the cure lies in doing things, in action. I've somehow got to get

Nelly interested and busy over something, if I'm to stop her dreaming. It's no use telling her to stop, or talking to her about the danger of it. That's what she says, and I know she's right, from my own experience." (p168)

Mary manages to arrange for Nell to work as an assistant in the children's home that Joy has also founded in the village, thus providing Nell with real children to replace the dream ones. She also encourages Nell to join the folk-dance class that she is teaching in the village. In later books Nell becomes nurse to Joy's children, reinforcing Oxenham's belief that mental ill-health does not preclude taking responsibility after recovery, and indeed that taking responsibility aids recovery. Mary also becomes a role model for and mentor to a former colleague in her typing office, Amy, in *Queen of the Abbey Girls*, and her newly developed ability as a role model and counsellor for girls and woman continues throughout the series, Mary remaining a central though secondary character until the end.

Later, in *The Abbey Girls Win Through* (1928), Mary realizes that she has further weaknesses in her character when Jen's mother dies shortly after Jen's father.

She loved Jen better than her life; but in Jen's direst need she had been unable to help her. She had failed her friend at her biggest crisis... "I'm just—just like a child. I haven't grown up properly. When a grown person's needed, I'm no use," Mary thought hopelessly. (pp71-3)

The solution in this case is to develop Mary's inner spirituality. Mary's craft — she becomes a published author for girls, acting as an adviser and role model through these to thousands of readers — and her dancing are not enough on their own to sustain her. Once she has developed her spirituality too, though, she becomes a strong and reliable character until the end.

MAIDLIN AND MUSIC

Along with Mary, Oxenham created a character with similar, but more complex difficulties in Maidlin, the niece of the Abbey's caretaker who had been brought up on a farm in Cumberland. Maidlin is adopted by Joy when she inherits a fortune from her estranged Italian grandparents — Joy is still only in her early 20s herself at this time, and has not yet married. Maidlin's father, whom Maidlin has never seen, was an Italian noble who fell in love with her mother when she was working as a maid in London.

Maidlin is first introduced in *The New Abbey Girls* (1923), so was already part of the circle when Mary was introduced in the following book. Initially, Maidlin's difficulties are presented as a fiery temper — that Oxenham, somewhat stereotypically, puts down to Maidlin's Italian heritage — along with extreme shyness that is exacerbated by social inexperience.

> "I can't say things! They're all shut up inside me!" Maidlin panted, expressing herself with difficulty even now. "I don't know why. I feel things, and think things, but I can't get them out. You all say such a lot, and it sounds so easy!" ...
>
> Joy laughed. "You poor kid! It has been hard on you to be plunged in among us so suddenly! And the other part of you is the Italian side, I suppose? The side that flares up like gunpowder, and

makes you do and say things you'd never thought of before?"

"I can't help it!" Maidlin whispered. "I don't know when it's going to happen. It is just like being two people, Joy." (Girls Gone By edition, pp195-6)

By the end of the book, Maidlin is settling down well and is devoted to Joy, with her shyness retreating to a more manageable level. Her father has died (heroically, of course) overseas, and she has become a permanent 'Abbey Girl'. This devotion to Joy, however, becomes the cause of her later and more serious mental health problems after Joy marries and goes abroad for a year. As the wedding approaches, Joy tells Mary:

"She looks at me with frightened eyes that hurt me, and she hangs on to me and follows me round, and watches me as if she were saying, 'How soon am I going to lose you?' I can't take her with me, but she's going to need a lot of comforting when I go." (p77)

Note that Mary has already become a trusted confidante and peer of Joy's at this stage in her development. Unable to bear life without Joy, Maidlin retreats to a dream world where Joy has remained at the Abbey.

"Maidie has built up a whole castle of dreams, of which the centre is Joy, here again with us. All day, and in bed at night, she dreams of Joy — what they'll do together; what Joy will look like; what she'll say and wear; every tiniest detail is planned out. Probably when Joy does come, poor Maidie will be so shy that she'll run and hide. But for the time being, she's happy in dreaming about it; and her work and health are suffering. Her mind's standing still; she isn't growing. She's sixteen; she ought to be developing in every way, but she's just where she was last May." (*Queen of the Abbey Girls*, pp302-3)

When this is eventually spotted by Jen after she returns to the Abbey following a family bereavement, the solution, as with Mary, is for Maidlin to explore her creativity, in this case through Maidlin taking singing lessons. This is, however, only of limited use. As with Mary, Oxenham does not offer Maidlin a 'quick fix'. Rather, from the time that Joy conveniently returns a widow from her honeymoon, Maidlin is portrayed as being torn between wishing to grow up and to become Joy's friend and confidante, and being afraid of adulthood and adult responsibilities and wishing to remain a child. This fear of adulthood haunts her and causes her recurring nightmares.

"She's growing up, and her deepest self is afraid, and wants to stay as she is. I should talk to her gently about grown-up life, and make her see it as a thing to hope for and to glory in; perhaps the fear will go, and the dream with it. But Maidie's an artist, and deeply sensitive; she's afraid of being hurt; she can't help it," Ann explained. "She's so responsive that every little thing moves her deeply. You'll find that she cares too much about trifles. Aren't you the same yourself?" and she turned quickly on Mary. (*The Abbey Girls Win Through*, 1928, pp115-6)

However, Jen points out to Maidlin that the widowed Joy now requires an adult companion rather than a third child — Joy having given birth to twins soon after returning home. This is particularly urgent as Jen herself is now married and, although Maidlin fails to understand this, expecting a family of her own. Maidlin quickly understands the possibilities:

> "I never wanted to grow up before," Maidlin confessed. "I hated the thought of it. Ros said it would be fun, but I couldn't see it. But I feel I want it now; I'm in a hurry to be grown-up! I want to get done with school and be ready to help Joy in al the things she does." (*The Abbey Girls at Home*, 1929, p180)

In continuing with this plot line in a number of further books, Oxenham crosses the line between portraying Maidlin's personal growth in depth and being repetitive with her story lines, although this is probably to be expected when she was producing popular fiction in volume. However, Oxenham is extremely skilled in the way that she describes Maidlin's continuing growth, and her readers clearly enjoyed returning repeatedly to the subject. Oxenham is particularly interesting in the way that she portrays *Joy* — a complex character in her own right — as wanting to keep Maidlin child-like throughout her widowhood, although she also has twin daughters of her own. This includes Joy deciding that Maidlin should not reach the age of majority until 25 instead of 21, although needless to say Maidlin goes along happily with this suggestion. Eventually, Maidlin runs away from Joy when Joy accuses her of playing up to the man who later becomes Joy's second husband, Ivor Quellyn, and this finally enables them to have an equal friendship (*Joy's New Adventure*, 1935). Maidlin repeatedly has to insist to Joy that she is no longer 'an infant' before this occurs, though.

Oxenham also portrays Maidlin's relationship with Rosamund, an informal 'adoptee' of Joy's who is a year older than Maidlin, with great delicacy. Initially Maidlin is jealous of Rosamund because she finds it easier to fit in with the jokey and relaxed nature of Joy's household than Maidlin does, but this quickly changes into a close friendship between them. Maidlin inevitably, though, becomes reliant on Rosamund — who has a decidedly non-'artistic' personality, although she loves beauty and crafts — with Rosamund helping Maidlin to understand her schoolwork and comforting her at night when she continually has bad dreams. Later, the difficulty and resulting pain that both of them experience as they grow up and separate before finding a new type of friendship is also portrayed in great depth.

Although highly sensitive and shy, from the beginning Maidlin is capable of acts of great courage when this is necessary to help a friend, and this must have inspired confidence in many of the books' shyer readers. It also illustrates Oxenham's belief that mental health problems do not prevent a character from acting boldly, and even heroically. Initially, Maidlin is spurred on to act when Rosamund falls out with a schoolmate but does not want the story behind their quarrel to become publicly known. If Maidlin refuses to become the school's May Queen, a position that she dreads occupying because of its public nature, then Rosamund's schoolmate will be next in line. At this point Rosamund will have to reveal what happened to cause them to quarrel, something she is anxious to keep private. For this reason Maidlin is prepared after all to become May Queen, even though she has not previously been prepared to do it simply to cause Joy pleasure.

Later, Maidlin is asked to meet a real Princess as part of her May Queen duties, and initially only agrees on the condition that Rosamund, the previous year's Queen, accompanies her. However, when Rosamund is called abroad to be with her dying mother, Maidlin decides that she can act alone after all.

> Jen and Joy looked at each other. Then they jumped, and stared at Maidlin, and then at one another again. For Maidlin was saying, in a clear, decisive voice:
> "I thought about that days ago, Ros, but I didn't want to worry you. It will be alright." (*The Abbey Girls at Home*, 1929, p171)

Oxenham later places Maidlin in a variety of situations where her courage continues to be tested. In *Biddy's Secret* (1932), the adult Maidlin takes control when she discovers that Mary's sister Biddy has secretly married in France; become pregnant (Oxenham underlines that it is strictly in that order); been abandoned by her husband; and had a baby. Maidlin helps to nurse Biddy back to health, and then with some difficulty persuades Biddy to accompany her home to England to confess and be welcomed back into the Abbey circle.

In *Maidlin to the Rescue* (1934), Maidlin discovers two younger cousins of whose existence she was previously unaware, Rachel and Damaris, and rescues them after the aunt who was bringing them up had died. This is despite their running away from Maidlin initially, believing that she had abandoned them; although they are desperate, they are still not keen for Maidlin to become their guardian until she has proven herself to them. Rachel and Damaris then become regular characters in the Abbey books, although Biddy, in contrast, soon returns to France.

Maidlin is finally acknowledged as an equal to Joy and Jen in *Maidlin Bears the Torch* (1937). Joy has remarried, and her husband Ivor Quellyn, a famous conductor, schedules Maidlin to make her London concert debut under her real name of Madalena di Ravarati. Needless to say she is a great success, and continues for the rest of the series to be a professional singer, specializing in oratorio but also remaining fond of folk songs. At the end of the book, Joy and her husband travel to New York, where he has taken long-term charge of an American orchestra. Maidlin is left in charge of the Abbey, becoming the Abbey 'Torch Bearer' — the 'torch' being "a spirit of welcome-and helpfulness-and kindness" (p204). Eventually, though, Maidlin marries another conductor and has a home and family of her own (*Maid of the Abbey*, 1943), cementing her adult status as a fully functioning equal of anyone's. This must have been extremely supportive and helpful for readers who identified with Maidlin's initial shyness and other difficulties, particularly but not only girl readers.

ROOTS OF REFORM

Overall, Oxenham's stress on the importance of nature, art and a supportive community to everyone's mental and emotional health reflects a belief in an holistic form of social support that has its roots in the social reform movements of the nineteenth century. In general, the genre of girls' school stories owes much to the nineteenth century, with authors reflecting the influences of the period when they themselves were girls rather than the time when they were actually writing — although this is more commonly true of the representation of schooling itself.

From the beginning of the nineteenth century, there had been a strong movement for reform of the treatment of people with mental health difficulties in institutional care. Referred to as 'lunatics' in 'madhouses', their care had been barbaric: it was common for chains and restraints to be used; and institutions were sited within stark, gloomy buildings. William Tuke, who lived from 1732 until 1822, was a Quaker who had a passion for reforming the system under which such people were held. He set an example in creating a private hospital in York. It not only dispensed with restraints, but also introduced the idea of therapeutic work, engaging residents in the tending and growing of produce within the institution's grounds.

This served to guide future reformers who were working in public 'asylums', but up until the latter half of the twentieth century, people with mental health difficulties were still kept away from the local community. The hospitals which evolved from the 'madhouses' in the 1900s were developed, in the main, in rural settings enclosed within areas of fields or countryside. The philosophy was served in part by the concept of the healing power of outdoor activity and the pastoral, informed by William Tuke, but also by the need to remove the inhabitants from any risk of contact with the general public.

Oxenham also grew up in a time when psychology was also emerging as a scientific discipline, having its roots in philosophy. The impetus for this came largely from Europe and North America, but in 1897 experimental psychology laboratories were established in London and Cambridge. Closely following, in 1904, came the launch of the *British Journal of Psychology*. Early psychologists perceived a need to unpick human behaviour from morality and knowledge: a new understanding of brain and spinal-cord function offered insights into how the body and mind functioned overall. There was a drive to create a scientific basis of understanding of behaviour by establishing provable, experimental theorums. Concepts of self and the relationships within the wider world were emerging rapidly as the twentieth century dawned. Psychologists in the early decades of the 1900s were struggling to medicalise mental health difficulties by creating scientific standards of diagnosis and treatments. The need to control symptoms was paramount in managing behaviour, and a range of medication and treatments were created to that end.

The first forty years of the twentieth century, when Oxenham was writing her most important 'Abbey' books, then saw psychology flourishing. Examples include with Sigmund Freud first publishing his works on psycho-analysis from 1900; Carl Jung separating from Freudian views in 1913 ('the Pixie' wrote about Jung and therefore can be supposed to support Jungian concepts); the development of Behaviourism in the same year; the introduction of Rorschach Testing in 1921; and the acceptance of Electro-Convulsive Therapy (ECT) as a formal therapy in 1938.

The late nineteenth century was also a period where the benefits of 'nature' in relieving poverty — and therefore disability and chronic ill health — became widely recognised by social reformers. In 1889 William Lever established Port Sunlight in the Wirral for the benefit of his factory workers, believing in the benefits of people living in decent housing away from the slums that dominated the industrial settings of his business. Other nineteenth-century philanthropists also felt impelled to contribute to the social housing and well-being of the poorer workers by building homes in what was perceived as being healthier rural settings. The relief of poverty was part of a plan to improve the health and quality of life of those less fortunate and to maximize standards of living. Port Sunlight in particular was in a geographic area that may well have been familiar to Oxenham when she spent time in and around Liverpool — the Wirral is mentioned in several later 'Abbey' books.

Oxenham creates her own model village in Rainbows, albeit on the Surrey/Sussex border, which features in 'Abbey connectors' *Daring Doranne* (1945) and *Margery Meets the Roses* (1947). Here she has the freedom to exercise her love of outdoor life and arts in a rural setting, and ensure that her characters live in idyllic surroundings within a community. There is an echo of the philanthropic provision of social housing by a rich benefactor, in this instance Doranne Hardie. Doranne inherits a large house and grounds from her aunt, who had abandoned it in favour of a small modern suburban house after her husband died. Doranne decides to build a village:

> "for people like you and me, who are longing to feel they have a home but can see no chance of ever finding one; people with tiny incomes who don't need to live in town...
>
> "I'll build a village of dear little houses, all different, with decent gardens ... and we'll hunt for the right sort of people, those who are longing for a home in the country. If they want cinemas and theatres they musn't come; we'll be miles from anywhere." (p144)

The houses are built with "extra small bedrooms", for:

> "I've a scheme for helping my villagers by asking them to board old people from Town, or invalids who can't afford holidays in the country. Much more friendly than a convalescent home, and no worry for me!" (p151)

As we have seen, Oxenham is unusual here in prioritising home care over institutional support, although Doranne also plans to hand over part of the big house to a London charity for use as a children's home. And in fact, in a later book the promised lodgers have become young airmen, while she creates another institutional wing of the main house for the old people with separate gardens.

In the last decades of the twentieth century, disabled people developed constructs by which to articulate the ways that they experience life in modern-day society. Contemporary thinking allows for the identification of the difficulties experienced by disabled people in living fully independent lives as being the social, environmental and attitudinal barriers that are faced within an inaccessible world. This is known as the 'Social Model of Disability'. When Oxenham was writing, though, the 'Medical Model of Disability' was dominant. Using the Medical Model, an individual is defined by their impairments or medical condition and treated accordingly; this in turn creates additional barriers to the fulfilment of independent living. In the example of mental health difficulties, someone who experienced 'day-dreams' to the level of disassociation from a shared reality would be regarded, using the Medical Model, as being unable to function independently. They would be seen to need psychiatric and/or therapeutic intervention, and would become diagnosed as mentally ill. If the treatment was effective then they would be considered as cured; otherwise they would remain chronically ill. Regardless of outcome, they would be regarded as unfit for future positions of responsibility, or for use as role models.

At the time of writing, then, Oxenham was adopting extremely radical thinking. Her concept of supporting people who were experiencing mental health difficulties within the community, and her emphasis on fresh air and activity that focused outside of themselves on to other people, were quite simplistic in psychological terms. This is not to say, though, that her beliefs suffered greatly from this; we can find many parallels in modern-day theory, and not just in the alternative models proposed by users/survivors of the mental health system.

As stated previously, Oxenham's treatment of physically disabled people seems to fall at least partly into the 'kill or cure' style of writing so characteristic of her time, although there are notable exceptions. Significantly different from the work of her peers, though, is her creation of characters who experience mental health difficulties, but who are also an integral part of the social milieu that she develops. These characters are well-rounded, and contribute actively as part of the fictional landscape of Oxenham's girls' and women's worlds. Their development is carefully staged and they don't drop away as redundant once the storyline moves on; rather, they move on as well. This would allow for Oxenham's writing to be considered as falling within the Social Model of Disability, and therefore make her unusual within a present-day context as well as significant within an historic one.

REFERENCES

Godfrey, Monica, *The World of Elsie Jeanette Oxenham and Her Books*, Girls Gone By, Bath, 2003.

Hubbard, Edward and Shippobottom, Michael, A *Guide To Port Sunlight Village*, Michael Hubbard, Michael Shippobottom, Liverpool University Press, Liverpool, 1988.

Keith, Lois, *Take Up Thy Bed and Walk, Death, Disability and Cure in Classic Fiction for Girls*, Taylor & Francis, 2001.

Porter, Roy, *Madness, A Brief History*, Oxford University Press, Oxford, 2002.

Ray, Sheila and Waring, Stella, *Island to Abbey*, Girls Gone By, Bath, 2006.

Stevens, Anthony, *Freud: A Very Short Introduction*, Oxford University Press, Oxford, 1989.

Stevens, Anthony, *Jung: A Very Short Introduction*, Oxford University Press, Oxford, 1994.

A full bibliography of Elsie J. Oxenham's books, along with those of the other 'major' girls' school story authors, is available online from Bettany Press at http://www.ju90.co.uk/prt.htm

MIDDLE PERIOD

VIII. CHANGES AT THE CHALET SCHOOL: ILLNESS & DISABILITY IN THE CHALET SCHOOL SERIES

JU GOSLING

INTRODUCTION

ELINOR M Brent-Dyer's 'Chalet School' series began in 1925 with the publication of *The School at the Chalet*, and ended in 1970 — a year after her death — with the publication of *Prefects of the Chalet School*, the series totalling 58 books in all. Among girls' school-story authors — and indeed among authors of other popular genres for girls, such as authors of pony stories — Brent-Dyer was unique in producing a series of such length. Of the best-known authors, Dorita Fairlie Bruce's 'Dimsie' series numbered only nine books; while Enid Blyton's 'St Clare's' and 'Malory Towers' series numbered just six each; and Angela Brazil seldom used the same characters in more than one book and never wrote a series as such.

Brent-Dyer is also unique in the longevity of her popularity: in the early 1990s, HarperCollins were still selling around 100,000 copies a year in paperback, and continued to publish them into the early years of the twenty-first century. In 2009, two international fan societies continue to flourish and the books are still being published, albeit now by a small press.

Elinor M Brent-Dyer was born Gladys Eleanor

May Dyer in a terraced house in South Shields on 6 April 1894. Her father, a former naval officer from Portsmouth who had come to South Shields to work as a surveyor in the shipyards, abandoned the family when she was only three. Her mother then lived as a widow, although Elinor's father did not actually die until 1911.[1] Brent-Dyer therefore grew up with her mother, her grandmother (who died in 1901), and her younger brother, Henzell Watson Dyer (b.1895). Henzell, apparently much loved by Elinor, died suddenly of meningitis at the age of 17 in 1912.[2] The themes of poor health, death and absence of family (particularly fathers and brothers) which are characteristic of the Chalet School series, quite possibly originated with Brent-Dyer's early experiences, which also included the death from tuberculosis in 1911 of her close friend and neighbour, Elizabeth Jobling, at the age of 16.[3]

SCHOOL AS THE GUARDIAN OF HEALTH

Brent-Dyer is believed to have conceived the idea for the Chalet School series following a visit to Austria with friends in the summer of 1924.[4] The first 13 books of the series are set in contemporary Tirol, near the village of "Briesau" on lake "Tiern See" — actually Pertisau and Achen See.[5] In the opening book of the series, *The School at the Chalet*, 24-year-old Madge Bettany travels to the Tirol to open a school, primarily for the sake of her 12-year-old sister, Josephine Mary (known as Jo or Joey), whose "health had been a constant worry to those who had charge of her" (pp15-16). Their parents are both dead, and Madge's twin brother, Dick, is about to return to work in India, where they were all born. The search for better health for Joey is therefore integral to the founding of the Chalet School, and the themes of health and illness remain constant throughout the series.

Madge begins the school with two pupils: her sister Joey and Grizel, the daughter of a neighbour in England. In the first week Madge enrols 15 more pupils and the school then continues to grow, reaching 33 pupils in the second book, *Jo of the Chalet School* (1926). By the ninth book in the series, *The Exploits of the Chalet Girls* (1933), the pupils number 105, and by the 18th book, *Gay from China at the Chalet School* (1944) there are 250 pupils. Madge's teaching career is short-lived, however, as she becomes engaged at the end of the second book, *Jo of the Chalet School* (1926) and marries at the end of the third book, *The Princess of the Chalet School* (1927), whereupon she retires from teaching. This was, of course, the norm in reality at the time, with all state-funded schools and many others operating a marriage bar against women teachers.[6]

Madge's husband, Jem Russell, is a doctor who has come to the Tirol to found a sanatorium for TB patients, and the sanatorium plays a key role in many of the books within the series. At first the couple remain close to the school, both geographically and emotionally. However, when Joey becomes an adult Madge is mentioned far less, and in the 21st book, *The Chalet School and the Island* (1950), she travels to Canada with her family for an extended stay. By the 30th book, *The Chalet School and Barbara* (1954), this separation has become permanent: Jem remains with the sanatorium in Wales, where it has relocated during the war years; while the school moves to Switzerland where a new branch of the sanatorium is to be headed by Joey's husband Jack.

Madge continues to appear periodically as a

visitor, but from the time she is married she never enjoys the ongoing relationship with the school that Jo does.

Jo is at the centre of the books. For the first 11 books she is a pupil at the school, becoming Head Girl in the seventh book, *The Chalet School and Jo* (1931). In the 12th book, *Jo Returns to the Chalet School* (1936), she returns temporarily to teach, and in the 14th book, *The Chalet School in Exile* (1940), she marries Jack Maynard, a colleague of her brother-in-law, who is both a doctor and a brother of one of the mistresses. Because of the links between the school and the sanatorium, Jack never works far from the school, and so Jo is able to remain associated with it throughout the series.

> "Jo's a married lady and a proud mamma of many [eventually eleven], and yet, in one sense, she's as much a part of the school as ever she was when she was Head Girl — or a sickening little nuisance of a Middle, for that matter. In my opinion, she'll still belong when she's a doddering old woman of ninety-odd, telling her great-great-grandchildren all about her evil doings at school!"
> (*Shocks for the Chalet School*, 1952, pp22-23)

Jo's health continues to be of concern throughout her teenage years. At best, she is unable to face a draught without catching a cold that threatens to turn into bronchitis or pneumonia. At worst, she faces a number of life-threatening episodes, beginning with the first book of the series, *The School at the Chalet* (1925), where Jo goes to find Grizel who has run away and they are caught in mist on a mountain. As a result, Jo loses consciousness; "the awful nerve strain through which the imaginative, highly strung child had gone might result in brain fever" (p301); and it is several days before it is known that she will live. Similar episodes are repeated throughout the early books. However, by early adulthood: "her years in Tirol had ended all that and she was now a wiry young person, who rarely ailed anything" (*The Chalet School in Exile*, 1940, p19). Jo continues to develop a fever easily as an adult woman, but is strong enough to be able to negotiate multiple births (two sets of twins and one of triplets) as well as single births with ease.

Although the character of Jo is central to the Chalet School series, she is not the protagonist in the sense that the series revolves around her. Rather, she embodies the spirit of the school ("Jo Maynard . . . now and always one of its [the school's] moving spirits", *The Wrong Chalet School*, 1952, p88), as well as the qualities that are held to be most desirable. The real focus of the series is instead the Chalet School itself, or the community it represents, to which Jo belongs: "Even when I'm an old lady with white hair, telling all my great-great nieces and nephews all about my wicked deeds, I'll never count myself as anything but a Chalet School girl" (*Jo Returns to the Chalet School*, 1936, p28); "I'm still, in part of me, what I shall always be — a Chalet School girl." (*The Chalet School and the Island*, 1950, p296).

Throughout the series, the distinguishing characteristic of the Chalet School community is its avowed aim to protect the health of its pupils. One of Madge's first pupils, Amy Stevens, is sent there to protect her health (*The School at the Chalet*, 1925, pp65-66), just as protecting Joey's health has been the reason why Madge starts the school. Later, when the sanatorium is founded nearby and Madge marries its head, Jem Russell, the school's function to protect its pupils' health becomes more explicit, with particular concentration on combating TB.

> So many of the girls had one or both parents at the sanatorium undergoing treatment, and the doctors were all of the opinion that prevention was infinitely better than cure. "Catch the children early, give them a good foundation, and we may save them," Dr Jem had said on one occasion. So plenty of milk, sleep, fresh air, and exercise were enforced at the school, and the girls throve on the treatment. (*The Chalet School and Jo*, 1931, p66)

This continues when the school later moves to England as a result of the war: "ever since the establishment of the two [school and sanatorium], great stress had been laid on the care of the girls' health. The school was planned with an eye to this, and the staff knew it" (*Gay from China at the Chalet School*, 1944, p62). "The prospectus laid emphasis on the fact that health was particularly guarded here" (*Carola Storms the Chalet School*, 1951, p177). The link with the sanatorium is only broken once in the series, when the school moves temporarily to a Welsh island. But by the 30th book, *The Chalet School and Barbara* (1954), both the school and the sanatorium have moved to the Swiss Oberland, along with Jo and Jack. The series then continued in its Oberland setting for another 16 years and 27 books, with the sanatorium closely linked to the school in all of them.

Inevitably, the continuing link between the Chalet School and the sanatorium invests more power in male characters than is true of other girls' school stories, where men may be almost entirely absent. The overwhelming majority of male characters are doctors, and the overwhelming majority of doctors are men. Only one main female character, Jem's niece Daisy, qualifies as a doctor, but since she marries another doctor almost immediately, Daisy soon leaves the profession again. The majority of patients, meanwhile, are women and children, and the physical proximity of the sanatorium to the school is a constant reminder of potential physical (female) weakness. Meanwhile male doctors are called into the school when characters suffer life-threatening illnesses or injuries, and spend the rest of the time treating TB patients, whose only chance of survival lies with the sanatorium staff. They are therefore seen as having a semi-god-like power over life and death. Susan Sontag points out that in typical accounts of TB in the nineteenth century, TB was represented as "the prototypical passive death"[7]. Patients were perceived as being extremely passive, leaving an image of the doctors who treated them as being extremely active and positive.

However, the sanatorium also functions to reduce men's power in the series. First, the sanatorium provides husbands in the form of doctors, and so the opportunity for former pupils and members of staff who marry to continue their links with the school after marriage. This enables them to maintain a self-identity within marriage, as well as to continue to appear in the series. Then, because of the nature of their work, men are usually absent from their family home, leaving women in control of the domestic environment. Lastly, it is men who are identified as carrying out caring, nurturing work rather than women, as Brent-Dyer rarely describes middle-class women carrying out childcare or domestic work. As with the whole of the content of the Chalet School, then, analysis reveals mixed and often contradictory messages that serve to expose the arbitrary and shifting nature of what it has meant to be 'female' in twentieth-century British society.

In reality, it is probable that there were English schools in the Alps where the children of sanatoria patients studied. Sontag has noted that "travel to a better climate was invented as a treatment for TB in the early nineteenth century", and TB continued to have a high mortality rate in Western Europe until the 1950s[8], with around 40,000 Britons contracting it every year. Elsie Oxenham, author of the 'Abbey Girls' series, describes a similar sanatorium in the Alps in her books, and creates "the big English schools, St Mary's and St John's, where children can be sent while their parents are under treatment".[9] It is also true that health was a consideration for many real-life parents when deciding to send their daughters to any type of boarding school. Sheila Rowbotham has written that: "at eleven off I went . . . to a Methodist boarding school in East Yorkshire, close to the sea. 'Healthy air,' my father said. 'Good for the chest, bracing.' "[10]

In the most explicit attempt to protect the girls' health, at the opening of *The Exploits of the Chalet Girls* (1933) the school opens an Annexe on the Sonnalpe close to the sanatorium. This remains until the Nazi occupation of Austria forces the school to move, initially up to the Sonnalpe and then to Guernsey. The Annexe is for delicate children who are felt to be better off in the fresher air and closer to the doctors, and the first teachers are old girls Grizel and Juliet. Despite being separated from the main school buildings, though, the Annexe is explicitly part of the school itself, for example having its own pages within the school magazine (p169). It also operates the same curriculum, as is made clear when the school moves to the Sonnalpe and the Annexe is then absorbed into it. There is no question but that 'delicate' girls are capable of the same intellectual challenges as the rest.

Perhaps it is not surprising, given Brent-Dyer's early life experiences, that she should be preoccupied with ill-health, particularly lung diseases. But her continual references to the school's function to protect its pupils' health portray a picture of fragile femininity. However, it is important to remember that the supposed fragility of girls' health had been of concern to educationalists during the late 19th and the first quarter of the twentieth century — the time when Brent-Dyer was being educated and then writing the first book of the series — with fears that giving girls an equivalent education to boys' would affect their general health and particularly their fertility.[11] These fears were supported by 'scientific' research. Felicity Hunt points out that one of the main ways that headmistresses combatted these concerns and preserved a full academic curriculum for girls was by concentrating "heavily on health and medical care and this included rules about dress, holding medical inspections and encouraging gymnastics and games".[12] It is possible, then, to interpret the stress that Brent-Dyer places on the school's function to protect its pupils' health as a means of extending the choices available to the girls rather than limiting them, and it is probable that she genuinely believed girls' health needed protecting more routinely than boys'.

ILLNESS OR INJURY AS A DEVICE TO IMPROVE CHARACTER

Given the school's relationship with the sanatorium, and the constant stress laid on the need to protect girls' health, it is not surprising that, within the series, illness plays a central role. Most frequently it is used as a plot device, functioning as a warning to those who resist being assimilated into the community. Illness or injury is explicitly caused by this resistance, either to the character in question or to another closely linked to them. (As, for example, when Jo becomes dangerously ill as a result of following Grizel when she runs away.) Brent-Dyer uses classic narrative structure in her use of a constant, in this case the community, whose calm is disrupted and then reinstated. The 'Illness/Injury' plot device essentially provides a vehicle for a character to change from representing undesirable to desirable qualities, thus enabling the reinstatement of the constant 'community'. It is not ill health, then, that separates a Chalet School girl from her peers, but bad character. Bad character may result in ill health, or ill health may be an essential part of a particularly *good* character.

Brent-Dyer's repeated use of the 'Illness/Injury' plot device is reminiscent of the morality tales popular in the late 18th and early 19th centuries, such as Sarah Fielding's *The Governess* (1749) and Maria Edgeworth's *Moral Tales* (1801). Morality tales formed the predominant genre in English children's books at the beginning of the nineteenth century, with the majority of authors being women.[13] A similar plot device was also a convention of nineteenth-century fiction, where illness symbolised a process of character change.[14]

With the exception of only two girls who are expelled in the course of the series, Thekla, who is seen to represent the spirit of "New Germany", and Betty, a girl who assists the Nazis when the school returns to England, all of the characters are seen as capable of reform within the community. (This is why the 'Illness/Injury' plot device is essential to the series.) Even the two aforementioned girls are described as improving in character later in life as a result of the ultimate punishment of expulsion from the community. In this Brent-Dyer is writing in the tradition of classic children's fiction, of which Alison Lurie has stated:

> a pastoral convention is maintained. It is assumed that the world of childhood is simpler and more natural than that of adults, and that children, though they may have faults, are essentially good or at least capable of becoming so.[15]

Brent-Dyer's use of the 'Illness/Injury' plot device is worked out most fully in *Eustacia Goes to the Chalet School* (1930). The orphaned Eustacia Benson is "the most arrant little prig that ever existed" (p9), having been brought up by professional parents with "great theories on how to bring up children".

> We have little difficulty in guessing the effects of those theories when we meet Eustacia for the first time one day in November, sitting in the drawing room at her Aunt Margery's, looking round it with a superior air, and mentally deciding how she would re-arrange the room, should it be given over to her." (ibid)

Eustacia is swiftly sent abroad to the Chalet School, since Madge is known to her aunt, who lives close to the Bettanys' old home in Devon. She protests, but her aunt ignores her.

> "You have upset the whole house in the short time we have had you. You have never once tried to think of anyone but yourself. You have told tales, been rude to the maids, behaved in a most

> unfitting way to both your uncle and myself, and are making the boys unhappy. ... You have repelled any show of affection, and you have made the whole house miserable." (p18)

Despite everything that the Chalet School does to try to change Eustacia's character, it is to no avail. "Eustacia was her ordinary smug self again; and so she remained until the terrible happening put an end to all feuds and hates, and a new Eustacia Benson was born who had very little in common with the old one." (p262) The "terrible happening" is, needless to say, a life-threatening episode. Eustacia decides to run away, not through unhappiness but in order to upset the school.

> It would be a splendid revenge, for it must hurt the School. She would write a note saying that it was mainly owing to Joey Bettany that she had done this; and they would have a bad time of it until they got news of her. (p276)

Unfortunately for herself, Eustacia does not understand the dangers of the mountain terrain that surrounds the school, and becomes trapped on the mountain during a storm that causes the river to flood, only narrowly escaping with her life.

> That wild scramble to safety had been achieved only at the cost of a sprained back-muscle, and the long hours of lying in a twisted and unnatural position had made matters worse. When Eustacia awoke from the long, deep sleep into which she had fallen just before Dr Jem came to tell the waiting women in the study that all should go well, it was to pain and helplessness such as she had never imagined before. (p311)

As a result, Eustacia is forced to lie flat for many months before she recovers slowly, and when she eventually returns to school more than a year later, it is to the Annexe. Unsurprisingly, her character reforms (literally) overnight as a result, and she is rechristened Stacie.

Brent-Dyer's treatment of Eustacia makes it clear that she is now fully included within the community, and does not have to wait for her recovery of good health and mobility in order to achieve this. Instead, she is moved into, not the sanatorium, but Madge's own home while she recovers, and she remains at the heart of the Russell family. Later, while still too unwell to attend lessons, she becomes editor of the Chalet School magazine, *The Chaletian*, and "relays of girls" are sent up at weekends to keep her company. Eustacia's back never fully recovers, and in middle age she moves into an annexe of Joey's home in Switzerland with her maid Bessie and occasionally acts as a teacher within the school, clearly still fully included within the community. In the interim period, she returns to Oxford where her father was a professor, and becomes a Classical scholar with an international reputation.

ILLNESS AS PURITY

The influence of the traditions of classic children's fiction can also be seen in other elements of the Chalet School series. The essential goodness and innocence of the character of the Robin, for example, is more than once used to help an older character to throw off undesirable qualities and reform. The Robin is first introduced in the second book of the series, *Jo of the Chalet School* (1926), as the extremely delicate daughter of an English friend of the Bettanys who becomes Jem Russell's secretary, and a Polish woman who has recently died of TB.

The Robin's pureness and innocence is associated with her delicacy — she is always decribed as being at risk of developing TB like her mother — and this is also a convention of classic fiction, in particular nineteenth-century romantic fiction. Susan Sontag points out that in nineteenth-century literature: "The dying tubercular is pictured as made more beautiful and more soulful."[16]

The Robin is described as an "angel-child" (Brent-Dyer, 1926, p36) with "such a lovely baby-face!" (p32), and the petting she receives "never seemed to affect her in the least" (*The Head Girl of the Chalet School*, 1928, p45). The Robin is so good that she is able on one occasion to intervene to bring Joey back from near-certain death, after Joey has contracted "pleuro-pneumonia" while rescuing another girl, Maureen, from an ice-covered lake.

(Note how once again illness is used as a plot device: in this case Maureen's lack of self-discipline brings down illness on both herself and Joey. Although Maureen recovers from her own "rheumatic fever" in the story, later in the series it is reported that she died young as a result of the after-effects of the incident.)

> Robin's eyes wandered past to the bed and its occupant. Joey lay propped up with pillows to relieve the breathing. Her black eyes were half-open, and her cheeks were scarlet. A tearing rusty sound came through her parted lips, and she was muttering to herself in low tones. The Robin ran forward and climbed up on to the bed. She possessed herself of the other hot hand, and leaned over.
> "Joey, I am going to sing you to sleep with

Mamma's song. You must close your eyes and go to sleep."

The black eyes opened a little wider, and the grown-up people in the room held their breath. Could it be possible that the Robin's baby voice was going to break the delirium where all else had failed? It looked like it. There was something in the black eyes that had not been there for five long days. (*The Rivals of the Chalet School*, 1929, pp169-170)

The Robin, who is described as looking "almost angelic" even during her teens (eg *The Chalet School in Exile*, 1940, p14; *The Chalet School Goes To It*, 1941, p18) eventually becomes a nun (*Joey Goes to the Oberland*, 1952, p16). Jo, Madge and their respective husbands are relieved because, despite Robin's health improving considerably, it is thought that Robin, unlike Jo, will never be strong enough to cope with the demands of childbirth.

CHARACTERS WITH LEARNING DIFFICULTIES

Away from the use of injury and illness to reform character, Brent-Dyer was particularly unusual in including some characters with learning difficulties within her stories. There is nothing sentimental about her treatment of them — the most prominent character, Jockel, is introduced in the following way in *Jo Returns to the Chalet School* (1936):

[Jockel is] a youth who helped in the gardens and attended to the cricket-pitches and tennis-lawns in season. Miss Wilson had always declared that he was slightly 'wanting'. At first the bewildered staff were under the impression that 'slightly' had become 'altogether'. He could only grovel there, mouthing at the ladies, and clutching the skirts of Miss Annersley, who happened to be nearest. (p252)

Jockel, it turns out, has come across the snow statues that the girls have been sculpting.

> Poor Jockel ... had suddenly come upon those hard-frozen images, and in the shock, his scanty wits had deserted him. The light had been streaming over them from the uncurtained staircase window, and, as Miss Annersley herself acknowledged, they had a ghostly look." (p254)

Jockel is only glimpsed next in *The New Chalet School* (1938), where he is set the unenviable task of scraping chewing gum off a door after some naughty children have covered the door in the stuff, and is described as being "not quite 'all there' " for his pains (p93).

In his following appearance, though, Jockel shows that he is nonetheless competent, brave and capable. In *The Chalet School in Exile* (1940), after the Nazis invade Austria, Jo is forced to flee for her life after she tries to defend a Jewish watchmaker from an angry mob. (Both the watchmaker and a priest who helps them are subsequently killed.) Madge and the school are able to follow in a more orderly fashion, but are forced to leave behind Jo's beloved St Bernard, Rufus. Eventually, though, Rufus reaches England, "emaciated, covered with bruises and cuts, and with his magnificent coat a dirty, bedraggled mat" (p321).

> He had been brought by poor Jockel, a half-wit who had been employed about the grounds of the

Chalet School at the Tiern See. Jockel had had as bad a time as his charge, and had contrived to get away, no one knew how. He had adored Joey, and knowing her love for the great dog, which she had rescued as a fortnight-old puppy from drowning when she herself was a wild schoolgirl of fourteen, had contrived to get him. The two had wandered through Western Europe, and had finally reached Bordeaux, where Jockel had fallen in with Cornelia Flower's father [i.e. the father of a pupil]. That understanding gentleman had engaged the lad as a servant, and sent Rufus over to England. (pp321-2)

Brent-Dyer therefore makes it clear that people with learning difficulties can use their initiative and overcome endless trials to achieve what would be a huge feat of survival for anyone. Later, Jockel is referred to as working for Madge and Jem when the school relocates to England (*Highland Twins at the Chalet School*, 1942, p78), something that Brent-Dyer no doubt considered to be a prized position. And in *The Coming of Age of the Chalet School* (1958) Jockel is once more back at home in Austria, working at the local hotel as a porter and able to drive a car at least well enough to be able to park it (p157), and greeted with enthusiasm by Jo and her friends when they arrive for a visit.

No other character with learning difficulties was to reach the prominence of Jockel, but in *Jo to the Rescue* (1945) we learn that Jo was to employ another character with learning difficulties in her holiday home. "Lily Purvis — her that's a bit daft — is to go every day to clean the steps and peel potatoes and such-like. Lily's rare and set up about it, I can tell you." (p9) Sadly, we learn nothing more of Lily — the only working-class character to be prominently featured in the book is Debby, who is a carer as well as a servant. However, the incident reinforced the message that people with learning difficulties are capable of working, and since those who are working class need to work, then 'good' employers should employ them. Perhaps it is needless to say, though, that no middle-class characters with learning difficulties, and therefore no potential Chalet School pupils, are ever mentioned. (Although it is hard work and good character, not intellectual ability or academic achievement, that is most valued at the Chalet School.)

PERMANENT INVALIDS

Brent-Dyer's emphasis on leading characters who are marked by 'delicacy' or disability was to reach its peak in *Jo to the Rescue*. This was unusual in being a story set away from the school; a plot device that Brent-Dyer had never used previously. (*The Chalet Girls in Camp*, 1932, featured the school Guides camping, and as such was part of the school activities.) Set towards the end of the war, *Jo to the Rescue* features the adult Jo and her three closest friends, Frieda, Marie and Simone, spending an extended summer holiday in Yorkshire with their young children and Jo's niece, Sybil Russell. In the same village is disabled twenty-three-year-old Phoebe Wychcote, living with her faithful servant and carer Debby, to whom she has to defer.

> If Debby ever left her, there was no one else to look after her, for she was singularly destitute of relatives. The long years of invalidism had left her timid and uncertain; and the death of her father, eighteen months before this, had taught her to cling desperately to her one prop. (p8)

Unknown to Phoebe at first, but known to Jo when she meets her, Phoebe's specialist doctor has just died too. Meanwhile Phoebe's "rheumatism" is out of control and flares up regularly, putting great strain on her heart. However, between attacks she is slightly more mobile than she was in her teens, being able to walk with crutches occasionally although she is largely dependent on wheelchair use. She also works whenever possible, sewing and embroidering items such as table cloths for sale.

> Phoebe had decided to try to add to their slender income by selling her work, and she was beginning to work up a small connection. The great drawback lay in the fact that she could never rely on being able to ply her needle at any time. When the cruel rheumatic pains attacked her fingers and wrists, as they sometimes did, she was helpless — unable, even, to feed herself. So she always had to warn her customers that she could never promise work for a certain date, though she always tried to get it done in the right time, often working when it was torture to hold her needle and the material. There was real heroism in the way she tried to overcome her disabilities, and Debby, watching over her with a gruff tenderness, could often have wept to see her struggles. (pp18-19)

Phoebe, though, is worried about becoming the stereotypical selfish invalid and discusses this with the village boy, Reg Entwistle, who has been her only friend until she meets Jo.

> "It's awfully easy to be selfish when you're a cripple, Reg. Ever since I was at that hydro and saw that poor Miss Emery, I've tried so hard not

to get like her. She didn't mean it, but she was horribly selfish. She wanted everything she could have for herself, and she never thought of anyone else. I should hate to get like that. And Father would have hated it for me." (p11)

However, Brent-Dyer makes it abundantly clear that selfishness is not inevitably linked to disability (and does not overstate Phoebe's 'heroism' either). Instead, the character in the story who is selfishness personified is the non-disabled Zephyr Burthill. Zephyr is the spoilt daughter of a wealthy man, and has become obsessed with obtaining the cello that belonged to Phoebe's father, who was a renowned concert performer. Debby believes that Phoebe should accept the Burthills' offer of £100 for the instrument, since the cello can be of little use to Phoebe, while the money would provide some security for them. Phoebe, though, is loathe to give the cello up, since it has enormous sentimental value for her.

At this point Brent-Dyer had a clear choice. She could have made Zephyr more sympathetic by the end of the book, and demonstrated that Phoebe, unable to become a professional musician herself, should then rightly give up the instrument to her. She could also have shown Phoebe to be selfish by refusing to do so, and linked this to her disability. In this she would have been typical, not just of her age, but of conventions that persist today. Instead, Brent-Dyer used Joey and her friends to demonstrate a very different approach:

> Jo read with growing indignation. "This is outrageous!" she cried as she finished and threw the letter down. "What right has he got to persecute you like this? The cello is yours. You don't wish to

sell. You've told him so, and that ought to end it. Besides how does he know that you'll never be able to use it? There are wonderful cures nowadays. It won't be long before the research people find something to put an end to rheumatism, I'm sure, and once it's discovered, you'll try it, of course, and may be quite well again. Then you could use the cello. And even if that doesn't happen, why should you be forced to sell, against your will, something that means more to you than anything else you have? It's simply disgraceful!" (p56)

The sanatorium doctors later make it clear that a cure is impossible, while Phoebe herself makes it clear to Jo that even if it were, she would never be able to play to concert standard now. Phoebe cannot keep the cello on the grounds that a cure will turn her into a concert performer herself. However, Jo and her friends make it explicit where Brent-Dyer's sentiments lie when they have a confrontation with the vicar's wife, who is on Zephyr's side.

"I have heard that, since you came here, you have made a great friend of Miss Wychcote. I trust you will try to make her see her conduct with regard to the cello in its true light, and show her how selfishly she is behaving –"

"I could never do that," said Jo quickly. "You see, I don't consider she *is* being selfish."

"No!" Marie chimed in. "The selfish one is the girl who is trying to make Phoebe give up her father's most prized possession, just to gratify a whim of her own. I am afraid, Mrs Hart, we all agree about that."

... "But that is silly," replied Mrs Hart. ..."Miss Wychcote could never make the use of it that someone who is in normal health can. I maintain that it is selfish to keep the cello to herself. If she wants to play, a cheaper instrument would surely be good enough for her." (pp202-3)

Jo and her friends have to defend the cello against burglars hired by the Burthills before it is finally safe, underlining just how strongly they believe that the cello is rightly Phoebe's, whether she can use it herself or not. Jo also manages, by the end of the book, to make Zephyr realise just how wrong she has been, and Zephyr apologies to Phoebe.

> "I'm not going to stay, but I did want you to know that I won't worry you about it any more. I'm – sorry – I was selfish – please forgive me." Zephyr's voice quavered and faded away. (p305)

At no point, however, does Brent-Dyer state that Zephyr should be sorry for Phoebe, and should allow her to keep the cello on the grounds that she is disabled. In fact, Jo makes it explicit from the first that the relationship between herself and Phoebe is equal, recognising Phoebe immediately as Nicholas Wychcote's daughter.

> "Vanna di Ricci told me after that he had a daughter who was about our age, she thought; but I never thought I'd have the luck to meet you!"
> The luck! Phoebe's lips suddenly quivered. She had hoped to be on terms of friendship with the newcomers; but she had never even dreamed of being so rapturously greeted. Jo saw it, and her eyes softened as she dropped into a nearby chair and bent forward.
> "Don't you call it luck for me? I admired his playing so much. I've always loved the cello, and

his was such wonderful music. I met him, and liked him personally. And now I've found his daughter." (pp21-2)

Instead, it is Zephyr that Jo pities, when Zephyr explains that her father has always given her everything that she wanted.

> "I can't imagine a more cruel thing to do to a child," said Jo soberly.
> "*Cruel?*"
> "Yes — cruel. It's given you a totally wrong idea of life. Don't you call that a cruel thing to do to a child?"
> ...Zephyr stared. Never in all her life had anyone spoken to her like this. This tall, graceful woman with the clever, sensitive face and lovely voice seemed to be pitying her — *her* — Zephyr Burthill, whose every want had been gratified as soon as it had been spoken. (pp104-5)

Jo eventually 'rescues' Zephyr by teaching her different values and introducing her to Robin, as she rescues Phoebe's schoolboy friend Reg Entwhistle, who has been longing for the opportunity to train for a profession. The title of the book, *Jo to the Rescue*, then, does not simply cast Jo as the rescuer of the disabled, passive victim: Zephyr and Reg are portrayed as being as much in need of rescue as Phoebe. Although it is understated, Jo also rescues her niece Sybil, through providing her with the opportunity to make good by helping Jo and her friends for the summer. Sybil's character had previously become corrupted through continual praise of her beauty (this did not come from her family or teachers, of course!), as well as her awareness of her position as the elder daughter of the Chalet School founder. Inevitably, this had resulted in the near-death of her younger sister Josette, when Sybil's arrogance and selfishness caused Josette to be scalded. Needless to say, Sybil has been reformed by the experience, and the summer completes this process, as Jo confirms at the end of the book.

> "She's very well, Madge, and has been a real help. I don't know how we'd have managed without her. She helped to look after the tinies, and gave a hand in the house, and was everybody's errand-boy. ... Sybs is a changed being." (pp294-295)

As the story ends, Brent-Dyer has two obvious choices when deciding Phoebe's eventual fate. Phoebe no longer has a specialist doctor to oversee her care, and so her care is taken over by the doctors at the sanatorium, headed by Dr Peters, who has "studied in America" (clearly then the epitome of medical training in Brent-Dyer's eyes!). Most authors of Brent-Dyer's day would therefore have finished the story by curing Phoebe. Brent-Dyer, though, only allows Phoebe's rheumatism to be relieved enough for her to be without the acute attacks of pain that strain her heart, and to be able to walk with sticks.

The other obvious choice, of course, would have been to let Phoebe's heart fail during one of the aforesaid attacks, and then decide that this was 'all for the best'. This would have fitted in very well with the normal literary conventions of 'kill or cure' for disabled characters. Brent-Dyer, too, had not shied away from killing characters off in the past, occasionally by accident — as in the death of Robin's father through a climbing accident — but normally through illness that the sanatorium doctors were unable to cure. Throughout the series, an occasional parent or other family member dies in the background, something that is portrayed as being quite natural. Brent-Dyer was not, then, at all afraid to show doctors failing to keep their patients alive when they can't be cured.

Instead, however, Brent-Dyer provided Phoebe with the same fate as her other favoured characters: marriage with a doctor — in this case, Dr Peters, who had been overseeing Phoebe's care. (Clearly, medical ethics were perceived rather differently then!) To underline that Phoebe is the equal of Jo's other friends, Phoebe is married from Jo's house just as Simone previously was, with Jo's triplet daughters acting as bridesmaids. Later, Phoebe becomes one of the doctors' wives who surround Jo when the school moves to Switzerland, and becomes a mother through adoption — her daughter Lucy later becomes the best friend of Joey's twin daughter Felicity, although by this time Phoebe herself is unseen. Phoebe is therefore portrayed as being quite able to lead a 'normal' life, despite continuing to need care and support. And it is worth noting that it is the husband, Dr Peters, who will provide that care and support within the marriage, not, as convention would normally dictate, the wife.

DELICATE CHILDREN

Jo to the Rescue, however, marked the end of an era for the Chalet School's treatment of illness and disability, although this was not immediately apparent. First, there was a four-year gap before the next book, *Three Go to the Chalet School*, was published in 1949, and unusually, this was acknowledged within the world of the story. The following book, *The Chalet School and the Island* (1950), relocated the series again, this time to a small island, "St Briavels", off the coast of south Wales. One change introduced was the delicacy of Joey's 'youngest' triplet Margot, who had previously been healthy, following an illness. In later books, Chalet School history was then rewritten to make Margot delicate from birth (this was more in keeping, of course, with the realities of multiple births than Brent-Dyer's original portrayal of all the triplets as being radiantly healthy).

From the time she is small, Margot is always portrayed as having a bad temper — and in 1945, in *Jo to the Rescue*, Jo had explained that: "I can't think where Margot gets her temper." (p255) But in 1949, and for the rest of the series, Margot's temper and her other character defects, including laziness, are linked to her earlier 'delicacy'.

> "When she was little she was so frail that no one ever thought they'd rear her. I remember," Biddy went on reminiscently, "Joey saying to me once, 'If she's to have only a short time in this world, I want it to be a happy one'. So no one made much fuss when Margot slacked and dawdled." (*The New Mistress at the Chalet School*, 1957, p25)

Margot's problems later become such that she puts both her own and other lives at risk: once when she and another girl nearly drown because she has been disobedient; and another time when she throws a heavy bookend at someone in a temper, knocking them out.

However, as Jo's daughter, Margot is eventually able to reform to the extent that she decides to become a medical missionary, while Jo's most delicate son, Charles, appears to be destined for the priesthood. In both cases, though, they become perfectly healthy first; the links between delicate health and idealised good character have gone for good by then.

Brent-Dyer's very different attitude after the war to the impact of ill health and disability on character can first be seen explicitly in the 'Island' books, with the introduction of Cherry Christy. Cherry is the step-sister of a new member of the Sixth Form, Dickie, whose father owns the 'big house' — formerly their home — that the school has been housed in. Cherry, though, does not attend school: she is recovering from polio, and her character has been radically and explicitly altered by the experience.

> Dickie was silent for a minute or two. "I'd better explain," she said slowly, at last. "Cherry's been ill, poor kid — I.P." Then, as the girls stared, "Infantile paralysis. It's left her very lame . . . it's made a change in her. . . she's been shy and — queer. . . If you see her, don't try to make friends, for I know she jolly well won't! Oh, I know it's idiotic and all that, but the doctor says it's part of the illness. It does change people a bit sometimes. He thinks that as the lameness gets better she'll come all right again." (*The Chalet School and the Island*, 1950, pp39-40)

It is not possible, then, for Cherry's character to improve while she is still disabled.

Now, it is the non-disabled girls who enjoy the moral superiority.

> Mary-Lou and her chums were a set of jolly youngsters, prepared to take life as they found it. They accepted Cherry's troubles without remark, and no one "stared" at her legs, though Vi Lucy hoped sympathetically that it wouldn't be long

before she would be rid of the irons.

"It means you can't play games or dance, or things like that, you see," she said. "I do call it horrid luck, Cherry. But when you come, we'll give you a hand when you want it till the irons are off." (p132)

Needless to say, Cherry is well on the way to being cured before her character alters sufficiently to join the Chalet School, although the reader never sees her as a schoolgirl.

Then, in her 24th book, *The Wrong Chalet School* (1952), Brent-Dyer began to set the scene for the school's final relocation to Switzerland, with references to the establishment of a Swiss finishing branch. By the next book in the series, *Shocks for the Chalet School* (1952), the branch was in operation, and was the subject of the following book, *The Chalet School in the Oberland* (1952). By the 28th book, *Changes for the Chalet School* (1953), it has been decided to move the bulk of the school to the Swiss Oberland, and by the 30th, *The Chalet School and Barbara* (1954), this has become a reality. Jo and Jack also move to the Oberland: Jack to be head of a branch of the sanatorium which opens near the school; Jo to continue to write and give birth in a house which is only divided from the school by a hedge with a gate cut in it. The link with the sanatorium, broken in the move to the island, also became a permanent feature of the series, which was to continue in its Oberland setting for another 16 years and 27 books.

Despite the continuing link with the sanatorium, though, the post-war Chalet books continued to treat the themes of health, illness and disability very differently to their forebears. There was never any question, for example, of re-opening the

Annexe: if girls were too 'delicate' to be assimilated into the mainstream under the watchful eye of Matron, then they did not appear at school at all.

It is possible, of course, that this was linked to the development of antibiotics as a treatment for TB; almost overnight, the old rationale for the real sanatoria disappeared. Brent-Dyer's sanatorium apparently continued to treat complications relating to TB, such as TB of the bones, but otherwise became more like any other (private) hospital. However, before the war girls were admitted to the Annexe for a variety of reasons apart from the threat of lung disease, so this in itself was not a reason. It is also true that the Swiss school was situated much more closely to the sanatorium than the Austrian school, so the benefits of opening an Annexe would be fewer — but then that could also have been a rationale for the explicit inclusion within the main school of much more 'delicate' girls than previously, which did not happen.

The change in Brent-Dyer's treatment of 'delicate' girls is explicit from the first of the 'Swiss' Chalet School books, *The Chalet School and Barbara* (1954). Barbara Chester is the sister of a number of established characters, but has never attended school herself because of her delicacy. On the basis of past books, Brent-Dyer might well have been expected to use this opportunity to introduce a new girl to the Annexe, or to create a character whose looks and personality were idealised and explicitly linked to their poor health. After all, now that the school was back in Switzerland, it was in a much stronger position to take girls whose health needs protecting again. But in fact Barbara has arrived at school because she has gradually become much stronger after an attack of measles, and never faces any dangers as a result of her health while at the school. Moreover, her character is explicitly stated to be better than anyone could expect of someone who has been an invalid most of their life:

> As the centre of attention in her family, with all the others taught to give up to her in every way, she had had every excuse for being selfish and self-centred. As Beth reflected now, it was little short of a miracle that she had grown up as sweet of nature as she was.
> "It's about the only time I've ever known measles to be a blessing in disguise," the elder sister mused. "If it hadn't been for that when she was ten, she might still be lounging about at home, the pet of everyone and getting more and more egotistical every day." (p9)

STEREOTYPES OF SELFISHNESS

The different treatment of 'delicate' girls post-war is seen most explicitly in the character of Leila Elstob, who is also introduced in *The Chalet School and Barbara*. Leila is the cousin of a Chalet School girl, Sue Meadows, but does not attend the school herself. Instead, she is being 'built up' for surgery at the sanatorium on her hip, which has been badly affected by TB, and her cousin Sue has been brought out to Switzerland with her for company. Unlike the Robin, Amy Stevens et al of the earlier Chalet School books, Leila fulfils all the stereotypes of the spoilt invalid, being "the most petted little piece of selfishness you could find anywhere" (p186-7). Sue, not Leila, is seen in need of protection by the Chalet School; without this interference, Sue's life will be too overshadowed by Leila's needs.

> She [the Head] had called at the Elisehütte to ask

Mrs. Elstob, Sue's aunt, to let the girl be a boarder for the rest of the term. They were at the beginning of winter and might expect other snowstorms just as fierce as the recent one. That would mean that if Sue remained a day-girl, she must lose a good deal of her work.

Mrs Elstob was not at all ready to agree. She pointed out that Sue was there, in the first place, to give her delicate cousin companionship which could not be done if the former were a boarder. Miss Annersley had done her best, however, for Sue's own sake and at last Mrs. Elstob had agreed that she should be a weekly boarder, provided she might come home for an hour each afternoon if it was fine, to amuse Leila. (p186)

Despite this, the Chalet School has every sympathy for Leila.

Indeed, they had contrived, among them, to bring a good deal of pleasure into her short, pain-filled life since the School had come to the Platz. Tiny gifts of no real value, notes, storybooks and many other things had gone along to the Elisehütte, During the winter, they had practised their skiing in front of her window to amuse her. The best of all had been the gift of the magnificent toy chalet made by one of the girls at Welsen, Tom Gay, for the Sale of Work at the end of the previous term, and won by Con Maynard in the competition for it. (*A Chalet Girl from Kenya*, 1955, pp129-30)

Most tellingly, in *A Chalet Girl from Kenya* (1955) Jo's triplet daughter Con acts to save Leila's life following surgery by calming her when Leila is restless and cannot sleep. But this all takes place at a distance: there is never any suggestion that Leila, who will clearly never be cured, will ever become a Chalet School girl. Instead (and unlike Phoebe), Leila is the object of charity, defined — and with her character marked — by her illness.

By the end of the 1950s, Brent-Dyer's treatment of disability as something that affects the mind as well as the body became completely stereotyped, and reached its peak in the character of Naomi Elton. Naomi, once in training as a ballet dancer, has been badly injured in a fire that also killed both of her parents. She arrives at the Chalet School as the first explicitly disabled new girl for some years.

> Naomi had been slowly getting to her feet and now Mary-Lou found herself looking down on a girl who was badly stooped with a crooked shoulder. But the face lifted to hers was lovely — almost as lovely as Vi Lucy's with cloudy fair hair framing perfect features. Dark grey eyes looked straight into hers as Naomi said, "How do you do?"
>
> It was a musical voice, but there was a hardness about it which rang in Mary-Lou's ears at once. The perfectly cut mouth was set in thin lines and there was a crooked twist to the smile which accompanied the words.
>
> "Hello, Naomi," she said, with her own delightful smile. . . She felt an odd repulsion to the girl mixed with the genuine pity that rose in her warm heart for anyone so terribly deformed.
> (*Trials for the Chalet School*, 1959, pp23-4)

Once again, the non-disabled Chalet School girls show their moral superiority, making every effort to include Naomi in their activities. It is Naomi's impaired character, not her physical impairment, that is seen to exclude her, but at the same time, both have the same cause — when Naomi is first introduced, her guardian writes to the school (p8): "Owing to the accident of which I have already spoken, I am afraid her mind has become slightly warped." Later Naomi herself explains:

> "I lost my father and mother and my power to dance all at once. Do you wonder," Naomi wound up, still in that bitter tone, "that I don't believe in God? Or if He really is there, then He just doesn't care?" (p104)

But:

> "If it was possible for me to be straight again and walk about and move normally, oh, Mary-Lou, if it ever happened, I'd believe in God again and love Him!" (p106)

It is not possible, in the post-war Chalet School, for Naomi to learn to love God without a cure. It is only when Naomi becomes involved in another life-threatening accident, and therefore experiences surgery that will virtually cure her as a by-product of this, that fundamental changes occur.

> "During last night's operation they were able to put right something that has been wrong ever since her first accident. When she is able to move about again, her lameness will be much better and she will be much straighter." (p223)

We understand full well that this will include her character. Naomi, though, fails to return to the Chalet School. Instead she spends an extended time in the sanatorium; time that, in previous days, might have been spent in an 'Annexe', or even, as with Eustacia in Madge's house, in Jo's home as part of the family.

'BETTER OFF DEAD'

Perhaps it is not surprising that Brent-Dyer now also appears to subscribe to the view that, if impairment can't be cured, then a character is better off dead. In her most explicit treatment of the theme, the disabled character is so unimportant as to be unseen, while all of the focus is on the non-disabled character who is indirectly affected. Jessica Wayne is a new girl whose mother has married a widower with an invalid daughter, Rosamund. "She can't walk. There's something wrong with her back and she's always either in bed or on her invalid couch." (*Mary-Lou of the Chalet School*, 1956, p133) When Jessica becomes jealous of the time that her mother spends with Rosamund, Rosamund remains at home — there is of course no Annexe now — while Jessica is sent to the Chalet School. Here Mary-Lou is able to show Jessica why she should pity Rosamund.

> "But don't you see," she said quietly, "that you are strong and well. You can play games and run about and garden and everything like that. You have all the fun of school and meeting new people and making fresh friends. You can go to the shops and choose your own materials for embroidery and knitting and — and raffia-work. You can pick your own books and visit the cinema — if you like cinemas and they let you go — and do everything like that. You have such lots, Jessica. But Rosamund has to depend on other people for every blessed thing. She can have very little choice. How would you like it yourself?"

... "Well, I suppose I should hate it, really," she said uncertainly.

"You *suppose*! You jolly well *know*!" Mary-Lou retorted forcibly. "Of course you'd hate it! You wouldn't be natural if you didn't!" (pp133-4)

And yet, of course, Phoebe had been in a similar situation, but at no point did Brent-Dyer suggest that her life was not worth living, even if a cure was impossible. Improving Phoebe's mobility was never even regarded as being a priority for her treatment: the priority was to reduce her pain and therefore the strain on her heart, in order to protect her life. Rosamund, though, is seen as having a life that is not worth living, and one where everyone including herself should rejoice in its coming to an end. By *The Coming of Age of the Chalet School* (1958), Rosamund has become worse, and towards the end of the book, Jessica is summoned back home to be at Rosamund's deathbed (quite how Rosamund's back trouble has led to her death is never explained). By now, Jessica loves Rosamund dearly, and Mary-Lou has to explain what is clearly the authorial view:

"If what you fear is coming to pass, won't it be best for Rosamund? She has only half a life as it is, and she's just a girl — our age, you said." (26-7)

"I know it's heart-breaking for you, but this isn't the moment to think about that. It's Rosamund you've got to think of. If you let her see you looking like that, it'll make her miserable. ... it's going to be so good for Rosamund! She'll be done with pain and weakness then. Isn't it worth while to know *that* for her?" (pp199-200)

Well, writing as someone with a spinal impairment and chronic pain, No!

FROM INCLUSION TO SEGREGATION

There is no easy answer to the question as to why Brent-Dyer treated her themes of illness and disability so differently in the post-war years. Undoubtedly, the discovery of penicillin made it more difficult to write convincingly about girls whose 'inherited' susceptibility to lung disease made it important to guard their health carefully. Penicillin, too, ushered in an era where it was believed that doctors would soon be able to cure everything. Perhaps Brent-Dyer believed that she genuinely lived in a different age to that of her youth, where she was forced to witness the death of both her brother and her best friend. The Chalet School's dedication to protecting the health of its pupils, and her belief in the curative properties of the mountain air, clearly reflected her desire for a different outcome for her fictional heroines.

However, even by the 1920s the idealised, tubercular invalid was a figure from the past, replaced with the eugenics movement and the ideal of a new, more robust human race. The horrors of the Holocaust, portrayed so much more vividly by Brent-Dyer than by any comparable children's writer of her day, might have been expected to usher in a more sympathetic treatment of the sick and disabled, not a complete about-turn. Likewise the post-war years brought in the first rights for disabled people, with the establishment of the National Health Service giving a right to medical treatment, and the introduction of a quota for disabled workers enforcing employment rights. These initiatives in many ways challenged the pre-war stereotypes of disabled people that Brent-Dyer had already rejected; it is hard to understand why she would now adopt them wholeheartedly.

However, it is undoubtedly true that many of the later Chalet School books suffer from being written much more quickly than the pre-war books: Brent-Dyer was now producing two or three books a year instead of one every year or two. She was also, as she became older, losing touch with contemporary girls' experiences, and relying more and more on her Chalet School 'formula'. Even her most committed fans find the Swiss books disappointing compared with the earlier books, and have remarked on how much slighter the characterisation is within them and how repetitious and unrealistic many of the plots are. Perhaps it is unsurprising, then, that Brent-Dyer's treatment of illness and disability became hackneyed and stereotyped too.

Brent-Dyer's personal life may also have had an impact on the content of her writing. After the war, the school that she was running from her home closed, and she never returned to teaching. However, she was still unable to make a living from her writing, unbelievable though this may seem to modern readers — the volume of Chalet School sales that was achieved with paperback publication came only in the final years of her life — while she had her elderly mother to support as well as herself. As a result she opened what was a de facto old people's home in her old school, taking in elderly lodgers while continuing to produce a book at least every six months (McClelland, pp238-51). The demands of these lodgers may well have reinforced cultural stereotypes of the exacting invalid, coming as they did to a woman who ideally would have lived only to write. McClelland points out that the realities of running a school meant that the quality of Brent-Dyer's school was light years apart from the Chalet School, and that it survived as long as it did only because it was based in an evacuation zone.[17] No doubt the realities of dealing with the sick and elderly were also far removed from the fictional sanatorium experience.

Ironically, if Brent-Dyer had continued to forefront the inclusion of 'delicate' girls within the Chalet School and given them even greater prominence, she might have survived the wrath of the post-war critics rather better than she did. The post-war critics heaped criticism on the girls' school story in all of its manifestations on the basis that the books were not 'realistic'. 'Realism', in all its gritty detail, became the hallmark of a 'good' book: realism, and the portrayal of a much wider range of social backgrounds than was seen to exist pre-war. Instead, Brent-Dyer attracted the full fury of the critics. Margery Fisher was typical when she wrote:

> In E. Brent-Dyer's stories about the Chalet School ... we have another clear case of fossilization ... These are survivals, and they must eventually suffer the fate of other books, creatures and tribes that prolong existence in a world that has passed them by.[18]

The death of Brent-Dyer in September 1969 only brought renewed attention to the genre of girls' school stories to celebrate its assumed demise. Nicholas Tucker's "Ditchwater at the Chalet School" was published in *The Times Educational Supplement* of 3 July 1970 to mark the posthumous publication of the final book in the series, *Prefects at the Chalet School*.

> So what is the appeal? ... Miss Brent-Dyer's special quality, other than the atmosphere of total belief in her stories, can only be described as an invariably plodding dullness, which obviously

must have attractions to her huge audience amongst children and "old girl" readers.

After all, who says that successful daydreams always have to be interesting? Perhaps for every youthful Florence Nightingale or Jean-Paul Sartre, both splendidly romantic daydreamers in their youth, there are equal numbers of dull daydreamers, who prefer things a little quieter. They would find admirable accommodation in the Chalet School . . . (p4)

Similarly, CS Tatham reflected in "Yesterday's Schoolgirls", published in *The Junior Bookshelf* of December 1969:

The recent death of Elinor Brent-Dyer marked the end of an era: or, perhaps more accurately, it drew a final line under an era that came to an end a long time ago. The 57th Chalet book [actually the 58th], published this autumn, is the last flicker of life in a type of book that has properly been dead for many years.

In fact, of course, the death of the Chalet School books has been predicted too often to be taken seriously; on the basis of past experience, they may still be being enjoyed into the next century. But it is interesting that it continues to be the pre-war books that are enjoyed the most: books where everyone is included, whatever their health status; and where impairment, if it affects character at all, only does so positively. The books that are enjoyed least are the ones where doctors can cure almost everything, where ill health warps character, and where death is preferable to ongoing impairment. Perhaps most readers, at some level, are concerned that, in the post-war Chalet School, they might be excluded too.

NOTES

1) *Behind the Chalet School*, Helen McClelland, Bettany Press, London, 1996, pp5-12.

2) Ibid. pp67-9.

3) Ibid. pp60-2.

4) Ibid. pp135-49.

5) Ibid. p141.

6) *Back to Home and Duty: Women Between the Wars 1918-1939*, Deidre Beddoe, Pandora, London, 1989, p82.

7) *Illness as Metaphor; AIDS as Metaphor*, Susan Sontag, Penguin, London, 1991, p25.

8) Ibid. pp74, 35.

9) *The Abbey Girls at Home*, Elsie J. Oxenham, Collins, London, 1928, p206.

10) 'Revolt in Roundhay', Sheila Rowbotham, In *Truth, Dare or Promise, Girls Growing Up in the Fifties*, Liz Heron (ed.), Virago, London, 1985, p197.

11) See Felicity Hunt [ed.], *Lessons for Life: The schooling of girls and women 1850-1950*, Basil Blackwell, Oxford, 1987, pp9-11.

12) Ibid. p9.

13) *The Oxford Companion to Children's Literature*, Carpenter, Humphrey and Prichard, Mari, Oxford University Press, 1984, p358.

14) For example, Marianne in Jane Austen's *Sense and Sensibility* (1811).

15) *Don't Tell the GROWN-UPS: Subversive Children's Literature*, Alison Lurie, Bloomsbury, London, 1990, pxiii.

16) *Illness as Metaphor; AIDS as Metaphor*, Susan Sontag, Penguin, London, 1991, p17.

17) *Behind the Chalet School*, Helen McClelland, Bettany Press, London, 1996, p226.

18) *Intent Upon Reading: A Critical Appraisal of Modern Fiction for Children*, Margery Fisher, Brockhampton Press, Leicester, 1961, p180.

REFERENCES

Beddoe, Deirdre, *Back to Home and Duty: Women Between the Wars 1918-1939*, Pandora, London, 1989.

Brent-Dyer, Elinor M, *The School at the Chalet*, W&M Chambers, Edinburgh, 1925.

Brent-Dyer, Elinor M, *Jo of the Chalet School*, W&M Chambers, Edinburgh, 1926.

Brent-Dyer, Elinor M, *The Rivals of the Chalet School*, W&M Chambers, Edinburgh, 1929.

Brent-Dyer, Elinor M, *Eustacia Goes to the Chalet School*, W&M Chambers, Edinburgh, 1930.

Brent-Dyer, Elinor M, *The Chalet School and Jo*, W&M Chambers, Edinburgh, 1931.

Brent-Dyer, Elinor M, *Exploits of the Chalet Girls*, W&M Chambers, Edinburgh, 1933.

Brent-Dyer, Elinor M, *The Chalet School in Exile*, W&M Chambers, Edinburgh, 1940.

Brent-Dyer, Elinor M, *Jo to the Rescue*, W&M Chambers, Edinburgh, 1945.

Brent-Dyer, Elinor M, *The Chalet School and the Island*, W&M Chambers, Edinburgh, 1950.

Brent-Dyer, Elinor M, *Carola Storms the Chalet School*, W&M Chambers, Edinburgh, 1951.

Brent-Dyer, Elinor M, *Shocks for the Chalet School*, W&M Chambers, Edinburgh, 1952.

Brent-Dyer, Elinor M, *The Wrong Chalet School*, W&M Chambers, Edinburgh, 1952.

Brent-Dyer, Elinor M, *Joey Goes to the Oberland*, W&M Chambers, Edinburgh, 1954.

Brent-Dyer, Elinor M, *The Chalet School and Barbara*, W&M Chambers, Edinburgh, 1954.

Brent-Dyer, Elinor M, *A Chalet Girl from Kenya*, W&M Chambers, Edinburgh, 1955.

Brent-Dyer, Elinor M, *Mary-Lou of the Chalet School*, W&M Chambers, Edinburgh, 1956.

Brent-Dyer, Elinor M, *The New Mistress at the Chalet School*, W&M Chambers, Edinburgh, 1957.

Brent-Dyer, Elinor M, *The Coming-of-Age of the Chalet School*, W&M Chambers, Edinburgh, 1958.

Brent-Dyer, Elinor M, *Trials for the Chalet School*, 1958, W&M Chambers, Edinburgh, 1958.

Fisher, Margery, 1961, *Intent Upon Reading: A Critical Appraisal of Modern Fiction for Children*, Brockhampton Press, Leicester, 1961.

Carpenter, Humphrey and Prichard, Mari, *The Oxford Companion to Children's Literature*, Oxford University Press, 1984.

Hunt, Felicity, [ed.], *Lessons for Life: The schooling of girls and women 1850-1950*, Basil Blackwell, Oxford, 1987.

Heron, Liz [ed,], 'Revolt in Roundhay', Sheila Rowbotham, In *Truth, Dare or Promise, Girls Growing Up in the Fifties*, Virago, London, 1985.

Lurie, Alison, *Don't Tell the GROWN-UPS: Subversive Children's Literature*, Bloomsbury, London, 1990.

McClelland, Helen, *Behind the Chalet School*, Bettany Press, London, 1996 (revised edition).

Oxenham, Elsie J, *The Abbey Girls at Home*, Collins, London, 1928.

Sontag, Susan, *Illness as Metaphor; AIDS as Metaphor*, Penguin, London, 1991.

LATE PERIOD

IX. MY SIBLING THE OTHER

REBECCA R. BUTLER

IN literature, as in life itself, relations between siblings can be rewarding, vexatious or a fluctuating mix of the two. This assertion applies in the field of children's literature as much as in any other literary genre. Examining books for children later in this chapter, we will encounter sibling relationships which are sometimes mutually supportive and gratifying, and sometimes fraught with tensions or even discord. But what happens if one of the siblings is or becomes disabled? Does disability change the sibling relationship in any fundamental way?

My working hypothesis for this chapter is that disability does add an important complicating factor to the sibling relationship. I will use the evidence contained in three books for children to test the hypothesis that disability makes the fictional sibling relationship more intense, more complex and, most significantly, more ambivalent. The three texts I have chosen to test this hypothesis are *Sleepovers* (2001) by Jacqueline Wilson, *The Gift* (2004) by James Riordan, and *A Different Life* (1997) by Lois Keith. Wilson's text is aimed at a readership aged around eight; Riordan's for a group of ten- to twelve-year-olds; and Keith's for an adolescent or young adult readership.

The study of sibling relationships in literature needs to be set in a particular context, that of the way in which siblings have been regarded in psychological studies. For the whole of the twentieth century, such a preponderance of emphasis was placed upon the parent-to-child relationship, and more specifically the mother-to-son relationship, that siblings were marginalised in both theoretical and clinical psychological studies. This imbalance has only recently begun to be adjusted.

SIBLINGS AND PSYCHOLOGY

The psychotherapist Prophecy Coles recently edited a book of essays entitled *Sibling Relationships* (2006). The book contains essays by a variety of distinguished writers who share the conviction of Coles that the excessive emphasis placed by Freud on parental relations left sibling and other relationships undervalued. Sibling relationships are now seen not just as a crucial element in the child's learning process, but also as a factor that influences the whole of society's world view. The sibling, where one or more exists, may play a crucial role in habituating the child to the experience of the other. Leonore Davidoff quotes a proverb cited by Sylvia Yanagisako in a study of Japanese-American kinship relations: "The sibling is the beginning of the stranger." (Coles, *Sibling Relationships*, p17)

Coles has a clear, if daunting, view of the difficulties faced when we try to place sibling relationships in a more definite context. "There is," she writes, "no general acceptance that our relationships with our siblings help to structure our psychic world." (p1) It is possible, argues Coles, that our relations with siblings are based upon purely destructive impulses such as hatred, the wish to murder and the fear of death. Or is it possible for siblings to share positive feelings? And where does all this leave the only child? One of the essays in the Coles book is by

Juliet Mitchell, Professor of Psychoanalysis and Gender Studies at Cambridge University. Mitchell argues that there is a crucial distinction between a weak trauma and a strong. 'Trauma', for Mitchell, has a strong and a weak sense. Weak trauma can be recovered from. Strong trauma, she believes, "does not change or develop, it is absolute for all time, it cannot be repressed or defended against." Mitchell argues that at the birth of a sibling the self is annihilated; one is "not oneself" but is "beside oneself" or "out of one's mind." (p9) If the birth of a non-disabled sibling is categorised as a strong trauma, to what category of trauma should the birth of a disabled sibling be assigned?

When I turn to the three fictional texts to be studied in this chapter, I will test these views of Mitchell. But care is required. It is not part of the purpose of this chapter to test the proposition that Mitchell's thesis is valid and useful to psychologists and psychotherapists. The question is whether it is a useful tool for analysing the relations of siblings in literature, and in particular in the three books I will examine. Literature has always been ahead of psychology in its recognition of the importance of the sibling relationship, as shown in fairy tales such as *Hansel and Gretel* and novels such as George Eliot's *The Mill on the Floss*. I will consider first the two texts intended for younger readers, turning later to Keith's text for more mature readers.

JACQUELINE WILSON'S *SLEEPOVERS*

"I always wanted to be part of a special secret club. It was almost as good as having a best friend." (Jacqueline Wilson, *Sleepovers*, 2001, p6)

Jacqueline Wilson's *Sleepovers* is a first-person

narrative, a rite-of-passage story. On starting at her new school, Daisy attempts to secure admission to a closed coterie of little girls: Amy, Bella, Chloe and Emily. Fortuitously, Daisy is equipped to make the group a perfect circle of "Alphabet Girls". The pre-existing members of the club have characters that are sharply defined, both in Wilson's text and with even greater precision in the illustrations by Nick Sharratt. In Sharratt's highly stylized drawings, for example, the girls all have distinctive hairstyles that reinforce their characteristics as defined in the text. Daisy also has a sister, Lily, who is also clearly depicted in text and image, as will be described.

Amy is the catalyst, the soundly based girl that everyone bounces ideas off. She is the most solidly rooted in reality. She confesses quite happily that she doesn't have a video player in her bedroom, though Chloe obviously regards it as an essential. Bella is the girl with the most voracious appetite, sharing out her chocolate at breaks but always making sure that she gets the most lavish share. Emily is the most approachable of the circle so far as Daisy is concerned, acting as her link to the group even before Daisy is fully accepted. Chloe is the style leader, the most fashion-conscious and the most averse to childish tastes. Chloe sets a standard in precocity that she expects all the other girls to match. The reader senses that this kind of posturing is alien to Daisy, and that she might therefore fail to be accepted.

When the girls begin discussing the arrangements for the first sleepover, which happens to be Amy's, Chloe volunteers that she won't have any trouble staying awake late since she often goes to bed as late as midnight (p7). Emily, with her customary lack of pretentiousness, states that she is regularly woken early by her baby brother crying for his bottle. The emphasis is clear. While Chloe tries to pretend she is more grown-up than she is, Emily establishes a link with her baby sibling. And when Emily engineers an invitation for Daisy to attend the sleepover, Chloe complains about the volume of Daisy's response. "Really, Daisy! You practically deafened me." (p8)

At this stage of the narrative it seems that Chloe's posturing is proving successful. Daisy's comment is that Chloe is "the one who tells everyone else what to do. The Boss." (p8) When the girls discuss the feasibility of having a complete series of sleepovers, Chloe says her parents let her do whatever she likes. Bella and Emily are fairly confident they can stage such a party. Only Daisy is left anxious and uncertain about the prospect of staging a sleepover party.

For Daisy has a secret, one that she might share with Amy, Emily and Bella, but definitely not with Chloe. Daisy has an elder sister, Lily, who is physically disabled. Lily is eleven years old, and is now attending a special school. "It's a special school because she has special needs. That's the right way to describe her. There are lots and lots of wrong ways." (p12) The children at Daisy's old school used to call Lily horrible names. She cannot be sure whether Chloe might do the same.

Daisy's meticulous regard for correct terminology is revealing. She is well-trained in enlightened expressions (although today the phrase 'special needs' is already falling out of favour). But the reader may suspect that other, less-praiseworthy sentiments may be at work below the surface. Would Daisy secretly like to sound as cavalier and uncaring as she suspects Chloe might? Might Daisy defuse Chloe's animosity in private conversation by using derogatory language such as Chloe later uses?

She may well be so tempted. Wilson has here constructed an outstanding example of the ambivalence that can mark the relationship between non-disabled and disabled siblings. It is revealing that Wilson feels it necessary to leave this ambivalence implicit, since rendering it explicit might divert her from what we shall increasingly see as a didactic aim.

The nature of Lily's impairment is never specified, though on the basis of the descriptions of her it seems most likely that she has an exceptionally severe case of 'spastic quadriplegia'. She is a wheelchair user and her speech is profoundly affected — in fact, she cannot utter words at all and, as depicted by Wilson, has a very limited range of vocalizations. Lily's physical limitations also trigger in her a range of emotional responses which to the outside world seem excessive. She gets bored and frustrated in situations where the non-disabled have a wide range of social experiences, such as shopping, and expresses her boredom in fits of irritation. She also suffers from irrational fears. Whenever she sees a teddy-bear, for example, she experiences panic. The reader sees that Lily's physical impairment has in this way encroached upon her psychological experience, a factor which of course complicates and imperils her sibling relationship with Daisy.

Inevitably Lily is excluded from some family activities which Daisy enjoys. Daisy, for example, goes swimming with her father; she is mastering the art of swimming without putting a foot down, and rides on her father's back as if she were a dolphin. The family dynamics of this situation are revealing. The girls' mother tries to involve Lily in the swimming and maintains the fiction that Lily is learning to swim well now that she is attending a special school, while Daisy asserts more realistically that Lily cannot swim at all, but is held in the water while she splashes a bit. Bella's sleepover is to include a swimming party. Daisy fears that the others will swim better than she: "Especially Chloe" (p30). Her father suggests that they might go for a practice swim before the party. Daisy agrees with one proviso: "Just you and me." If Daisy is to make serious progress towards being a competent member of the group, Lily must be excluded. Later Daisy is seized with guilt and asks Lily if she really enjoys swimming. As far as she is able, Lily claims that she does enjoy it.

Daisy's hopes for membership of the circle are overshadowed by uncertainty. Is the sister of a disabled girl even a feasible candidate for membership? Her doubts make it difficult for her to be open with the others about Lily. Until quite late in the story she doesn't even reveal that she has a sister, though when it is her turn to stage a sleepover the truth is bound to emerge. The criteria for membership of the circle are never explicitly stated. There is no book of rules. But these criteria can be construed from what is said, mostly by Chloe. The first and most important criterion is apparent age. Chloe wants to be seen as an adolescent or even as a young adult, but certainly not as a child. Possessions are another criterion. Chloe suggests that everyone of her age should have a video player in her bedroom (p9). Being fashionable is essential; at Daisy's party Chloe turns up wearing a sparkly new T-shirt, make-up and high heeled shoes.

All these criteria pose a serious dilemma for Daisy. Though Lily is older than she, Lily is seen as trapped in an endless form of infancy. Though Lily is older than Daisy, throughout the story we see the strong trauma of her birth endlessly repeated to

Daisy. In Daisy's eyes, Lily has no use for possessions, other than for a few utilitarian objects like her wheelchair. And fashion is meaningless to her. What would she do in high heels? All Daisy's efforts to conform to the norms of the group, norms which are mainly established by Chloe, drag her further away from Lily. And when Daisy escapes from the ambience of the group, she finds herself more and more alienated from her sibling as Chloe places her under relentless pressure to conform. When Daisy first becomes a candidate for membership of the group, Chloe is punished by a teacher for making too much noise. She blames Daisy and tries to disqualify her as a candidate. Chloe fabricates every reason she can to exclude Daisy from her party, and concedes defeat only when all the others say they won't attend without Daisy (p50).

Lily represents a threat to the independence that Daisy wants to achieve as her passport into the group. She also complicates the already tangled nexus of connection between the girls and the parents — at one point, Chloe tries to flirt with Daisy's father. Lily adds an element to this network that is alien, unpredictable and somewhat menacing. Whenever there is a competition for attention within Daisy's family, Lily will always win it. Her physical needs become paramount. When Lily starts screaming in the shop where Daisy is buying a gift for Amy, the shopping expedition must come to a premature end — although ironically the episode ends with Daisy hastily purchasing something more expensive than would usually be contemplated, turning Lily's pressing claims to her own advantage (p17).

Lily is a burden that Daisy must carry into the Alphabet Girls' gang. If they accept Daisy, they must accept Lily. The difficulty these young girls face coming to terms with extreme disability is severe enough, even without the scheming of Chloe.

The way that Wilson depicts the disabled sibling Lily, and the way that her depiction is strengthened by Sharratt's imagery, are highly controversial. Lily is depicted in the narrative not so much as a disabled person, but as a mere collection of symptoms. Her vocal expression consists of nothing but "Ur ur ur ...", endlessly repeated. When Daisy claims to be able to attribute meaning to these sounds the reader must take her word for it: no supporting evidence is offered in Wilson's text.

It is a matter of fact, based on extensive experience, that however seriously disabled people may be, they can nearly always find some means of communication, with the eyes in particular being a potent mechanism for communication. But Lily, according to Wilson's text, has no such facility, and lacks access to any of the communication technologies now commonly used by people with speech impairments. Sharratt also depicts Lily as a victim, especially during the crucial shopping scene, where Lily's face is contorted and darkened with frustration, her hands clutched helplessly across her chest. The fact that the reader learns nothing of Lily's feelings or aspirations through any means other than Daisy's interpretation, places Daisy in a position of unrestrained power over her sister. The reader knows nothing of Lily that is not mediated by Wilson and Daisy.

Wilson now confronts her young readers with a supremely ironic twist. As has already been stated, Daisy has dreaded throughout that having a disabled sibling will prejudice her chances of being accepted in the group. Up to this point Lily has been a potential embarrassment to Daisy, not a support. But Daisy's fears about how her friends would respond to her sister turn out to be largely misplaced. For when Daisy has her own sleepover and the girls are brought face to face with Lily, all the girls but Chloe respond with sympathy and understanding. Chloe cannot handle Lily. She mistakes her for a ghost and wets herself. According to Amy, Lily is "special because she's got special needs" (p111). But Chloe sees her as "this totally batty, loopy maniac baby sister who screams all the time" (p110). Chloe's inability to deal with Lily leads not just to her forfeiture of the leadership, but also her expulsion from the group. Lily is the litmus test that members of the Alphabet Girls must pass, and Chloe signally fails.

There are two possible interpretations of the denouement of *Sleepovers*. Anyone who has had contact with disabled people, especially disabled young people, is likely to find Wilson's depiction of Lily unsatisfactory in the extreme. Lily is not established as a character in the narrative at all; she is merely a cipher used to test the tolerance and humanity of her non-disabled sister's friends. This action, testing the response of Daisy's friends, is more or less the only action for which Lily is responsible throughout the narrative. The situation is guaranteed to irritate any reader sensitive to the issues of disability, simply because it reflects so clearly a good deal of what disabled people experience in the world. If this interpretation stands alone, then Wilson must be judged to have depicted a disabled character in a particularly insensitive manner. And this would be a surprise, given Wilson's standing as a sensitive and intelligent writer. It is nevertheless a conclusion to which the text initially drives even a reluctant critic.

There is however an alternative interpretation. It is possible to argue that viewing Lily as a mere cipher is a failing into which even her well-meaning sister has fallen; that seeing Lily as a mere bundle of symptoms and not as a real person is genuinely how Daisy sees her. What happens to Chloe may then be seen as opening Daisy's eyes to the real person concealed within the bundle of symptoms. In ancient Greek drama Aristotle described the moment of anagnoresis, when the scales fall from our eyes and we suddenly see a character or a situation as it truly is. Perhaps when Lily causes Chloe to fail her test, the reader and Daisy see for the first time that within Lily there is a powerful and decisive character, capable of diverting the whole narrative into another channel. In the end the group of girls includes Lily but not Chloe, an outcome that would have been unimaginable at the outset.

How does a critic balance and evaluate these two interpretations? My own view is that the latter interpretation, the one more favourable to Wilson, lacks credibility for two reasons. First, it casts Daisy in the role of an unreliable narrator, which may be a device too sophisticated for a book for young readers. Second, the evidence required to support the second interpretation is deficient. If Lily has within her the latent power to exert a decisive influence on events that go far beyond her family circle, then I cannot believe that these powers would remain unnoticed for all the years that precede the opening of the book, as well as for most of the narrative span of the book.

The reader's reaction is fundamental to a moment of anagnoresis. The reader should be momentarily nonplussed, but then quickly realise that the denouement actually follows on logically from earlier suggestions. If Wilson had really meant to contrive a moment of anagnoresis, it would have been easy for her to embed a hint or two in the earlier text that there was more going on in Lily's mind than her sister gave her credit for. I see no such hints in the text, nor any evidence that a subtext has been constructed with this end in mind. Sadly, I conclude that Wilson has indeed allowed her disabled character to remain nothing but a cipher, thus robbing the sibling relationship of much of the emotional power it might otherwise have carried.

JAMES RIORDAN'S *THE GIFT*

We have seen that in *Sleepovers* the selfish and vain Chloe, though scarcely a likeable character, has a dominant influence that persists until the last few pages of the book. James Riordan's book *The Gift* (2004) is also dominated by a thoroughly unpleasant character, the mother of the first-person narrator and her disabled twin. Tracy Smart is deliberately aimed to offend the reader's sensibilities from the moment that she is introduced. She names her twin daughters Fee and Bee, to defy the registrar who thinks he knows better. She engineers her own pregnancy at the age of fifteen to escape from school and is "the envy of her mates" (p1). She regards the regular production of children by various fathers — she is on her third partner and fifth child — as a shrewd method of increasing her entitlement to state benefits, and thinks of shoplifting as a normal way of providing for her family. She sells access to the children to their fathers: pay the bills and they can see the children.

Worst of all, she refers to Bee in the most insulting manner conceivable, calling her "Dopey spastic" (p78). When she learns that the computer Bee needs might be used for electronic shoplifting, she comments "Tha' dimbo could come in useful ar'er all." If a writer constructed a model of the unmarried mother designed to fit the picture created in the most reactionary tabloid newspapers, then Tracy Smart would fit it exactly.

Perversely, yet wholly convincingly, the frightful inadequacies of their family background create a bond between the twins. They are supposed to share a sixth sense. "You look ar'ter 'er, Fee. You know wha' she's on about. Buggered if I do." And indeed there is a bond between the twins, which develops more strongly as the narrative unfolds.

> As we grew up, we developed a sort of sisterly sense, special to us alone. Sometimes it was just a glance or touch or thought. She'd look at me or touch my hand, and I instinctively knew what she wanted. It was uncanny.
>
> We also developed a secret code. Only I could understand words that were just grunts or whinnies to others. (p5)

This is exactly the kind of intuitive dialogue that is so conspicuously missing between Daisy and Lily in *Sleepovers*. The question naturally arises whether this relationship between the girls is realistic, based on instinctive sympathy and devoid of conflict or competition, or whether it is an over-romanticised view. This question will be answered when we reach the end of our consideration of Riordan's book, in the light of the way in which the narrative and characterization unfold.

In any case, the two girls find refuge from their catastrophic family background in different ways. Fee allows herself to be drawn into the circle of the sports club, attracted by something as old-fashioned and ill-suited to her context as team spirit. Bee seeks her self-realization in poetry, writing verse which she allows her sister to pass off as her own for as long as circumstances permit.

Riordan uses an intermediary figure to link the very different aspirations of the two sisters. He is Grandad, the father of the twins' father. He is "the weirdo" who has worked to attain an education and letters after his name. He subscribes to old-fashioned values that would easily embrace team spirit and the urge to win a foot-race. But he also cherishes cultural values and, once he knows of Bee's poetic talent, is the natural person to turn to for a computer. When Fee ends the telephone conversation that will produce the computer, Bee has a little smile "playing at the corners of her mouth" (p23). She can follow the maneuvering that goes on within the family better than her mother thinks she can.

A critical turning point in the book arrives when Fee is obliged against her will to visit Bee's school. She agrees to go only because Bee exerts irresistible pressure on her. She imagines a draughty hall full of vacant-faced kids "catching flies", with a jolly fat woman teaching them to sing. Instead she finds an attractive building, with well-organised functional units and, of course, pupils with a vast array of different impairments. The school band performs creditably, reminding Fee of her own brief career playing the recorder, a career terminated by her mother's loud complaints of "I can't 'ear me programmes" (p12).

The ambivalence that Fee feels towards her sister is memorably underscored. Fee is pleased that Bee is receiving proper care and attention and it is assumed by the school that she and the other disabled pupils have a valuable life to lead. But when she contrasts Bee's situation with her own life, educated in an inferior school building and haunted by an endless list of family chores that includes caring for Bee as well as the youngest children, she cannot help but feel jealousy.

It is, incidentally, a considerable authorial feat on Riordan's part to have captured so accurately the atmosphere of a 'special needs' school, together with the community spirit that drives such establishments, sometimes creating a spirit of optimism hardly (to be honest) justified by the objective prospects of the pupils in a world prejudiced against disability. Riordan manages to capture both sides of this ambivalent picture.

There is, however, a serious question to be asked about the characters of *The Gift*. They can be seen as representing warring forces in modern society. The mother is a supreme individualist, greedy, amoral and shameless. The girls come from a deprived background, but are struggling to develop and fulfil their aspirations. A careful reader must ask the question whether Riordan has produced a genuine novel or a work of socio-economic commentary, campaign literature on behalf of the inclusive society.

In my view, the character of the mother is exaggerated, a piece of pastiche. She would be at home in a half-hour TV soap. But the characters of the twins are more highly developed and more credible. The reader learns to care about them as the novel advances, regarding Bee as a person and not just an assemblage of symptoms and needs. It is the development of the twins' characters that saves Riordan's book from being a didactic exercise. And if it does fall into the didactic trap at all, at least we can claim that it teaches understanding and acceptance of disabled people.

In short, as the story unfolds Bee becomes less and less a mere symbol of the 'Other', and more and more an equal participant in the narrative. This process gives point to the deliberately ambiguous title of the novel. Is it Bee's gift for poetry or Fee's gift for fast running that is being celebrated? The answer is of course that it is both, and the inner gift of any individual.

As the perceived strong trauma of having a disabled twin recedes for Fee, so the trauma that both Fee and Bee face together becomes stronger. Their mother's attitudes and behaviour are the trauma, repeated daily and incessantly. Tracy Smart threatens to decamp the whole family to York on the day before Fee's sporting championships and Bee's poetry competition. Tracy has no good reason for transporting her family to the north, except that the shops there will be unaware of her reputation as a shoplifter. In reality, of course, Tracy is in flight from her daughters' aspirations, which threaten to lift them out of the cycle of dependency and dishonesty that frames her life. Her plan is foiled by a conspiracy between Bee and her disabled friend Charlie. When the non-disabled teenagers have abandoned hope, the disabled save the day. Decisive action by the disabled, and the close bond of the sisters, have combated the strong trauma of a ruthless and unprincipled mother.

Including in a novel poems that are the supposed product of one of the characters is a difficult task, and one that has defeated some famous authors. The poetry attributed to Bee in this novel is actually the work of a young disabled poet named June Craven. The verse is simple and unadorned: its main virtue is rhythm. Riordan uses the poems skilfully and integrates them well within the text. The reader can easily accept that they are the poems of the fictional Bee. As the book closes an audience is moved to tears by Bee's poem.

Let people know how I feel
Letting people know
People like me are still real
Now I can show
That I have a voice
I have opinions
I have a choice
We all have options. (p116)

For the first time, perhaps, the non-disabled audience members recognise that a disabled person may have a promising career as a writer. This moment is calculated to stir emotions in anyone who has an inclusive society at heart, but we must also admit that it is highly contrived: "And, for the first time, no one noticed the wheelchair." (p117).

However, overall I find James Riordan's Bee a totally convincing character. She is disabled, but proves to be both capable and resolute. I find that people who don't know me well automatically express amazement that anyone in a wheelchair can achieve academic distinction – as if combining disability and intelligence is somehow impossible and contrary to nature.

CONCLUSION FOR THE YOUNG READERS' TEXTS

My hypothesis is that, while the relationship between any siblings may be rewarding or fraught, the extremes are more severe when one sibling is or becomes disabled. I would argue that both the Wilson text and the Riordan text support my hypothesis, but in ways that are less than wholly satisfactory. While Daisy aspires to become an accepted member of the Alphabet Girls, her disabled sister lurks in the background. She has the capability, when revealed, to spoil everything for Daisy. In fact, however, Lily provides the test that separates the worthy from the unworthy members of the club. Chloe's vanity, superficiality and babyishness are revealed by her reaction to Lily. But, as argued above, the otherwise satisfactorily ironic conclusion is spoiled by Wilson's failure to establish Lily as a character earlier in the book. In other words, the fraught dimensions of the Daisy/Lily relationship are established more convincingly than the rewarding ones.

In Riordan's book it is a case of Bee and Fee *contra mundum*. They are faced with a bad mother of epic proportions, who seems to derive satisfaction from thwarting them. Riordan depicts them coming together in an unlikely partnership to achieve their goals, with the disabled twin demonstrating an unsuspected degree of cunning and resolution. In contrast to Wilson's book, Riordan does depict the two siblings as forming a partnership in which from the start the disabled sibling plays an active role. Thus the rewarding aspects of the sibling relationship are in this case properly established. It must be admitted, however, that Riordan casts a sentimental aura over the denouement of his book, and the partnership is a little contrived and unconvincing.

LOIS KEITH'S *A DIFFERENT LIFE*

Lois Keith is a disabled writer who set herself the explicit goal of improving the way in which disabled characters are portrayed in children's literature. Her work includes critical studies, other non-fiction and fiction. Libby Starling, the protagonist of Keith's novel *A Different Life*, is one of the most precisely defined and fully developed disabled characters to have appeared in recent children's literature. Accordingly Libby's relationship with her younger brother Robbie is of relevance to this examination.

At the beginning of *A Different Life* (1997), Libby is a 'normal', non-disabled teenager. She has the usual range of preoccupations about her appearance, her body image and her prospects. There is a boy, Jesse, in whom she is interested. But does Jesse like her? Methodically Libby lists her fifteen-year-old preoccupations, which significantly include: "When was Mum going to stop seeing Robbie as the sweet, little, innocent perfect child and me as the difficult, moody teenager?" (p3)

We see that the agenda Libby initially establishes with her sibling is one where discord and competition for attention and approval are prevalent. And the competition for approval is one that Libby sees herself quite clearly as losing at this stage. However pressing these routine questions of teenage life may have seemed, though, they soon sink into unimportance. On a seaside school outing Libby hopes to make some impression on Jesse. She seems to have succeeded when he playfully pushes her under the water while they are swimming. But either as a result of swallowing polluted sea-water or in some other way, Libby becomes ill and is left paralysed from the waist down.

One of the most distinctive features of Keith's writing is her use of irony. She has the keenest possible awareness of the tricks that life and a narrative can play on people. Here we see Libby gaining a sudden and huge advantage in the competition with Robbie for attention, albeit one she would be happy not to have gained, by becoming immobile and in a sense more childlike than her younger sibling. Later we see Libby conducting a different campaign, one in which she strives for attention and respect as an adult individual who is disabled, rather than just as a victim. It is of course inevitable that, during this transformation, her sibling relationship with Robbie changes too. Keith, as we shall see, charts this transformation with skill and insight.

Libby and her brother have a morning ritual: he enters her bedroom and climbs into her bed while she pretends to be fast asleep. When at last he prises open her eyes, Libby pretends to have no idea who he is or what their relationship is. Though he knows that this is a game, Robbie manifests increasing levels of tension until Libby ends it, stating his name, age, address and relationship to her (p24). It is interesting, and significant in the light of what is to happen, that the ritual depends upon a fantasy: Libby has during the night metamorphosed into a person who is a complete stranger to Robbie. This game can be held to represent a ritualised and harmless re-enactment of the strong trauma of a sibling's birth as depicted by Mitchell. Moreover the re-enactment is physical, bringing brother and sister into close bodily proximity with each other.

THE ONSET OF DISABILITY

Libby indicates that even before the onset of her disability she was growing intolerant of Robbie's intrusions into her private sphere. Her mother insists that Robbie is just a baby and should be shown some tolerance. Libby reflects that he is big for a baby, and expert too at getting his own way (p26). On the morning when her illness begins, Libby simply cannot tolerate Robbie in her bed. Robbie is disappointed, even more so when Libby begins to vomit and he is exiled from her bedside.

We see here how the contest for attention is waged by competing degrees of incapacity: Robbie deserves tolerance because he is a baby, Libby achieves privacy by failing to control her gut.

As Libby grows weaker, Robbie is not even allowed to ask her where he can find the gift that she brought him from the seaside. In Mitchell's terms, we may state that Libby has now been reborn as a helpless and dangerously needy sibling, her demands for care and attention suddenly eclipsing his. If Libby experienced the arrival of a young brother as a strong trauma, Robbie is certainly suffering a similar fate as his older sister becomes as helpless as a baby. The identity game must now begin again on new terms, as the new Elizabeth Alice and the new Robert Richard have to be identified and related.

As Libby begins her long campaign, first to find out what is wrong with her and then to cope with its ramifications, Robbie is her staunch ally. Trying to reach the bathroom after a series of strange and frightening dreams, Libby collapses. Significantly, her doctor finds the first evidence of lack of feeling in her legs. She is to be taken immediately to hospital (p37). Libby reverts to infancy, calling her mother Mummy, as two enormous people load her on to a stretcher. Robbie hands her Morris, his much-loved toy rabbit. Morris has shared Robbie's bed every night since he was two. He will make Libby "feel better when you feel sad". Libby realises that she loves Robbie "more than I'd ever done before. I was sorry for all the times I'd been cross and impatient with him."

The sibling bond has been strengthened by adversity. But how brittle is this relationship? Can it be formed into something permanent? Robbie's affection certainly endures when he visits Libby in hospital. He brings her a little old-fashioned suitcase full of such presents as a toy stethoscope and an alarm clock with a pig that oinks on the hour. Libby is suffering in the aftermath of a botched lumbar puncture. Robbie examines Libby's hydrating drip and asks whether the canula hurts. Without waiting for a reply, he bends to kiss her hand better. Even as late as Libby's sojourn in the rehabilitation centre at Pinner (p294), the person she misses most is Robbie. The feeling is mutual. Robbie will not read his "reading book" to anyone but his big sister.

THE INTRUDER

If a child faces a situation where a sibling becomes disabled, probably the least welcome development of all is for that sibling to strike up a relationship with a disabled friend, as Libby does with Brian. The fact that Brian is young and male, and so potentially a surrogate little brother, makes matters even more challenging for Robbie. Brian is three years old, with a cute face and curly red hair. His upper torso is covered in plaster, which makes the reader suspect he has a spinal problem. Robbie sees Brian as an immediate threat. In the hospital Brian is just concluding a long, inconsequential but strangely restful soliloquy about his cats when Robbie is left in Libby's room while their mother sees a doctor (p120).

Keith very tellingly compares Robbie's reaction to that of a cat spotting a stray tom on its territory. Robbie accuses Brian of stealing Libby's hairbrush and tries to eject him from the room. As Brian leaves the room, Libby explains that his family live far away and he turns to Libby for company. But Robbie is impenitent.

"He's always in here, I hate him. He shouldn't be in here all the time. He's not your little brother, I'm your little brother!" (p123)

Libby invents a game using her wheelchair as a taxi to placate Robbie. But we suspect the damage goes too deep to be so easily repaired. When Libby is allowed to leave hospital for Christmas provided that she promises to engage in a regular routine of exercise, she cannot bring herself to tell Brian that she is leaving him, but he learns the truth from the staff (p155). Libby buys Brian a Christmas gift, then guiltily sends her mother out to buy a present for her brother.

When Libby becomes disabled, the effects on her and her sibling are complex. New demands are imposed upon Robbie, and also upon her, but new opportunities to display themselves in a flattering light also arise for both siblings. At the outset, as we have seen, Robbie responds well to these new opportunities, even sacrificing his most beloved toy to comfort his sister. Libby, in contrast, is initially so absorbed in her new predicament that she has not much attention for anyone else. Her whole family seem in some way to fail Libby. Her father becomes absorbed in the question of how Libby became ill, and whether the pollution of the water can be established as the cause. He is immersing himself in this technical question because he cannot face what has happened to his daughter. Libby's mother is the great manager, the organiser who can resolve any problem by effort and thought. But now she, too, has come face to face with a problem that effort and thought cannot resolve. In this context, Robbie's efforts to soften the blow that has fallen on his sister seem objectively ineffectual and even pathetic.

We should, however, make the effort to view

Robbie's gestures from his subjective viewpoint. Robbie has been accustomed throughout his short life to viewing himself as the needier of the siblings. Suddenly, the roles are reversed. When Robbie has a need, it is likely to be instantly over-shadowed by a need of Libby's, for rest, for privacy or for almost anything that runs counter to Robbie's needs. We observe that Robbie is coping not only with a fundamental shift in his relationship with Libby, but also with changes in the attitudes and behaviour of his parents towards their children and towards each other. Emotional upheavals are going on all around Robbie, and he has to deal with them as best he can.

If we read Keith's text carefully, we see that Robbie's efforts to conform to this new situation mean little to Libby. But the magnanimity that they reveal in a small boy is truly impressive. All these challenges Robbie can meet more or less satisfactorily so long as his sister is sick and removed from his domestic space. But in this case Libby's sickness will prove temporary, and will give way to a permanent disability that is something other than sickness. When the sick and hospitalised sister becomes a determined young woman competing in a wheelchair for attention and priority in Robbie's own home, the situation will change again as Robbie faces another strong trauma.

THE SIBLING TURNS AWAY

As Libby begins to adjust to her different life, to her life as a capable person who uses a wheelchair, the dynamics within the family change fundamentally (p188). The trigger for these changes is a television programme about Libby. Libby had hoped that making the programme would give her a chance to enunciate her aspirations for the future. Instead it depicts her as a wounded victim, surrounded by a family bravely sacrificing themselves for her benefit. Libby is outraged. She is tired of the cause of her illness being investigated by her father as if she were a question in a science exam. She is tired of having to be treated like a baby, carried upstairs while she waits for the house to be adapted. Libby hugs Robbie to demonstrate to him that he is not included in the implied rebukes. But she is conscious that yet another aspect of the sibling relationship has been exposed: Libby is actively using her brother as a barrier between herself and her mother and father.

Though this passage is expressed in unemphatic prose, it is a turning point in the sibling relationship. Libby's gesture towards Robbie looks positive and inclusive. She seems to be maintaining her warm sibling contact. However, Libby and the reader know that it is nothing of the sort: Robbie is being used to help establish the distance Libby needs from her family. Eventually the reader senses that Robbie will recognise this device for what it is, a way of fending off parental interest. There is a danger that he will come to associate seeming kindness with exploitation, and respond accordingly.

Libby's device works, at least in the short term. Her parents no longer gaze at Libby with anxiety all over their faces, or give a brave little smile when she catches them doing so. Libby's view is that all the members of her family have been scared of her, as if she were "an immobile rocket, fizzing and fizzing but with nowhere to go off." (p188) Of course, Libby's relationship with Robbie is also changed. He stops behaving "like the model child" (p190) and becomes "naughty and irritating". Robbie deliberately waits until he knows Libby is in her room. Then, with a grim expression on his face and his lips tightly closed, he gathers up all the gifts he has made to Libby — including Morris the rabbit and the little suitcase — and repossesses them. The look he gives his sister as he does so is intended to convey to her that she is the guilty party. Libby is not the only one to be targeted by the new, troublesome Robbie. He begins to make a fuss about his meals, to refuse to go to bed on time and to monopolise the choice of TV programmes.

What is the explanation for this rapid shift in Robbie's behaviour? If we accept that in Mitchell's terms Robbie has experienced a strong trauma as his big sister becomes a helpless invalid, so we may conclude that her embarkation on the road to a 'different life' devalues his experience. He has given his all to a cause that in the end proves undeserving. As she often does, Keith has hinted at a major issue with a seemingly minor episode. What do disabled people expect of the world? In principle they wish to be treated as equals. But they also need help sometimes from the non-disabled. Keith uses a sibling episode to launch a process that will involve everyone: Robbie is acting as a forerunner for the whole family who have to learn to redefine their relationship with Libby.

LIBBY'S METAMORPHOSIS

The television programme creates an interest in Libby's situation among friends who have been in danger of forgetting all about her. Perversely, however, this interest has the effect of pushing Libby deeper into her shell. Eventually it is an invitation from the social worker Barbara which entices Libby out of the house. Barbara is Jesse's aunt, a determined and effective young Black woman who uses a racy wheelchair. She will set

Libby an example in independence and aspiration that will in time change the course of Libby's life.

Yet even as this process begins to unfold, the disgruntled sibling acts to spoil it. As Libby manipulates herself into the front seat of the car and her mother folds and stows the wheelchair, Robbie complains that he is never allowed to sit in the front seat any more (p192). Libby's choice of words is revealing: Robbie is "whining". The disillusionment is taking place on both sides of this sibling relationship. His mother silences Robbie with "a look that could kill a python". When the car reaches Barbara's flat, Libby is worried that her mother might come in and take the time that Libby wants to spend with Barbara. Ironically, Robbie saves her the worry. He is playing up so badly that his mother daren't leave him in the car. Libby will have Barbara to herself.

Robbie perhaps feels some presentiment that another and even more serious distraction is to come into his sister's life, leaving him even more estranged from her in ways that he cannot possibly match. Libby's relationship with Jesse becomes romantic. They kiss in the middle of a maths revision. Libby looks in the bathroom mirror to see what she has become.

> I could feel him still with me. I hoped that he had seen what I saw now, a smooth oval face, big green eyes, my mouth full and my hair smooth and shiny. I was in love with this new idea of myself. (p326)

The new Libby now volunteers to do something that her mother has been asking her to do for ages, to work with Robbie making a card for their grandparents' golden wedding anniversary. Libby explains this behaviour to herself by saying that she wants "to be nice to everyone ..." (p326) Yet though this gesture seems on the surface to be well-intended and inclusive to Robbie, Libby hastens to correct this impression. "Poor Robbie, I wasn't much use to him." While he is engaged in the world of scissors, glue and paper, Libby is inhabiting a world of romantic fantasy. A gesture that seems to embrace Robbie actually does nothing of the sort.

At the opening of *A Different Life*, the relationship between Libby and her little brother is clearly depicted. Libby is the controlling influence, determining how dealings between the siblings should be transacted. Though Libby is worried that she is seen as the troublesome teenager while Robbie is the perfect child, there is little doubt where the power resides. Indeed, it could be argued that Libby's ability to trouble her parents is a measure of her power. The list of teenage preoccupations given by Libby right at the beginning of the book makes it clear that she has many other issues on her mind, involving her friends, her fashion consciousness, her academic work and her popularity. The same is not true of Robbie. The reader has the impression that Libby is more or less the only centre of gravity Robbie has. Quite suddenly, the relationship shifts. Now Robbie becomes the key player in Libby's daily life, and given the way that her parents' confidence slips away, he is the only support who can be thoroughly depended upon.

The new balance of power is in Robbie's favour, and he wields his power benignly. But two further developments weaken his grip on power. First, Libby realises that she is not confronted by a binary choice. She is not confined to being either a non-disabled young woman or a helpless cripple. There is a space between the two, a space that can contain a determined young woman in a wheelchair with aspirations and accomplishments of her own. In this space Libby and her family and her friends must build a way of life.

Robbie cannot easily adjust to this new reality. He needs the simple power structure in which either he or his sister has the dominant influence. The ambivalence of the new sibling relationship robs him of his confidence. Note that when Robbie comes to repossess all the gifts he made to Libby, he makes quite certain that she is watching him do so. He needs her to witness his declaration that the closeness of the past is no longer on offer.

CONCLUSION

These three contemporary novels all portray a disabled sibling playing a significant role. When the denouement of Wilson's book comes, it is Lily (earlier a potential embarrassment to her sister) who acts as the litmus test which Chloe fails, losing Chloe her place as the leader of the group and even her membership of it. In James Riordan's book we see twins with very different aspirations, one attempting to write poetry, the other taking part in foot races, bound together by the shockingly inadequate family background they share. They must help each other or fail. They are depicted as having a strong intuitive relationship and spiritual resources to share when they need to. When Bee disappears on the eve of her poetry competition and Fee's sports day, Bee turns out to have a gift for intrigue that shapes events around her to a much greater extent than anyone may have expected. Meanwhile Lois Keith describes the physical and emotional voyage that her disabled character must undertake, sometimes in harmony and sometimes in conflict with her younger brother.

Both Wilson and Riordan have an important message for young readers and try, with varying degrees of success, to adapt this message for their audience, but their self-imposed didacticism creates tricky authorial problems for them. Keith starts at a different point. She has a vision of reality based in part on her own experience, and in part on the detailed knowledge of the disabled world that any disabled person acquires. Her characters are three-dimensional, not archetypal. She strives to convey that vision in all its subtlety to an older readership.

Earlier I referred to the work of Juliet Mitchell as quoted in Prophecy Coles's book, and the distinction between a weak trauma and a strong. It is Mitchell's hypothesis that the birth of a sibling represents a strong trauma, one that is irremediable for all time. Mitchell's distinction is presumably a useful one for psychologists. It may be that psychologists, placing heavy emphasis on a structural model of the human psyche, are more inclined to favour water-tight categories and the pursuit of taxonomy than are writers and readers. But it must be admitted that the evidence contained in these three books does not support the theory that the presence of a sibling (in these cases a disabled sibling) results in a trauma which can be firmly categorised as strong, or indeed classified in any other way.

My working hypothesis, outlined at the start of this chapter, was that disability makes the sibling relationship more intense, more complex and, most significantly, more ambivalent: that in short such relationships are each a unique product of the characters of the siblings and their circumstances. They cannot be fitted into uniform categories. I believe the evidence contained in the three books that I have considered does substantiate this hypothesis. Libby and Robbie, Daisy and Lily and

Bee and Fee enact just the complex and ambivalent rituals we should expect. And the ambivalence which is present in the relationship between any pair of siblings is in these texts made more profound and more significant for the reader by the disability of one of them.

REFERENCES

Coles, Prophecy, ed, *Sibling Relationships*, Karnac, London, 2006.

Eliot, George, *The Mill on the Floss*, (first published 1860), Penguin Popular Classics, London, 1994 edition.

Keith, Lois, *A Different Life*, Livewire, The Women's Press, London, 1997.

Riordan, James, *The Gift*, Oxford University Press, Oxford, 2004.

Wilson, Jacqueline, *Sleepovers*, Random House, London, 2001.

Founded in 1994, Bettany Press specialises in books about 20th-century girls' popular fiction, together with reprints of rare titles and original fiction for both girls and women.

**For details of our books
and how to order them,**

**visit our website at:
www.bettanypress.co.uk**

**or write for a catalogue to:
Bettany Press, 8 Kildare Road,
London E16 4AD.**